The Practitioner Inquiry Series

Marilyn Cochran-Smith and Susan L. Lytle, *SERIES EDITORS*

Teacher Narrative as Citical Inquiry: Rewriting the Script
JOY S. RITCHIE & DAVID E. WILSON

From Another Angle: Children's Strengths and School Standards
MARGARET HIMLEY WITH PATRICIA F. CARINI, EDITORS

Unplayed Tapes: A Personal History of Collaborative Teacher Research
STEPHEN M. FISHMAN & LUCILLE McCARTHY

Inside City Schools: Investigating Literacy in the Multicultural Classroom
SARAH WARSHAUER FREEDMAN, ELIZABETH RADIN SIMONS,
JULIE SHALHOPE KALNIN, ALEX CASARENO, and the M-CLASS TEAMS

Class Actions: Teaching for Social Justice in Elementary and Middle School
JoBETH ALLEN, Editor

Teacher/Mentor: A Dialogue for Collaborative Learning
PEG GRAHAM, SALLY HUDSON-ROSS, CHANDRA ADKINS, PATTI McWHORTER,
& JENNIFER McDUFFIE STEWART, Editors

Teaching Other People's Children: Literacy and Learning
in a Bilingual Classroom
CYNTHIA BALLENGER

Teaching, Multimedia, and Mathematics: Investigations of Real Practice
MAGDALENE LAMPERT & DEBORAH LOEWENBERG BALL

Tensions of Teaching: Beyond Tips to Critical Reflection
JUDITH M. NEWMAN

John Dewey and the Challenge of Classroom Practice
STEPHEN M. FISHMAN & LUCILLE McCARTHY

"Sometimes I Can Be Anything": Power, Gender, and Identity
in a Primary Classroom
KAREN GALLAS

Learning in Small Moments: Life in an Urban Classroom
DANIEL R. MEIER

Interpreting Teacher Practice: Two Continuing Stories
RENATE SCHULZ

Creating Democratic Classrooms: The Struggle to Integrate Theory and Practice
LANDON E. BEYER, Editor

Teacher Narrative as Critical Inquiry

REWRITING THE SCRIPT

Joy S. Ritchie and David E. Wilson

WITH RUTH KUPFER, CAROL MacDANIELS,
TONI SIEDEL, AND JOHN SKRETTA

FOREWORD BY BONNIE SUNSTEIN

Teachers College, Columbia University
New York and London

Published by Teachers College Press, 1234 Amsterdam Avenue, New York, NY 10027

Library of Congress Cataloging-in-Publication Data

Ritchie, Joy S.
Teacher narrative as critical inquiry : rewriting the script / Joy S. Ritchie and David E. Wilson with Ruth Kupfer . . .[et al.] ; foreword by Bonnie Sunstein.
pp.   cm.—(The practitioner inquiry series)
Includes bibliographical references and index.
ISBN 0-8077-3961-8 (cloth : alk. paper).—ISBN 0-8077-3960-X (pbk. : alk. paper)
1. Teachers—United States—Biography. 2. Education—United States—Biographical methods. 3. Teaching—United States. I. Title. II. Series.
LA2311 .R58   2000   371. 1'0092'2—dc21   00023415

ISBN 0-8077-3960-X (paper)
ISBN 0-8077-3961-8 (cloth)

Printed on acid-free paper

Manufactured in the United States of America

07 06 05 04 03 02 01 00   8 7 6 5 4 3 2 1

Contents

Foreword

A few years ago, among the browned and dusty papers in my mother's storage cartons, I found an old report card. "Bonnie tells too many stories," my second grade teacher wrote in perfect 1950s cursive. "She is a smart girl, but she needs to stop telling stories and get to her real work." The remainder of my school years reflected this concern among my teachers and taught me that stories did not blend very well with the "real work" of school.

As a new college student in a very selective Honors English I class at the University of Pittsburgh, I turned over the onionskin of my first weekly essay to view my professor's response. I'd read the assigned book, crafted an essay on my new graduation typewriter, and submitted the package with swollen freshman expectation and a fancy paper clip. "This is a narrative piece. Your mind wanders all over it. It is too creative; not a critical analysis of the work in question. This is not the business of an English class. D."

More than three decades later, I've finally collected the knowledge and given myself the courage to recognize that my teachers may have been mistaken, that my "real work" is tied to telling stores. And for all those years, my "real work" has been, in fact, the "business of an English class." Despite my teachers' efforts to socialize me into the rules of school appropriateness, I've never been able to stop myself from telling stories and writing them—personal ones and professional ones, despite the humiliations they've afforded me. And I've never been able to stop listening and reading those of others. Stories have shaped my skills as a teacher, a writer, and a researcher.

As Dave Wilson and Joy Ritchie illustrate, telling our own stories—and then revisiting them to see what they mean—is a courageous and revolutionary act, far from the marginal position it occupies in the research community. Stories catalogue our triumphs and inventory our humiliations. Storytelling is an act in which we take control, and from which we make meaning out of the disparate chunks of our lives. It is, ironically, an act that is not always valued in school. And no wonder. Stories separate us from one another. Our personal narratives make us unique. Like children from the same family, we know they should not be compared against others or even against themselves. We cannot measure stories on anyone's scale, not even our own. We cannot disconnect stories from the tellers, the tales, the audience, or the times and places in which we tell them.

In her novel *Stones from the River,* Ursula Hegi (1994) offers us Trudi, marginalized and feared in a small German village because she is a dwarf, a *"zwergin."* Throughout a life that spans two world wars, Trudi spins her own stories, collects those of her townspeople, and dispenses published stories at her father's pay library where she works. As she develops into adulthood, she learns to use stories to understand what others do to her, what she does to others, to analyze the triumphs and humiliations of family, community, nation, and world—at peace and at war. As she matures, even her relationship with her beloved Rhein River changes, and she comes to learn how. Early in her life, Trudi understands the power of her stories like she understands the river, but without quite understanding what to do with them:

> Trudi would hold those pictures in her mind throughout the decades to come, and without even being near the river she would always know how it looked. She could close her eyes and picture the Rhein from the dike or close up from her favorite place on the jetty. She knew exactly how high the water could rise around the willows; knew the swift change of color—from moss green to molten black—and how the sun could shine on the surface so hard that it would blind you if you stared at the river; knew the pattern the current formed around the rocks in late summer, while early in spring they lay submerged. . . .
>
> It was like that with stories: she could see beneath their surface, know the undercurrents, the whirlpools that could take you down, the hidden clusters of rocks. Stories could blind you, rise around you in a myriad of colors. Every time Trudi took a story and let it stream through her mind from beginning to end, it grew fuller, richer, feeding on her visions of those people the story belonged to until it left its bed like the river she loved. And it was then that she'd have to tell the story to someone. (Hegi, 1994, p. 73)

Decades later, through two love affairs and four deep friendships, gaining success in others' eyes in spite of her physical condition, living inside bombings and the Nazi invasion, enduring mental illnesses, ugly deaths, poverty, and starvation, Trudi is still at the pay library dispensing and collecting stories and lending books. But along with her maturity, she realizes something deeper, more analytical; something at once more personal and universal:

> Now the purpose of her stories had changed. She spun them to discover their meaning. In the telling, she found, you reached a point where you could not go back, where—as the story changed—it transformed you, too. What mattered was to let each story flow through you . . . It would still begin by feeling drawn to secrets, but she could curb the urge to tell, let it settle into something that nurtured the fragments of life which fell into her way, until a story was ready to unveil itself. (Hegi, 1994, p. 505)

What we can do with stories, which this book shows in the very stories it tells, is what Trudi learns. We can curb the urge to merely tell our secrets, and let the real story unveil itself. We can turn them over and inspect them, understand them in light of who we've become, and work hard (yes, the "real work" of school) to recast their meaning. When we take the time to do that, we theorize our stories (and hence our selves) into our pedagogy, our politics, and our practical lives.

I invite you to join six of our colleagues as they take us on a journey of critical analysis (yes, "critical analysis") identifying where and how their stories fit into their lives at school. These are not altogether pleasant journeys; they are at once intimate and discomforting. You'll see over-functioning adults decrying their lack of time to do anything thoroughly, people marginalized by their intelligence, their parents' issues, their middle-class guilt, their sexual orientation, and even their desires to mentor their students. You won't read one story from one person, nor a set of standard "case studies." As you read, you'll live out the complexity of many stories as they create each teacher's life—in that teacher's own voice. You'll watch as each teacher reshapes the stories and you'll be able to lurk in the forming of each teacher's pedagogy. In short, this book shows us how to make our stories become the "real work" of school, the "business of an English class." Dave Wilson, Joy Ritchie, and their Nebraska colleagues Carol, Toni, John, and Ruth offer us, as John points out, "an invitation to belong" to an emerging tradition of using personal narrative to create professional pedagogy.

Using narrative for learning is not a new idea; stories are essential to the human condition. Folklorists have long known that people use stories to both teach and resist tradition, whatever their culture. *Verbal art* (Bauman, 1977) and *performance theory* (Goffman, 1959; Turner, 1986) are terms used in anthropology and sociology to describe the symbolic features of storytelling. Stories, like other cultural events, present and re-present a culture to itself (Handelman, 1990). Performance of verbal art invites participation in symbolic experience: signs, as folklorist Simon Bronner (1998) writes, "of identity-forming intensity, of sincerity, of really being alive" (p. 461).

In my own research collecting teachers' stories at a summer writing program (Sunstein, 1994a) and in a teacher's room (Sunstein, 1994b), I realized that what people often term a "transformation" is not really a transformation at all. In fact, it is an affirmation of the self that's already there, a gradual recognition of "really being alive." As Carol writes, "For someone who had defined herself by fulfilling others' expectations and who had let others control her life, this looking within for meaning, knowledge, and awareness seemed radical indeed."

Joy Ritchie, Dave Wilson, and their colleagues show us not just *how* the rigor of analyzing personal narrative works, but *that* it works. It offers teachers—inside our own culture—a way to "sincerely and intensely form our identities." In short, it helps us make our own signs of "really being alive." This book advances our research on "reflective practice" and explains in detail why we must not stop telling stories, to ourselves and to each other. I wish I could tell my second grade teacher that I am really very much alive and getting on with my "real work," but that I'm still telling stories. The difference is that now I know what some of those stories mean.

                                                        Bonnie Sunstein

Acknowledgments

Throughout our work we have appreciated the ongoing cooperation and enthusiasm of the prospective and practicing teachers who participated in the study and of our colleagues in English and education who encouraged our work. Among our colleagues, Robert Brooke provided response to early drafts; Rick Evans and Larry Andrews generously welcomed participant observers into their classrooms. We are indebted to Carol MacDaniels, Sue Dauer, Sheila Reiter, and Kenneth Peterson, who conducted interviews and served as participant-observers in early phases of the project. We are grateful to Pam Grossman for her generosity in helping us develop our research protocols at the outset of our study and to Cindy DeRyke, who provided valuable assistance in preparing final drafts of the manuscript.

Our original study was supported by grants from the National Council of Teachers of English Research Foundation, the University of Nebraska-Lincoln Research Council, the University of Nebraska-Lincoln Vice Chancellor for Graduate Studies and Research, and the University of Nebraska Layman Fund.

We are grateful for the forbearance with which John Skretta, Carol MacDaniels, Ruth Kupfer, and Toni Siedel responded to our requests for yet another draft of their chapters; they have contributed invaluable insights to our ideas about teacher development. Finally, we are grateful for the patience and support of our partners, George Ritchie and David Smith, who endured our talk about narrative and teacher development when we were rafting the Tatshenshini River, hiking the Wind River Range, or just driving to the movies.

1

The Interplay of Subjectivity, Experience, and Narrative in Teacher Development

But we cannot move theory into action unless we can find it in the eccentric and wandering ways of our daily life. I have written the stories that follow to give theory flesh and breath.

—Minnie Bruce Pratt, *S/HE*

The narrative of teacher development we present in this book has been evolving over 10 years of collaborative work with teachers. Research on teacher learning and change has, until recently, focused primarily on content knowledge and pedagogy; it has too often excluded personal development in considering professional development. We argue that the development of a professional identity is inextricable from personal identity and that when personal and professional development are brought into dialogue, when teachers are given the opportunity to compose and reflect on their own stories of learning and of selfhood within a supportive and challenging community, then teachers can begin to resist and revise the scripting narratives of the culture and begin to compose new narratives of identity and practice. They can begin to author their own development.

REFLECTIONS ON OUR OWN PERSONAL AND PROFESSIONAL DEVELOPMENT

This book examines both the multiple ideologies that "script" teachers into their personal and professional identities and the processes that allow teachers to resist and revise those scripts. As we, Dave and Joy, reflect on our own professional development as English teachers, we recognize how thoroughly the personal and professional have converged in our own experience and also how our personal and professional lives have been shaped by larger social narratives and ideologies.

Joy

"How did you get derailed into teaching high school English?" asked one of my colleagues who had been on the committee that recommended my hiring. I didn't say what I might have: that I hadn't been derailed at all but had been on the very track considered appropriate for a woman in the late 1960s and early 1970s. I became a high school English teacher without much conscious reflection, but I realized later that my decisions were influenced by specific social class and gender narratives. Neither of my parents went to college, but convinced by post–World War II narratives of upward mobility and prosperity, they simply assumed that my brothers and I would and that our lives would be quite different from theirs. Like other women my age, I had few models of women in careers, and the only women I knew who had careers were teachers. The two I knew personally were my sister-in-law, Judy, who was in an English teacher education program, and her mother, Geraldine, a junior high social studies and English teacher. When I finally had to declare a major in college, I chose English because I'd been successful in my advanced placement high school classes and in several undergraduate literature classes. I was also drawn to art history, but I couldn't imagine what women art historians did. Although I didn't consciously recognize it at the time, both literature and art history embodied forms of literacy and culture linked to a higher social class identity than those I might have taken on had I chosen other acceptable paths for women by going to nursing or secretarial school. I'd bristled when my father said that my husband's graduate education would probably take precedence over mine because he would be the "breadwinner." Following another appropriate track for women, I had married as an undergraduate. I followed George, my husband, when he went to Europe for a year of study, putting my undergraduate degree on hold, and then returned to finish my undergraduate education in New York, where he was then a student, too.

On the day of my final senior seminar on James Joyce, the ROTC and members of SDS (Students for a Democratic Society) were skirmishing on the campus of Columbia University, where I was a student. The social context of the civil rights and antiwar movements of the late sixties and seventies—as well as the gender and social class roles that I had internalized—led me into teaching and continued to influence my development as a teacher. When my husband began a doctoral program at Indiana

University, I began a master's program in English, still following the proper gender track, but also—by starting my own graduate studies rather than working to support my husband's—beginning to resist my father's assertion. It was also the only next step I could see. During my first semester, then–Secretary of State Dean Rusk visited campus to speak about the war in Vietnam. George went to the speech along with other students protesting U.S. foreign policy. Although I also opposed the war, I didn't go because I was preparing a presentation for my literary scholarship seminar on some Tennyson letters from the university archives I'd been assigned to annotate. I cared much more about the war than I did about Tennyson, but I was not acting on my beliefs.

That was one of the moments when I began to wonder what purpose these graduate studies really held for me. Shortly after, I read a column by Joseph Featherstone in *The New Republic* describing Jonathan Kozol's *Death at an Early Age* (1967) and other radical educational critics. His idealistic, activist image of the teacher allowed me to consciously consider teaching as a way to put my idealistic political views into professional work that might also allow me to find a job. Getting a teaching certificate along with a master's degree was also a way to realize the new feminist slogan I was hearing, "The personal is political," and to bring my personal and professional lives into some sort of continuity.

My first year of teaching English in a newly integrated high school in North Carolina (where my husband took his first academic position) felt like an exhilarating emergence into voice and selfhood. During six years of college, I had become an increasingly quiet, "good" student in large, impersonal, almost entirely male classes in which I was the silent, passive recipient of the professors' monologues. Little in my educational experience asked me to articulate my ideas or feelings to fellow students or to the professor, and the two or three teacher preparation classes I had been required to take did little to help me develop a theory of teaching. Like the shy introvert who becomes a stand-up comic, I blossomed as a teacher in my own classroom. I loved my students, and even the most difficult seemed to respond to me. I learned most about being a teacher from conversations with my new colleagues and with Judy, my sister-in-law, who had been teaching for three or four years. One colleague, Phyliss, drove with me to a dusty warehouse in Virginia to collect overstocked paperback books for our classroom libraries; another benevolent friend gave me $100 to start a collection of Black literature and women's literature for our students, and Phyliss collected paint and art supplies for us to use in a team-taught interdisciplinary art and creative writing unit. I began to more consciously and deliberately reshape my teaching to allow students' active engagement and play with language in the hope that they would find the relevance and excitement of reading and writing for their lives.

After two years of teaching in North Carolina and another four years in Nebraska (where George had taken another university position), the institutional pressures to conform to rote, atomistic conceptions of literacy instruction became too tiresome to counter. And with a new son, I needed more flexibility. By then, beginning a Ph.D. didn't seem to be jumping the gender track at all, but rather was like taking the next train that at least some women around me were also taking. In my doctoral program, reader-response, feminist, and progressive composition theories gave me the theoretical language I needed to critique many of the assumptions about writing and literature I had developed from the formalist approaches of my own education. Participating in Nebraska Writing Project workshops, first as a student and later as a facilitator, enabled me to reexamine my own experiences as a reader and writer as well as to think critically about my teaching practices and my students' literacies. For the first time, I also became a writer, writing about my father's death and my family history and writing with and about my son, rather than writing only literary critical essays. Later, when I began a tenure-track position, I became a researcher in a women's literature class, a project that also brought me back to my own personal history as a woman and allowed me to reintegrate my personal life with my professional identities and to look at and revise the narratives that have shaped my life.

This awareness has allowed me to continue to reflect on the intersections and tensions of my identities as a woman, a mother, a wife, and teacher. A few years ago, a graduate student came to me ostensibly for advice about her graduate program. Instead she said, "What I really want to know is, can we, I mean women, really do what you're doing? Is it really possible for me to have this life? I mean, can we have it *all*, like you do?" Her question took my breath away, in part because it felt so wrong. My life is full of compromises, losses, and contradictions that she couldn't possibly see. But her question also remains an important reminder for me. Just as my educational and career tracks have been influenced by complex cultural assumptions, so are my students' responses to me as a teacher shaped by gender and other cultural narratives. I'm continually led to consider the possible implications for my students of my identity as a white, middle-class, heterosexual woman, how these factors influence the dynamics of my classroom, my interactions with students, and students' perceptions of my authority. With this continuing awareness, I can more consciously resist and revise the positions I and my students might otherwise assume for me as a teacher.

Dave

In high school when I told my guidance counselor that I wanted to be a teacher, he replied, "That would be a waste of your intelligence," and talked me into writing "pre-law" on my college applications. Once in college I switched to English, having heard from an uncle that that would be good preparation for law school. And ever prudent, I later added education as a fallback plan.

In the first education course I took, I was hooked by our graduate instructor, a young man who talked about teaching, relevancy, and social change. Later, when it came time to student teach, I joined a special inner-city program that held out the promise of crossing racial and class boundaries. From there I exported my idealism to a teaching assignment with the Peace Corps in Afghanistan, and later to religious and public schools in the United States.

Even with an emerging social consciousness, an effort at teaching for change, and multiple teaching sites where both might seem welcome, my teaching style was rather traditional. While my first education course had kindled my idealism and given me new goals for teaching, it hadn't offered me a new pedagogy. My funky young grad assistant did most of the talking, and gave quizzes, tests, and points like almost all of my other teachers had.

My conceptions of teaching were rooted in my childhood, where I was the eldest son of a teacher and a teacher's aide (the one time I skipped a class, I ran into both parents). Early on in my school career, I remember returning home each day to offer my younger siblings and teddy bears a dose of what I'd gotten. I'd line them up in rows, threaten them for silence and order, and reward them with recess. Much later I remember sitting around our dining room table on hot summer evenings with my whole family, in front of our one window air conditioner, helping Dad grade his multiple-choice driver's ed exams ("Ten is C").

Teaching for me was about power, order, and authority. I never felt so much like a teacher as I did when I gave an exam and would walk up and down silent rows of students, their heads bowed in concentration (or resignation?).

The longer I taught, however, the less satisfied I grew that my teaching was leading to change; my students seemed little different when they left my classes than they'd been when they'd entered them. But I had no vocabulary or theory with which to voice or frame my frustrations. My own teacherly development began when I moved back across the country to rural Iowa and found myself teaching with a department chair who asked me tough questions ("Tell me, Dave, have all of your worksheets made your students better writers?"), engaged me in real dialogue about learning and teaching, introduced me to thoughtful colleagues around the state, and sent me off to the Iowa Writing Project and the Bread Loaf School of English. It was in those last two settings that I finally experienced as a student not just talk of teaching for change but a new pedagogy for change.

A few years later, full of questions, I left my classroom for a doctoral program. I also left because I couldn't reconcile my emerging sense of myself as a gay man with my role as a teacher in the rural Midwest. Within a year of commencing full-time graduate work I had written and published an article on adolescent literature and homosexuality, finally beginning to integrate my sexual orientation with my sense of myself as a teacher. Course readings, dialogues with my classmates and mentors, and my new role as a teacher educator, later as a writing project instructor, and still later as a researcher in classrooms and in the writing project provided me with broader experience, community, and a vocabulary and theory for better understanding the lack of fit between my beliefs and practices.

The longer I teach (the older I get), the more my personal and professional identities seem to become integrated. Recently, as part of a peer review of teaching project, a colleague observed me teach. In our follow-up conference she noted, "Dave, you come across as a big brother in your classroom, just like you do with your colleagues and your family." I was surprised. While I'm well aware of the role I play in my own family, I hadn't been aware of the ways in which this role had seeped from my personal/familial interactions into my professional/teacherly interactions. Given my new awareness, my next challenge is to decide if I want to accept this role or resist and revise it.

OVERVIEW

Our own professional autobiographies and our work with preservice teachers have confirmed for us the impossibility of living outside ideologies of culture, gender, and literacy. Although the versions of our lives we've constructed here are shaped in relation to the themes of this book, they nevertheless illuminate for us the inextricable connections between our personal and professional development. When added to the even more detailed narratives Carol MacDaniels, Toni Siedel, John Skretta, and Ruth Kupfer have written, our narratives are indicative of the multiple and complex interplay of the personal and social in teacher development as they become visible to us when we engage in ongoing reflection, critique, and revision of those narratives. And they demonstrate the necessity of allowing those narratives to be read in dialogue with many other such narratives in order for us to see the multiplicity of paths teacher development may take. We cannot continue as teacher educators to shape programs, classes, or descriptions of teachers that ignore the interplay of personal and professional identity or that exclude multiple opportunities for teachers to engage in critical reflections upon this interplay in their own development. Nor can we suggest that teachers will develop along the lines of a single homogeneous paradigm.

In this book we argue that when preservice and experienced teachers study writing, reading, and pedagogy in contexts that also encourage them to actually write and read and compose their ideas and histories, then pedagogical or "content" learning takes on new meaning as it becomes connected with their ongoing development as people. The interplay of multiple and often conflicting narratives of professional and personal history, we believe, can provide the catalyst for reflection, critique, and "re-vision" that initiate and sustain teachers' capacity to resist confining cultural narratives and to write new narratives of teaching and living, thus recomposing themselves as teachers and as individuals.

THE CONTEXT OF THIS STUDY

This book is in large part the story of what preservice and inservice teachers have taught us about the importance of narrative as we have listened to their stories over the past 10 years. For the first three of those years (1989–92) we conducted a formal study investigating the growth of knowledge of English and teaching in 25 prospective English teachers. This project, "The Development of Knowledge of English and Teaching in Preservice English Teachers," was funded by grants from the National Council of Teachers of English (NCTE) Research Foundation, the University of Nebraska-Lincoln Research Council (UN-L), and the UN-L Chancellor for Graduate Studies and Research. The full study involved multiple interviews over six semesters, participant observation in four key courses (Composition Theory and Practice, Linguistics for the Classroom Teacher, Learning in the Classroom, and English Methods), observations of these students in their field-based preservice teaching experiences, analyses of their writing, and observation in their first year of teaching. We designed this project around the assumption that we could learn most about preservice teachers' developing conceptions of English and teaching by asking them, over the course of several semesters, to tell us the stories of their experiences in K–12 and college classrooms, stories of their writing and reading lives and of teachers who had significantly influenced them. Many of our research questions implicitly asked participants to construct narratives, often about parts of their educational lives they had never examined or "composed" before. For example, we asked questions like, "Who would you identify as the best teacher you've ever known? Why? Can you think of particular instances of good teaching? Tell us about specific incidents in that class that helped shape your understandings of teaching English." And we often asked our participants to loop back and reconsider stories they had told us earlier in light of new experiences. For example, during a semester of practicum, we asked questions like, "Two semesters ago you told us about the best teacher you'd ever had. How do your experiences in practicum help you reconsider or better understand why that teacher was so good?"

While we counted on the revelatory power of teachers' stories for us as researchers, our understanding of the importance of narratives in teaching and research also became much more complicated. We did not set out to collect narratives from teachers, but as we listened to their responses and reviewed the transcripts, we were drawn most to the narratives that emerged. We also soon suspected that composing stories of literacy learning for our project was having a crucial impact on these prospective teachers' understandings of teaching and of English. Answering our questions was not just providing us with data; it was also providing them with opportunities to articulate and reshape their understandings. Our protocols had become a pedagogy.

Subsequent to this three-year study, we continued to follow and have regular, more informal conversations with several of the teacher participants and to draw in other teachers and prospective teachers as we imagined ways to apply what we were learning about the importance of narrative, collaborative reflection, and writing for teacher development. Among these teachers are the four contributors to this book: Carol MacDaniels, Toni Siedel, Ruth Kupfer, and John Skretta. Carol and John were a part of the original cohort of preservice teachers we studied; in addition, Carol served as an interviewer and participant-observer for our initial project. Toni and Ruth were master's-degree students in English education. We have remained involved with the professional lives of these four teachers as they continue to take graduate courses from us, help us in various professional development efforts, serve as cooperating teachers for our preservice teachers, and aid us in continuing to think about the potential of narrative in teacher development.

With support from the UN-L Vice Chancellor for Academic Affairs— and after our original study—we established a collaborative professional development project that pulled together 25 teachers (including Carol and Toni) from eastern Nebraska to reflect on the forces that had shaped them as teachers and to articulate their teaching autobiographies and their present beliefs and understandings of teaching and English.

Our narrative in this book has been shaped by the interplay among various narratives: preservice and experienced teachers' narratives of their own learning; the narratives that we—Joy and Dave—have brought to our listening from our own experiences in English and education; and the theoretical narratives that have shaped our understandings. In this chapter we address several overlapping issues:

- exploring issues of identity and subjectivity
- applying theories of subjectivity to teacher development
- experience and theory in teacher development
- narrative in teacher development literature
- problematizing narrative in teaching and research
- narrative as action
- narrative in our research

Although we see all of these crucial issues as interconnected, here we briefly outline the theoretical assumptions concerning each of them in order to help readers understand our perspective more clearly in the stories that follow in subsequent chapters.

EXPLORING ISSUES OF IDENTITY AND SUBJECTIVITY

Identity/subjectivity as a central issue in teacher development emerged for us as we listened to preservice teachers compose and revise their narratives of learning and as we later continued to listen to their narratives of professional development as they moved into their first few years of teaching. When we began this study, our understanding of identity/subjectivity was much less fully examined and less complicated than are our current understandings of the political and ideological forces that shape us as teachers and as persons. Our earlier view of teacher identity was loosely linked to the liberal humanist tradition and constructed teachers as unique, autonomous individuals. Throughout the book, we use both terms: *identity* and *subjectivity*. We are aware of the different theoretical implications of these two terms—that "identity" is much more associated with a more traditional humanistic, Enlightenment, notion that sees the self as rational, unified, singular, simple, autonomous, and consciously self-chosen, whereas "subjectivity" connotes the postmodern under-

standing of the individual as socially constructed, complicated, fragmented, contradictory, and fluid. We naïvely thought of teachers as autonomous agents who, when immersed in a carefully designed English
teacher education program, would then be "transformed" through that
experience into the kind of teachers we had envisioned in designing our
program. We even used such language in our first conference presentations and journal publications from the study. We can now see the difficulties in our simplistic view of identity, our use of "conversion" metaphors, and our assumption that preservice teachers would be and could
be converted from their positivistic, "current traditional" notions of language and learning to our progressive, student-centered notions. In particular, we did not yet see fully the powerful array of ideologies that had
already shaped students' views of teaching and language, or how the
very transformation we sought was also an attempt to regulate, control,
and shape teachers and was part of yet another ideology of education,
one that we were not making visible to ourselves or to our students.

We were, then, viewing the choices available to preservice teachers
in simplistic and binary terms. They could, we imagined, remain entrenched in traditional conceptions of language and teaching, which conceive of reading and writing as linear, silent, solitary processes best
taught in steps through the mastery of discrete skills, with an overall
focus on form and correctness by teachers who see their task as the authoritative transmission of information. Or our preservice teachers could
be transformed/converted to our process-centered, progressive model,
which conceives of language learning as lifelong, socially mediated, interactive processes best taught by teachers who view their task as creating contexts for their students to engage the word and the world and
make sense from that engagement. We failed to take into account the
array of contending social and political ideologies calling out to them via
their own experience in schools, the stories and advice of family and
friends, and cultural representations of teaching and literacy learning.
We failed to take into account a postmodern, complicated view of subjectivity and the self. And we also saw teacher development as a linear,
rational or cognitive process, without recognizing both the ideological
and the personal forces shaping our students and us (for example, the
effects of white male privilege that John Skretta explores in Chapter 7 or
the role Ruth Kupfer's identity as a lesbian has played, which she explores
in Chapter 8). Just as the humanistic view of the writer and language
learner often fails to see students as sites of contradiction, as being
scripted by conflicting social and political forces, we also failed to see
preservice teachers as similar sites of contention.

We have benefited from what has become in the last decade a commonplace critique of the Enlightenment view of identity in English and composition studies. Similarly, expressivism, a term that has come to suggest a focus on the development of voice through process-oriented, student-centered pedagogies, has too often been conceived as apolitical, failing to take into account the realities of race, gender, and class that shape language learning. Expressivism has been criticized for leaving students unprepared to analyze and address conflicting and repressive positions. In its calls for liberatory education, expressivism often fails to acknowledge its own ideological and potentially prescriptive authority and the position of those who become subject to that "liberation"; and it does not take into account the multiple, fragmented, and overlapping positions of individuals and the way those positions are controlled through discursive narratives of education, gender, and class (see, for example, Myers, 1996; Jarratt, 1991). Similar critiques have been made about the psychological-cognitive bias of educational psychology as it continues to influence teacher education. Colleges of education have often presented the teacher as a rational agent whose pedagogical decisions emerge from a single intellectual position provided by teacher education. This thinking has also dominated and restricted thinking about how teachers develop because it always posits "individual" needs above the "social" rather than seeing them as interrelated (McWilliam, 1994). Education's embrace of individuality contributes to an uncomplicated view of teacher agency and learning.

We can now see the ways in which our earlier view also drew on the assumption that the teachers we worked with would be shaped by the rational discourses and experiences of English education (through the theories we presented in carefully chosen texts, classes, and field experiences). But as our project progressed, we were moving away from this idealistic view of individual student as autonomous and unconnected to broader contingencies of history and language. For example, we began to find Bakhtin's (1975/1981) theoretical perspectives useful to theorize the competing and conflicting ideologies that shaped our students' concepts of language and learning. And implicitly we did understand the power of political and ideological forces in shaping our own lives and the lives of our students, although we had a less well articulated understanding of ideology even as we acted on an understanding of its power in our practice. In our teaching each of us sought to acknowledge and work against ideological narratives surrounding masculinity and femininity, for example. Feminist and gay and lesbian rights issues had brought us to this political understanding. Joy taught a women's literature mini-class in her high school in the 1970s, and Dave was writing about gay and lesbian literature for adolescents. But we did not as clearly see how our own positions were part of larger ideologies of identity. Nor did we see how preservice teachers were also contending with multiple issues of identity.

APPLYING THEORIES OF SUBJECTIVITY TO TEACHER DEVELOPMENT

We began our study of teacher development just as postmodern and feminist theories of subjectivity began to have much more play in our field. As our study evolved, we started to view students and ourselves in a much more complicated light. First we began to see more clearly our own ideological positions and the way they often came into conflict with other powerful educational ideologies. For example, the conflicting and hierarchical relations between English and English education, between literary studies and composition, between college and K–12 teachers, and between educational psychological views of learning and anthropological/linguistic views produced conflicts for us and for our students. Students often experienced competing conceptions of reading in their adolescent literature class and in their British literature class and vastly different conceptions of writing in their university composition theory class and in the ninth grade English class in which they observed and taught during their practicum. As these conflicts became evident to us in the narratives preservice teachers constructed of their experiences, we saw how the narratives of teaching in our culture are embedded within much more powerful ideologies of identity. For example, at several key points in our research we noticed that teachers who had seemingly been "transformed" or converted to constructivist perspectives on language learning while they were preservice teachers were pulled back toward the educational ideology of the schools in which they were teaching. In these teachers' stories we saw the multiple ideologies of schooling and personhood as they intersected in teachers' lives. No longer could we point to a single set of opposing ideologies, but instead we were beginning to see how multiple ideologies of gender, race, and class, along with ideologies of authority and the meaning of education and the role of the teacher, all intersected to form powerful narratives "calling out" to the teachers with whom we were working.

Our present understanding of subjectivity in teacher education is informed by feminist theorists and their translation of Louis Althusser's theories of ideology and the processes by which an ideology produces people who conform to a set of social norms. Althusser's work (1971) has enabled feminist and other theorists to critique social structures that

seem to be "natural" or given. He argues that "ideological state apparatuses," the discourses, institutions, and social practices that comprise social life, "hail" individuals and provide the constructs by which they
come to recognize themselves (or misrecognize themselves), in Althusser's terms. For example, the pervasive 1950s image of family as found in
Life, Look, and television shows like *Father Knows Best* promoted an ideology of family that called out to us, telling us what we ought to aspire to
and how to define ourselves, making us blind to the real-world variations
in family configurations. We found especially relevant to teacher development Althusser's description of the process by which language and other
social rituals are internalized and become the source of our understanding and definition of ourselves. The social rituals of 12 or 14 years of
schooling become the source of preservice teachers' definitions of learning and of their own identities as teachers. Narratives of teacher authority
and control were powerful in shaping Dave's conception of himself as a
teacher, for example. Joy failed to question her position as a silent, "good"
student in her education because it seemed consistent with narratives in
the culture concerning women's behavior. Because of the powerful sense
that institutions and their rituals are just "natural," "the way things are,"
it is difficult to find the gaps and contradictions through which to open
a critique of those dominant perspectives.

Feminist theories, which have extended and qualified Althusser's
work, provide insight about critical strategies for critique and resistance.
They also resonate with our belief that human subjects, while constituted
by powerful ideologies, nevertheless also have the means to resist, revise,
and subvert the prescriptions of ideology. As we have watched teachers
develop over several years, we've come to see, as Judith Butler (1990)
suggests, that if we conceive of teacher subjectivity as an "effect that is
produced or generated" (p. ix) by multiple institutions, discourses, and
practices, new possibilities also open up for agency. The understanding
that human identity isn't "natural" or something fixed or essential, but
that it is always an effect or construction of complex and competing
forces, allows much more play and possibility for intervention. In Butler's
(1990) argument about gender construction she speaks of gender identity
as "performances" of cultural scripts and argues that cross-dressing or
other forms of gender play are ways to highlight the constructedness of
gender and to subvert those constructions. Further, she says, "Construction is not opposed to agency; it is the necessary scene of agency, the very
terms in which agency is articulated and becomes culturally intelligible"
(p. 147). If women can also understand their identities as constructions
rather than as solely natural or innate, they can resist and subvert those

cultural scripts and begin to write new versions, new roles for themselves that in fact more truthfully and fully represent the varieties of female gender expressions.

What Butler (1990) argues for women, then, we also see as potentially true for teacher identity. Teachers need opportunities to see teacher identities as performative, as "effects" or constructions rather than as natural, inevitable, or essential. For example, Toni Siedel, who tells her story in a later chapter, was able to make sense of her situation at school when she saw that the authoritative "scientific" language of expertise in traditional writing instruction was being used in her school to diminish her own authority as a young female teacher. As she began to analyze that authoritative discourse through the perspective of progressive theories of language learning and later through feminist theory, she gained both a theoretical and an experiential standpoint from which to deconstruct and then to subvert and resist those narratives (Hennessy, 1993; Weedon, 1987). In other words, she saw that a theory, a narrative of language learning—not an absolute truth—was being used to attempt to determine how she taught and how she thought about her authority as a woman. When she could view it as a construction, as an "effect" of ideology, she could critique it, analyze it, and make decisions about its relationship to her as a feminist teacher. John Skretta, in a later chapter, makes similar moves as he writes about his identity as a white middle-class male.

When teachers come to see that they reside as teachers and persons at the intersections of various educational, gender, and social class ideologies, they then can make decisions about who they will be, about what identity they choose to "perform," as Carol illustrates in her later chapter. This process occurs over time and, we argue, is supported by the dialogue and reflection made possible when teachers compose narrative representations of their ideas and experiences. That process is never finished or fully complete, but is an ongoing process that requires a supportive climate of reflection and dialogue to sustain it. The teacher narratives in this book—those written by Toni, Ruth, John, and Carol—suggest to us that when teachers can consciously locate the sites of their resistance to prescriptive ideologies of personal and professional identity, they have the possibility of intervening in them and contesting them.

EXPERIENCE AND THEORY IN TEACHER DEVELOPMENT

As teachers and scholars, we value the material, experiential, local, daily lived experience; we believe that attention to practice is important. But we also believe that experience—whether in our personal lives or in our classrooms—does not provide us with "authentic" uncontested truth. All experience is interpreted, valued, and felt through particular perspectives. The problematic relationship between theory and experience/practice has also remained a constant question in this study. In academic circles over the past decade, theory has often held a privileged position over experience or pedagogy in literacy and English studies, and too much attention to experience has been demeaned for its lack of critical rigor. Add to that the common assumption that teachers often reject theory as too abstract, too difficult, and too removed from experience or practice, and the theory/experience dichotomy becomes more vexed. Our study has helped us see how this binary also shapes the dilemmas that arise for students and teacher educators. It has become more crucial for us to attempt to establish a reciprocal, dialogic relationship between theory and experience in the opportunities we attempt to provide our students.

The problem is not that experience—either in the accidental apprenticeship or the deliberate apprenticeship in teacher education (or in one's personal life)—is too personal or local, and therefore invalid. The problem is that experience is often left untheorized. Without the opportunity for critical analysis of experience, teachers and students have no way to see how their experience is itself constructed in and through language and through institutional and cultural ideologies. Indeed, it is a central premise of this book that the reconstruction and reconsideration of experience through narrative is crucial for teachers to achieve critical literacy. Teachers need theoretical language to help them see the competing and conflicting narratives of learning and teaching. As we will see in Toni's narrative, she needed the authoritative language of theory to critique the authoritative theories that attempted to shape her pedagogy as a beginning teacher, just as she needed feminist theories to help her critique the narratives that situated her as a female in the culture.

In understanding the value and the limitations of teachers' uses of experience, we have found the work of feminists Joan Scott (1992) and Rosemary Hennessy (1993) particularly useful. Both address experience as a construct, but they suggest ways to continue to value experience as a source of knowledge while also suggesting ways to theorize experience in order to make it a more critical and revisionary tool. In her essay "Experience," Scott (1992) says:

> When experience is taken as the origin of knowledge, the vision of the individual subject (the person who had the experience or the historian who recounts it) becomes the bedrock of evidence upon which explanation is built.

Questions about the constructed nature of experience, about how subjects
are constituted as different in the first place, and how one's vision is structured—about language (or discourse) and history—are left aside. (p. 25)

Scott (1992) reminds us that experience should be encountered not
as truth but as a construct or representation mediated by culture, context,
history, and language, and that seeing it this way can serve as the catalyst
for further analysis of the conditions that shape experience. But Hennessy
(1993) adds an important critical strategy for ensuring that experience is
not narrowly read: any critical theorizing of experience must be continually recontextualized in a reexamination of the relationships between personal and group history and, of further importance, they must be read
in relation to the critical discourses of "others" (p. 99). Hennessy is suggesting that one's individual experience cannot be analyzed or understood in the most comprehensive terms until it is placed in a larger context. Experience is seductive because it seems so immediate, so authentic,
and so grounded. But experience is not neutral or authentic. As John's
story demonstrates, the experience of white male middle-class teachers is already embedded in and shaped by language and the politics
of whiteness and class and must be read against the grain of "others'"
experiences—women, Black, lesbian, poor, wealthy, or disabled students
and teachers. This requires a much different critical context than one that
simply elicits and validates experience without also providing the recon-
textualizing theory to reexamine and revise those experiences. In this
book, it is the multiple nature of four teachers' experiences, read in dialogue with each other, that provides opportunities to reread the complexity of teacher development.

At the beginning of our study, we thought of teachers' development
as linked to their position as rational, "experiencing" individuals, and
although we understood that preservice teachers needed a theoretical
foundation, we may have placed more emphasis on providing them with
crucial experiences to shape their learning, even though we realized that
in our own development as teachers we needed a language and a set of
theories about language and learning to help us set goals and to interpret
experiences in classrooms. We did not at first see that we needed to help
students analyze and interpret the contradictions between the experiences we were providing them and their previous experiences in their
"accidental apprenticeships," their countless hours spent as students in
K–college classrooms.

We found, however, that preservice teachers were often still enthralled by their prior experiences in a particular high school English
class that had become for them *the* experience on which they based many

of their assumptions about teaching. The conceptions of English and teaching they constructed from that experience often interfered with their ability to consider alternative models for teaching English, and thus they resisted any new theory or practice, even when they felt it had transformed them as readers or writers.

We came to realize that neither their accidental nor their deliberate apprenticeships had provided students with a language, a set of theoretical constructs, to allow them to see the assumptions behind the competing practices they were immersed in. And furthermore, they had not had opportunities even to recognize and articulate the conflicts, much less the conflicting theories that created them. No one had asked them: "What assumptions about learning, about language, reading, or writing, are at play in a given practice?" "Why did your teacher teach as she did?" "How might others in your school or class have experienced that same learning environment differently?" Because they couldn't see the conflicts or their own particular perspectives, they either resisted new theories or pedagogies or simply practiced an additive model of learning in which one could endlessly add new strategies or methods to one's repertoire.

We also found that even when preservice teachers had opportunities to theorize their experience and had acquired a metalanguage, some theories were simply more powerful than others, depending on the institutional context in which the preservice teacher was working. Their prior experience or the experience of others with whom they were teaching at the moment often carried more authority than all the meta-awareness and theoretical understanding. For example, even when preservice teachers had claimed that their experience in a reader-response literature class was empowering and life-changing, we found that they often invested more authority in text-centered approaches to teaching when they found themselves in a particular school culture that privileged more formalistic approaches. But that is not only because students lacked a strong theoretical background or because they failed to theorize their experience. The choices they finally made as teachers were more complicated. Other theories and other experiences—those having to do with their identities, their dreams, their sense of belonging, their relationship to the community— often won out, as we demonstrate in Chapter 3. As a result, we had to consider why some experiences were more valued or powerful than others.

Some of the students with whom we work actively resist theory, saying that they simply want to know what to do, to be told what will or won't "work" in classrooms, and that they don't want to read a lot of philosophizing or theorizing about it, because what counts is the immediate day-to-day decisionmaking they must do. Experienced teachers, too, are often hostile or cynical about theory because they feel as though they've seen it all before. For them, theory is yet another attempt by those with more power (university researchers and theorists or administrators) to impose another mandate on them, seeking to control and regulate their practice. Experienced teachers also create an "ideal" versus "real" dichotomy in which theory is abstract and acontextual, incapable of being useful in the real contexts in which they see themselves working. These concerns are genuine. As feminist philosopher Sandra Harding (1991) and others have argued, experiential claims made by people whose life experience has always been marginalized, as teachers' often has been, often are devalued and dismissed by dominant perspectives that are deemed more objective or scientific. The teacher-research movement has been one attempt not only to help teachers reclaim authority for their experience, but also to ground it in theory.

But the risk is that teachers and researchers, ourselves included, hold onto a theory/practice or theory/experience dichotomy that limits our thinking about what controls and regulates practice. For many teachers, theory is not something to talk back to. In Bakhtin's (1975/1981) framework, theory can function like "authoritative discourse," which like religious or legal texts is fixed and powerful and demands our allegiance. When teachers talk back to theories, making them "internally persuasive discourse . . . half ours and half someone else's" (pp. 345–346), theories can be dynamic, can lead to productive dialogue and generative reflection in the way that teachers like Toni, Carol, Ruth, and John have done.

In addition, it is important to see that preservice and inservice teachers who seem to want only to talk about immediate practice, about "what works for me" or what has "worked" for others, are not lacking a theory. They are basing their assumptions about "what works" on a set of theoretical assumptions, albeit unconsciously, or without articulating them clearly. And it is as misguided for us to think of teachers as lacking theory as it is for teachers to think of themselves as not needing or using theory. It is true that we researchers, given the context in which we operate, our reward systems, our teaching loads, often do have access to knowledge, to theories, to a metalanguage or set of metanarratives about teaching and language learning to which teachers have not historically had access. On the other hand, we often lose contact with the very K–12 classroom contexts that would allow our theories to be more consistently informed by experience. Or we present theory in a way that makes it seem "authoritative" rather than dialogic, not enabling us to talk back to it and use it to strengthen our work. We need to be reminded and to help students understand that rather than being "real," fixed, and empirically established, the meaning of experience *and* of theory must be continually open to revision and dialogue as the participants, the contexts, and the perspectives change, as narratives are revised and retold.

NARRATIVE IN TEACHER DEVELOPMENT LITERATURE

The confusing and contradictory narratives of teaching and literacy in our culture often construct teachers' identities and practices in ways that subvert their real potential to develop as teachers, diminishing their authority and undermining potentially powerful conceptions of teaching, literacy, and selfhood. Students bring these unexamined narratives with them into a teacher education program and into their teaching careers. They constitute an "accidental" apprenticeship in teaching, as in Dave's experience of grading his father's multiple-choice exams around the dining room table. They interact with other authoritative narratives of language and pedagogy to shape teachers' practices in schools.

We recognize that narrative has become omnipresent in educational research and, more specifically, in the literature of composition, literacy studies, and teacher development. As Maxine Greene says, "The sounds of storytelling are everywhere today" (in Witherell & Noddings, 1991, p. ix). This impulse has developed from the significant anthropological turn that our discipline has taken in the last decades, marked by the publication of Heath's *Ways with Words* (1983) and by the early case studies of Emig (1971), Graves (1983), and Calkins (1983). It also was prompted by the emergence of feminist theories of knowledge such as *Women's Ways of Knowing* (Belenky, Clinchy, Goldberger, & Tarule, 1986) as applied and complicated in books like *Stories Lives Tell: Narrative and Dialogue in Education* (Witherell & Noddings, 1991), *Educating Feminists: Life Histories and Pedagogies* (Middleton, 1992), and *Learning from Our Lives: Women, Research, and Autobiography in Education* (Neumann & Peterson, 1997).

We see an evolution in the use of narrative. Earlier, teachers' stories were dismissed as mere anecdote; they often remained unexamined, unproblematized, and untheorized. Then, with the emergence of work like that mentioned above, narrative gained force as a research methodology. It often provided the most compelling and persuasive form in which to present ideas about teaching, because stories, like teaching, are rich with context and peopled with individuals. In focusing on the stories of six beginning teachers, Grossman (1990) gives life to the complexities of content and pedagogical knowledge in English among beginning teachers and the role of subject-specific coursework in contributing to their knowledge and beliefs about English. Ruth Vinz (1996) in *Composing a Teaching*

Life uses narratives of her own and several other teachers' lives as prompts to readers to research and reconsider the stories of their own teaching. In *Inside/Outside*, Cochran-Smith and Lytle (1993) document how experienced teachers engage in inquiry and dialogue to reexamine their schools, their teaching, and their students. In this project, teachers narrate their experiences in reflective journals, student case studies, and anthropological inquiry into the culture of their classrooms and schools. Many of these books that employ narrative as a form of research draw from cultural criticism and the critical pedagogical perspectives of Freire (1986), Giroux (1983), and others from postmodern or feminist theories.

More recently, with a growing understanding that teachers embody their knowledge in narrative and as a part of the move to value teacher knowledge and teacher perspectives, teacher narrative has become a tool for teacher development. Rather than dismissing teacher stories as "mere anecdote," teacher educators have come to use stories, inviting preservice and inservice teachers to tell, reflect on, and dialogue about stories from their teaching lives. We now have many excellent books documenting the ways in which teachers have been prompted to tell stories of schools, classrooms, and students, documenting teacher thinking and learning in a variety of settings (for example, Hollingsworth and Cody's *Teacher Research and Urban Literacy Education*, 1994, or Gitlin et al., *Teachers' Voices for School Change*, 1992). These collections of stories function in at least two ways: first, they serve as ongoing justifications for the importance of teacher narrative (for example, Jalongo & Isenberg's *Teachers' Stories: From Personal Narrative to Professional Insight*, 1995). And second, many of these books also serve as persuasive arguments for reform of schools and document the processes by which teacher change can occur. Teachers' stories are used as evidence to support arguments. But they also function collectively to provide our discipline with a rich, thick, varied mosaic of schools, students, and teachers' lives, perhaps aiding attempts to break out of educational straitjackets. In Wasley's *Stirring the Chalkdust: Tales of Teachers Changing Classroom Practice* (1994), Wilson's *Attempting Change: Teachers Moving from Writing Project to Classroom Practice* (1994), and Hynds's *On the Brink: Negotiating Literature and Life with Adolescents* (1997), the authors show teachers in the midst of change and arguing for change.

Our book parallels, overlaps, is indepted to, and builds on these other works in several ways. As we listened to the stories that we prompted teachers like John, Carol, Toni, and Ruth to tell, narratives became more than products for our consumption as teachers and researchers. They became a catalyst for revising our own thinking about teacher development. We also came to see more specifically that narrative can become the means by which teachers can resist and revise the prescribed narratives and roles of their personal and professional lives. The stories teachers construct about their own experiences as learners, and about their lives and their students' lives within and outside educational institutions, can become what feminist theorist Teresa de Lauretis (1984) calls a "critical instrument" illuminating the ideologies—the stories—by which their lives and teaching practices are constructed. Such narrative investigation allows teachers to connect professional learning and their practice as teachers with their ongoing development as people. In that active use of language, identity and practice may be revised and forged anew. Narrative, then, is not merely a precursor to revision and change in teachers' lives; in forcing us to compose, articulate, and reinterpret our lives, it can move us toward action.

PROBLEMATIZING NARRATIVE IN TEACHING AND RESEARCH

We also recognize that narratives in teacher education have sometimes been romanticized; after the initial writing or telling of the story, they often fall short of the next crucial step: critique or problematizing. Those of us who use narrative in teacher education must ask: What is the context in which the story is told? Where are the gaps, the silences, the tensions, the omissions? What narratives from other lives might contradict or complicate our own? Who is privileged by these narratives? What positions and relationships do they reinforce?

There are further problems in using narrative in our teaching or our research. The narrator is tempted to reinvent her past in order to give meaning to her present. In constructing narratives of our practice and our experience, we often selectively recall past behaviors in order to make them consistent with our current situations, attitudes, and understandings. Also, most storytellers want to please their audience, and if we as their teachers are seen as a primary part of their audience, then to what extent are preservice or inservice teachers shaping their narratives consciously or unconsciously to please us? The teacher, like the researcher, inevitably intrudes—shaping through questions, tone, nonverbal cues, pauses, interruptions, and encouragement—the students' (or the research participant's) responses.

Pedagogies that rely on narrative have also been challenged recently for feminizing teaching and for lacking rigor. While students may feel supported and nurtured in classrooms in which their own stories are privileged, thus creating relationships between students and teachers, recently there has been considerable discussion and debate about feminized or maternal pedagogies (Schell, 1998). In these pedagogies that value collaboration rather than competition, that attempt to promote nurture rather than conflict, and that displace authority from teacher to students, the teacher becomes one who establishes caring, supportive, and interdependent relationships with and among students. But critiques of such approaches argue that they do not confront and promote but instead suppress differences in the classroom, that they support white middle-class values, and that they fail to prepare students to critique repressive positions. Others see them as potentially exploitative because they may feed into the teachers' needs and desires rather than those of students. And still others, especially women, believe that such pedagogies of "care" jeopardize women teachers, whose authority is often already called into question by virture of their gender alone (and further questioned if the teacher is a minority or young woman) and who may find white majority students further questioning their authority if they seem nurturing or soft (see Jarratt, 1991; Yee, 1991). Schell (1998) argues that this strain of "maternal" caring pedagogies has reinforced the feminizing of teaching and thus continues to shore up the low status of teachers in a culture that sees the feminine as less powerful and less valuable.

NARRATIVE AS ACTION

Despite the problematic nature of narrative, and its often reductive use in education, we continue to see it as a critical instrument, a form of language as action for revision of teaching and self. This is not a new idea, of course. That sense of narrative is as old as Western culture—from Plato's *Phaedrus* (1973) and *Gorgias* (1960) to Augustine's *Confessions* (1991), to Paulo Freire's *Pedagogy of the Oppressed* (1986) and Audre Lorde's (1984a) "Transformation of Silence into Language and Action." But despite the long history of this conception of language, narrative as potential action, it has sometimes been difficult for us in English education to enact that in our pedagogies.

One vital model of how narrative serves as a form of action is in the theory and pedagogy of Paulo Freire (1986). Freire's theory and method set forth the process of *conscientization*, learning or knowing as a process of both reflection and action. In order to come to understanding or knowlege, individuals have to name or identify their own lives and realities. For the peasants with whom Freire worked, the process involved the literal naming and writing of the words around which their lives revolved. For students and teachers, it also involves the active naming and narrating of the concrete realities of lives in and out of classrooms. That naming and narrating become a way to produce generative themes or issues in one's life and work. In this book, for example, John's theme of masculine privilege emerged in writing and rewriting his experiences for our study and later for our book. The narrative itself is a form of interpretation, analyzing, and finding meaning, and, as Carol argues later, it becomes the first step in locating the tensions and unspoken silences in one's life. In Freire's (1986) pedagogy, the *conscientization* process enables learners to gain access to the power of the alphabet. Through articulating the word, learners can then also gain access to the power to read the world around them, extending the interpretive power of language and building the possibility for action. We argue that in teacher education, this process of naming and reading their world and their words gives teachers access to the power of reflection and reinterpretation—and thus to resistance and revision.

Even as Freire's work in Brazil was beginning, American feminists were employing a version of this process in often maligned consciousness-raising groups, a process that in fact was linked to action in many women's lives, and which feminist theorists as diverse as Teresa de Lauretis (1984) and Carolyn Heilbrun (1988) argue we cannot do without. Still other literary theorists and cognitive psychologists have explored the impact of reading and telling stories. For example, Paul Ricoeur (1983) says that stories are models for redescribing the world, and David Lodge says, "Narrative is one of the fundamental sense-making operations of the mind" (quoted in McEwan & Egan, 1995, p. 141). Reading our students' stories enables us as teachers and scholars to glimpse the sense that our students are making. And it's also important for our students to make sense and to do it overtly, so that they can then examine, critique, and revise that sense. The active use of language in constructing written and spoken narratives makes that possible.

Telling the story of one's life is often a way of stepping back and making it an object of reflection, of spectating on one's life. Cognitive psychologists call this decentering; it allows one to step outside the busyness and make of it all some meaning, some sense. Huberman says:

> When decentering is in play, there emerges the real possibility of unfreezing one's current vision of oneself and moving it to another place, cognitively speaking. For some phenomenologists, and for many critical theorists, interactive interviewing around teachers' autobiographies is a royal road to attitude change and, from there, to a sort of emancipation from the grooved ways of thinking about one's work . . . Exploring one's life as a teacher can, and often does, open up alternative ways of reconstruing ways of acting and being in the classroom and, from there, of shaping another career path. (Huberman, in McEwan & Egan, 1995, p. 131)

There is a vital link between narrative and human action. McEwan and Egan (1995) say:

> In form, a narrative is basically extended language configured in such a way that its earlier embodiment in life becomes revealed . . . Narrative . . . takes shape . . . as a rhythm that ultimately springs from patterns implicit in human life and action. (p. vii)

The potential for teacher change—teachers revising their conceptions of and practices surrounding language learning—is not located in programs or classes that do something *to* teachers or give teachers new methods or information. Instead, change is made possible and becomes sustainable when teachers gain critical perspective on how their identities have been constructed by/in the culture and how the cultural narratives of teaching have shaped their personal and professional subjectivities. When teachers use writing and reading to name and interpret their own histories, the narratives they compose can begin to reveal the contradictions and conflicts among their own complex subjectivities. Recognizing those contradictions makes it possible for teachers to resist and revise the hegemonic narratives of teaching and learning that position them as teachers and as individuals. In turn, as the teachers in this book suggest, they may more fully understand the social and political implications of literacy for students and help students use writing and reading to become self-reflective and critically literate citizens.

NARRATIVE IN OUR RESEARCH

Our personal and professional lives are articulated and defined by narrative. They are also woven together by the narrative communities in which we work. It makes sense to us now, in looking back on our work together, that we focus this book, in part, on the multiple uses of narrative in teacher development. Narrative as a way of knowing has long been a focus of our work as teachers and researchers, and it has been the glue of collaboration and friendship. Early on in our collaboration we discovered that Joy often came to our work sessions expecting to immediately begin writing. Joy mentally shifted gears as she walked the two blocks from her office to Dave's. Dave, on the other hand, always seemed to need to start our work sessions with catch-up stories about what was happening in other areas of our professional and personal lives. We talked about classes we were teaching, our lives as then-untenured faculty members, departmental politics, our students, and our families. We began to see that this talk was not unrelated to the research we were doing, that in fact we were using narrative to make sense of our lives inside and outside the academy, and to assert our identities. When we began working together, we had only met each other recently. Our conversations allowed us to introduce ourselves and our histories to each other as a way of establishing an individual identity so that we could forge a collaborative identity and relationship. This, we now believe, enabled us to work together better in spite of our differing styles and the seemingly inevitable distance between an English department and a college of education.

Our focus on narrative in teaching and learning also makes sense to us because we both began our careers as secondary English teachers and grew up in the discipline surrounded by the work of theorists who argued for the principal role narrative plays in learning. We each have observed the interpretive power that writing stories of life experience has had for students, young and old, in our writing classes and in summer writing projects and institutes. We have experienced firsthand and have witnessed in others the "conversion" teachers and students experience when they are given permission and the opportunity to write what is important to them, when writing becomes a means of naming, interpreting, and revising one's life. As we've continued to theorize and problematize the function of these narratives and to become suspicious of conversions, we've also grown to see the ways in which even these conversion stories are already written by the culture, are not just the expression of an authentic inner self, and how as teachers we can encourage students to examine and critique their own life narratives and their conversions.

Narrative had also been central to our research. Before we began this study, we had each already conducted ethnographic research in which we had elicited, recorded, and retold the narratives of those who had participated in our research. We valued the narrative form of research that fleshed out rather than stripped away the rich contexts in which students' and teachers' understandings emerged, and we believed in the reliability of stories as data. While narrative had been central to our lives as teachers and as researchers, we had either not fully theorized or had undervalued the uses of narrative in teacher education and change. We had also not yet complicated our understandings of narrative, its reliability and its complex psychological, social, and political purposes.

We want to acknowledge some of what we've learned about the nature of stories as we collected, interpreted, and reconstructed them, turning them into our own research narratives. We realize that there is never one true story, one true or neutral perspective on experience. We acknowledge that we may have shaped students' stories from the initial utterance when we first devised the questions for interviews, influenced them by the pose we struck as interviewers, by the relationships we developed with students during interviews, and later by our work with them as colleagues. We recognize that what we were asking students to do was not risk-free. Although we were not asking for intimate details from their lives, even in composing one's literacy autobiography painful and delicate matters are exposed (childhood estrangement, divorce, teenage pregnancy, single parenthood, interracial relationships). John, Toni, Ruth, and Carol—and also David and Joy—have experienced the alienation that also comes from telling one's story (or having it told by others), from placing one's life in a frame and then reinterpreting it. As Grumet (1991) says, telling our stories "requires giving oneself away" (p. 70).

Given the potential risk in telling stories, we also want to acknowledge that some stories cannot be, should not be, and are not complete. This is true for multiple reasons: first, we might not know the whole story; second, we might not be willing to face or address the whole story; third, it might be unwise or we might be unwilling to share parts of our story with others. Because stories are not innocent, we also recognize that we cannot afford to read them or rewrite them naïvely or carelessly. Just as there is no "true" story, there is no single "true retelling" of a story. The stories here are a version of stories we listened to. We've taken them from their context and reframed them, recontextualized them, often in a theoretical frame the original teller of the story might not even have considered. Our retellings of the narratives students told us may misrepresent or interpret their experiences in ways they wouldn't recognize. The "I" speaking in a transcript we reread in writing this book no longer exists as that same "I," just as the "I" or "we" writing these words will no longer exist by the time the manuscript is published. We may seem to label or "fix" these narratives in some static category, even though we suspect that our participants and we ourselves may not recognize or want to own the words uttered last year or last month. Many of these stories bear the imprint of several years of reflection and revision. Where possible, we allow those who participated in the research to speak for themselves, including their transcribed words, and sometimes we ask those participants to write their own stories or rewrite ours.

We also learned again that the space between the self that tells and the self that listens is fluid (Grumet, 1991, p. 70). Sometimes we felt we were keeping a respectful distance from the stories students told us. But stories are seductive, persuasive, permeable. They pull us toward them: they may even take us over. From the tapes and transcripts of interviews, from the pages of journals and student writing, certain stories called out

to us and drew us in. The stories we include in this book are not inno-
cently or objectively chosen; they are stories that we found illuminating
and emblematic of the issues that teachers confront in their learning and
development. They were stories that moved us, that we found compelling
because they resonated with our own understandings of language learning and teacher learning. In some cases, we realize that these are the
stories in which we feel deeply and personally implicated, stories that
may have explained something to us about our own experiences as
people and as teachers.

We recognized this most forcefully as we wrote about Carol as a case
study, a version of which is now Chapter 4. As we also considered the
transactional nature of interpretation and the always subjective nature of
our ways of reading the word and the world, we had to consider why we
were using Carol's story. Why did Carol's story become for us an iconic
narrative about teacher education? The identifications and transferences
at work in any act of reading were also part of our reading of Carol's
story. Although we suspect that Joy's shared experience with Carol as a
woman growing up in the 1950s and 1960s and Dave's experience as an
outsider growing up gay in a small town may be implicated in our reading of Carol's story, we can never fully comprehend the connections we
are drawing on. In ways of which we were at first unaware, we now recognize that Carol's story, as we heard it, resonated with our own stories and
became yet another way for us to understand our own development as
teachers and as people.

As researchers, we can't escape being implicated in the narratives we
gather to do our work. The writing of Ruth Behar (1996) and others has
helped us to understand the way we've been pulled in by these stories.
Our research, like our teaching, brings us into intimate contact with lives,
developing close relationships that Carol described as "caring" and
"love." We find ourselves captivated by and transformed by these lives.
As surely as our contact with Carol, as she claims, helped her "transform"
her life, she has changed us. We might have attempted to maintain the
stance of objective researchers, but we believe that to do this would be
to deny the nature of the relationships that narrative ways of knowing
presuppose and bring about. We need to make ourselves vulnerable to
these stories and to those whose stories we use.

We recognize that ethical issues of care and representation must also
be considered in the research narratives we write. The narratives we construct and reconstruct here about teachers and preservice teachers are as
much about us as they are about the participants in our research. Gelya
Frank (quoted in Behar, 1993) describes what may occur when researchers

are involved in collecting data about the lives of other people, as we often are. She says interpreting materials from another's life may be thought of as

> a process that blends together the consciousness of the investigator and the subjects, perhaps to the point where it is not possible to disentangle them . . . In some sense the reporting of data may represent a personal portrait of the investigator as well. The portrait would take the form of a shadow biography, a negative image. (p. 320)

As researchers using stories in our work, we need to remind ourselves of the very nature of stories; they are not neutral objects. They invite us—even command us—into relationship with the teller. The borders of stories are fluid and permeable; stories always become something else, the same story yet different, changed and transformed by the teller and by the hearer. In our selection and use of them, they draw us in, implicate us, revise us. Because of the relational, rather than rational nature of knowledge that comes with stories (Noddings, 1984) and because of the speculative and generative nature of stories, they demand that as researchers we continually reexamine the stories we tell and consider our responsibilities to those who tell us their stories.

On the other hand, we want to point out that it was the collaborative nature of our work—the constant negotiation of interpretation with others—that has made self-reflexivity and self-scrutiny more possible and that has highlighted for us the interpretive nature and multiple meanings of all the stories we collectively tell. It is the stories of the teachers in our study and other new stories we continue to compose together that continue to teach us about ourselves and about teaching. We watch semester by semester as our conversations and the stories they hold about teaching allow us to reflect on and reinterpret our classrooms. These converging— sometimes contradictory—stories keep moving us to revise our own assumptions about learning, to resist our internalized ideologies about ourselves as teachers. We know readers of these narratives will put them in still other perspectives; we hope they will use them to think about themselves, their research, and their teaching in order to keep open that potential space that allows us to maintain a dialogue between theory and experience.

2

Dual Apprenticeships: Conflicting Narratives in Teacher Preparation

> We live our lives through texts. They may be read, or chanted, or experienced electronically, or come to us, like the murmurings of our mothers, telling us what conventions demand. Whatever their form or medium, these stories have formed us all; they are what we must use to make new fictions, new narratives.
>
> —Carolyn Heilbrun, *Writing a Woman's Life*

At the beginning of our study of preservice teacher development, we had thought of our students' university experiences as a somewhat unified and deliberate apprenticeship, one that we and our colleagues carefully provided in courses like Composition Theory and Practice, Adolescent Literature, and English Methods and in well-selected placements in practica and student teaching. We had hoped that upon completion of this deliberate apprenticeship, our students would have experienced and subsequently composed for themselves an understanding of writing, reading, and language learning as complicated personal and social processes. We had hoped that they would develop an understanding of themselves as teacher-learners and of the importance of their students becoming their own teachers. And finally, we had hoped that they would develop a broad vision of education—of the philosophical, ethical, and political purposes of education that would allow them to resist and revise traditional conceptions of English and teaching.

We discovered, however, that in addition to the deliberate apprenticeship, there is another, "accidental" apprenticeship that plays a much more significant role in determining preservice teachers' understandings of writing, reading, and language learning; their understandings of themselves as teachers; and their visions of education. This other apprenticeship is longer, extending from preschool to young adulthood. This other apprenticeship is more pervasive, involving almost every class these students have taken, almost every teacher with whom they have interacted, and countless media representations of teaching and schooling. Finally, this other apprenticeship is more powerful. It is not the experience of their deliberate apprenticeship in a few teachers' college and English department courses that shapes their understandings. Instead, it is more likely their intense and prolonged accidental apprenticeship that most determines what these students do as teachers and who they believe themselves to be as teachers. In reality, it is even more complicated than that. It is not their experience—either in their deliberate or accidental apprenticeships—so much as it is the meanings they construct from those experiences as they are also filtered through their personal and social contexts.

This chapter examines the ways in which the meanings constructed from both the accidental and the deliberate apprenticeships interact to shape preservice teachers' understandings of teaching, learning, literacy, and self. First, we examine conflicting narratives of teaching and learning in our students' accidental apprenticeships. Next we discuss the cultural scripts that shape accidental apprenticeships. In the third section, we look at the role that our students' experience in traditional classrooms plays in their accidental apprenticeships. In the fourth section, we describe our students' potentially transformative experiences in their deliberate apprenticeships. Next we explain the ways in which our students' emerging sense of the interpersonal dynamics of learning offer them new narratives of teacher identity. Finally, we begin to explore the limited and incomplete nature of students' tentative revisions of the powerful cultural narratives of teaching to which they had been subjected.

CONFLICTING NARRATIVES OF TEACHING AND LEARNING IN ACCIDENTAL APPRENTICESHIPS

Our research has developed within the context of contemporary critiques of American education by Michael Apple (1982), Henry Giroux (1983), and Paulo Freire and Donaldo Macedo (1987), who argue that the practice of education in America is part of a larger social narrative that promotes a positivist ideology of knowledge, teaching, and learning, one that continues to conserve and reproduce the status quo. This ideology continues to promote belief in authoritative knowledge as a product of rational modes of thought and objective inquiry that can be contained and imparted to others. Giroux and Freire in particular analyze the position of teachers in that process, a position that continues to be little more than that of assembly-line workers who carry out prescribed tasks, attempt to achieve specified quotas (covering the subject matter, meeting outcomes), and generally reproduce knowledge rather than create it. The teacher, like her students, is expected to fit into the power structure without rocking the boat. Giroux and others claim that in recent years, "teacherproof" textbooks and a variety of accountability and standardized assessment strategies have further "de-skilled" teachers, weakening their ability to be critical decisionmakers.

In contrast to the pervasive positivist orientation of schooling are progressive philosophies of knowledge and teaching. While we acknowledge that these progressive reforms take many forms and are now also shaped by such varied perspectives as social constructionist, cognitive psychological, poststructuralist, critical, feminist, and cultural theory, a common element is a belief that knowledge is partial, fluid, and situated in the knower and the social/political context in which he or she is located. In linguistics and language and literacy studies, it has become commonplace to say that learning is an active process of construction by the learner. We learn to speak, read, and write in meaningful interactions through which we construct knowledge of reading, writing, and speaking. While positivism presents knowledge as authoritative and "given" and thus conceals the power relations in which it has been produced (what feminist theorist Donna Haraway (1988) calls the "god trick"), progressive perspectives make the relationship between the knower and the known more visible and indeed part of the process of inquiry.

At the beginning of our initial study, when we asked students to describe their important learning experiences, almost all of them pointed to one or two occasions in or out of school in which reading and writing became constructive, creative activities directly connected to growth in their personal and social lives. Many of these experiences occurred in K–12 or university classes with teachers who, in contrast to "de-skilled" teachers, were actively involved in the ongoing construction of knowledge, maintained a critically reflective posture, and believed that literacy instruction must become part of a contextualized, personal and interpersonal dialogue that creates possibilities for growth and understanding. So vivid and powerful were students' descriptions of these experiences that we began to identify them as "transformative." We were optimistic that students were beginning to use these experiences to reconceptualize writing, reading, and teaching as they became teachers.

At the same time, we noticed discord in students' responses. When we asked them about their conceptions of teaching, or about their understanding of the processes of learning to read and write, their answers often seemed contradictory and fragmented and only reflected partially, if at all, the transforming experiences they had described to us. At first we attributed this confusion and contradiction to the fact that these were just inexperienced students still sorting things out for themselves. But as we continued to interview these students, read their writing, and observe them over a period of several years, we realized that the confusion had not just been theirs; it had been ours as well. Our understanding of what potential English teachers need and how they learn had also been fragmentary and contradictory. Like them, we had failed to examine critically our own learning experiences and to use those experiences to help shape their preparation in our English department and teachers' college courses.

We are both teachers whose teaching has been transformed—or, more accurately, has evolved—because of our work in writing projects, our attempts to realign our teaching in writing workshops, our ongoing reading of contemporary scholarship, and our collaborative teaching and research. But that evolution did not occur easily nor as the result of a single isolated course, nor even a series of courses. It occurred over several years of clarifying and developing our beliefs and practices within communities of teachers and researchers. Nor are we finished learning. We are still changing and developing as we explore the implications of theory and practice in our fields. Yet we assumed that preservice English teachers could be changed and empowered with three or four classes in the English department and teachers' college. We, like our students, often defaulted to narrow notions of how potential teachers learn, rather than critically examining our own and our students' experience and allowing that to guide our work with these students.

We believe there is a great deal we need to understand about the beliefs and assumptions that our students construct from their apprenticeships. This study has reminded us that positivist assumptions that suggest that knowledge exists independent of knowers and can be broken down into discrete, quantifiable pieces still dominate American classrooms, though, as students' accounts suggest, alternative perspectives arising from social constructionist, critical pedagogy, cultural theory, progressive, and feminist perspectives are also present, if sporadically, in their K–12 and college experiences. Dan Lortie (1975), Pam Grossman (1987, 1988, 1990), and Deborah Britzman (1991) point out that socialization of teachers begins in childhood in the thousands of days that children and young adults spend in classrooms. Lortie (1975) estimates that by the time a student enters teacher education, she has spent 13,000 hours observing teachers. Our students described some of those experiences to us, but neither we nor they had probed those experiences for how they might influence their beliefs about teaching and learning. Nor had we clearly understood how those prior experiences in schools, their years of hearing and seeing popular cultural and folk representations of teaching and schooling, and our students' identities as gendered and classed individuals interact with their deliberate apprenticeships in university courses and practica.

As we began thinking and writing about our students' dual apprenticeships, we slipped easily, as they do, into binary categories for describing those apprenticeships—traditional and positivist, on the one hand, and progressive, student-centered, and interactive, on the other. We recognize that it is simplistic and reductive to posit two monolithic paradigms, one "traditional" and the another "progressive." It's very easy to equate traditional, behaviorist philosophies and epistemologies with the accidental apprenticeship, and constructivist, whole language, or critical pedagogy as the other, deliberate apprenticeship we provided. These are seductive conflations, because to some extent they hold. Our students did report that most of their experiences in their accidental apprenticeships were in traditional classrooms and most of their deliberate apprenticeships were in constructivist classrooms. We realize that within both of these paradigms, a variety of epistemologies exist. And from any one epistemology, a variety of pedagogies might be implied. Within a progressive paradigm, a teacher might take a cultural studies, a reader-response, or a feminist approach to the classroom. It's also true that while we might want to label as "traditional" a teacher who uses lectures as her primary teaching strategy, a student—given her unique relationship with that teacher—might experience that classroom in a way that we would expect from a more progressive or student-centered classroom. Furthermore, any two students might experience one teacher in different— even contradictory—ways. We have had different students describe the same class as "personally empowering" and as "chaotic" or "coercive." Clearly, while it's useful to create such categories, they don't always reflect the complexities that shape teachers' decisions or students' experiences, and we risk creating caricatures of teaching.

CULTURAL SCRIPTS OF TEACHER IDENTITY IN ACCIDENTAL APPRENTICESHIPS

Powerful cultural and personal narratives surround prospective teachers and shape their emerging identities as teachers. These narratives are a part of what we came to call the accidental apprenticeship. In fact, the accidental apprenticeship is no accident. It is only accidental to teacher

education. It is not accidental in the culture; it's part of an ideology of
regulation and control, part of our socialization in very specific epistemologies and discourses surrounding schooling and literacy. We found
that these traditional assumptions about the roles of teachers, the nature
of language learning, and the purposes of education are not housed
solely in schools and universities but are pervasive in the wider culture.
As Lightfoot (1983) suggests, these narratives are promoted in *Time* and
Newsweek, in popular literature like Pat Conroy's *The Water Is Wide* or *The
Prince of Tides*, in television sitcoms like *Welcome Back, Kotter* or *Mr. Rhodes*,
and in films like *Dead Poets Society, Dangerous Minds*, or *Mr. Holland's Opus*.
These depictions of teachers and schools have become so commonplace
that they often become intertwined with students' memories of their own
teachers.

In *The Lives of Teachers* Lightfoot (1983) highlights the way stories
about teaching in the popular media create one-dimensional portraits of
teachers that are mere caricatures of the real complexity of teachers' lives
and work.

> These caricatures presented in the popular press echo many of the stereo-
> typic perceptions of teachers left over from our childhood memories and
> experiences in school. Our adult recollections of teachers exaggerate the ex-
> tremes. We yearn for and idealize the special teacher who changed our life
> and gave it purpose, and we denigrate the memory of poor teachers who
> wasted our time and damaged our spirits. (Lightfoot, 1983, pp. 65–66)

She also cites a *Time* magazine article about a dedicated teacher who
sweeps her classroom floors and scrubs her students' desks daily, calls
students' parents at night, spends her own money to purchase pencils
and paper for her students, and stands at the chalkboard drilling them
on sentence diagrams. Such a story reduces the teacher to an unrealistic
caricature, but one that nevertheless becomes a cultural script defining
teachers and good teaching. A "good" teacher is a veritable warrior for
standards, order, and control, and a self-sacrificing saint. This and other
similar caricatures project contradictory visions of teaching that our students clearly have internalized. On the one hand, teachers are often idealized as dedicated, creative, caring, and valiant in the face of massive
changes in the culture, and on the other hand, they are characterized as
inept technicians, burned out and besieged by the difficulties of teaching
and powerless in the face of complex social change (Lightfoot, 1983). John
Skretta, one of the teachers in our study, described in a conversation with
us the seductiveness of Jonathan Kozol's (1967) portraits of teachers as
social activist martyrs. While John found Kozol's portraits compelling,

he eventually began to resist Kozol's portraits because he saw them as caricatures that also translate into teacher-as-victim. Although he sees himself as a social activist, John did not want to embrace Kozol's incomplete portraits for himself. Few depictions of teachers capture them as whole beings or suggest that teachers' lives, personalities, and characters are connected to the work they do in classrooms. Thus teachers and preservice teachers have limited and impoverished cultural resources from which to draw as they construct an identity for themselves.

In our conversations with students in our study we found many who drew on the culture's stories about teachers—from film, fiction, and television—when asked to describe themselves as teachers. Students recalled influential images of the teacher at the chalkboard diagramming sentences, or sitting at the big desk reading out vocabulary words. From the naïve *Welcome Back, Kotter,* they were persuaded that they can be a friend to students and teach them by dispensing glib wisdom. Or from the protagonist in *Dead Poets Society,* they were persuaded that if they are dramatic enough, they can turn their students into passionate literati. Many were persuaded that if they as teachers are excited enough, their students will "catch" that excitement, too. All of these popular images had been compelling to students and had made their way into their conceptions of teaching.

While these naïvely positive images of teachers' dramatic power to change and influence students' lives are very important in shaping preservice teachers' images of teaching—indeed, in drawing them into teaching and giving them energy and idealism—other stories of teachers' failures and lack of power are equally influential. As our students read about and experienced various versions of student-centered, collaborative, and critical pedagogies in courses like Composition Theory and Practice or their literature courses, they often challenged these pedagogies with stories of other experienced teachers in order to convince themselves that such nontraditional pedagogies could not be successful except in the most idealistic setting. Their response was often: "It won't work." "What if they won't let me do that at my school?" "I can see how this would work with upper-level or gifted students, but not with junior high students." "These students must have been from upper-class families." Our students talk to former teachers or friends or relatives who are teaching, and their stories about needing to maintain control, about "dysfunctional" students who need "structure," and about authoritarian administrators who monitor and control the curriculum become further evidence of their own future powerlessness as teachers. These folk narratives colonize our students, diminishing the value and power of their own experience as students within progressive, student-centered classes.

Our understanding of the power of these narratives comes from Marxist, poststructuralist, and psychoanalytic theorists who highlight the role of discourse and symbolic forms in the production of human subjectivity and the powerful ideological force of education, religion, media, literature, and other social institutions. As we mentioned in Chapter 1, Althusser (1971), for example, describes the process by which individuals internalize the ideologies of the culture as similar to what occurs when we hear ourselves being hailed while walking down the street. Stories of teacher identity hail preservice teachers, and they mistakenly recognize themselves as addressed by these identities and roles they offer. Preservice teachers internalize and begin to act in accordance with the scripts these hailings or narratives provide. As Heilbrun (1988) asserts, the stories the media, other cultural institutions, and family and friends shout or whisper about teacher identity, about teachers' roles in classrooms, about the nature of language learning, and about the nature of knowledge and authority are so much a part of the fabric of our culture and schooling that they are nearly invisible. They are so pervasive that they seem to be natural, a given—difficult to see, name, resist, or revise.

ACCIDENTAL APPRENTICESHIPS: NARRATIVES OF PRESERVICE TEACHERS' EXPERIENCE IN TRADITIONAL CLASSROOMS

Memories of previous teachers were another especially powerful part of the accidental apprenticeship shaping our students' formative identities as teachers. As we pursued our study, many of our interview questions invited students to compose their academic biographies. Their stories about their prior and present experiences in classrooms—elementary, secondary, and university—suggest that most of their experience has been in what we might call traditional or behaviorist-oriented classrooms. This should not surprise us, given the work of Henry Giroux (1983), Herbert Kliebard (1973), William Zeichner (1983), and others who conclude that education programs in this country are dominated by an orientation that breaks learning into skills and then focuses on methods to teach mastery of those skills. These students' descriptions of these classrooms also coincide with descriptions Arthur Applebee (1981, 1989a, 1989b), Applebee, Langer, and Mullis (1986), and Gerald Graff (1987) have given us of the state of secondary and college English instruction. Despite reformist rhetoric and process pedagogies, little seems to have changed in many schools and classrooms.

The stories of teaching and learning that students construct from their relationships with teachers reveal the variety of impulses that shape their decisions to enter the profession and the identities they take on as prospective teachers. As Waller (1932) and Lightfoot (1983) suggest, most of these decisions are not rational. "Personal history, early identifications with respected teachers, perceptions of appropriate women's work, and fears of institutional barriers all combine to shape decision making" (Lightfoot, 1983, p. 245).

It is important to emphasize that the images of teacher with which students enter preservice education, while taken from the culture and from their own previous experience, are complex constructions—or as Waller (1932) says, caricatures—resulting from the complicated psychological and social contexts of students' lives.

> This is an idealized and not a factual portrait [of the teacher], because the memory will not hold all the flesh and blood of human beings for so long a time; the general impressions remain, but the details fade. The idealized conception tends to become a caricature, because a real enmity exists between teacher and taught, and the memory transmutes the work of memory into irony. (Waller, 1932, p. 59)

John Skretta said when we asked about teachers who had influenced his decision to teach: "I guess in some ways I'd want to be an amalgamation of all those ideal teachers I've had who had a great deal of knowledge and could communicate well with students." It's not just a combination of John's two favorite teachers and Robin Williams or Jonathan Kozol (1967) that John or another preservice teacher is imagining. The images of teacher and teaching that students construct are their *interpretations* of the significance of those memories, reconstructed and reinterpreted through the lens of their own personal histories, their personalities, and culturally inscribed desires. For example, John's image of himself as teacher may have some origins in his reading of Jonathan Kozol and his experience with two favorite high school teachers and three college mentors, but as he suggests in his own narrative in a later chapter, these influences are also transmuted and translated by his own identity as a white male, the eldest son of an upper-middle-class Catholic family.

In some respects, despite the overfamiliarity of teaching in the culture, the images of teachers and teaching that students bring with them are incomplete. Their 13,000 hours of observation are grounded in a student perspective in compulsory contexts and generally allow them to see only classroom performance. Teaching is reduced to method, activity, and management: lecture, study guides, quizzes, worksheets, tests, grades, discipline. This method/activity/management-as-ends model of teaching "reduces the complexity of pedagogical activity to a technical solution" (Britzman, 1991, p. 47), overlooks pedagogy as a means for larger educational purposes, and conceals the theories in which methods are grounded.

Preservice teachers' long accidental apprenticeship of observation—again based as it is in their roles as students—is also charged with issues of power and control. K–12 students find themselves in compulsory attendance; observation is a kind of survival skill that enables students—from a vantage point opposite that of teachers—to learn to avoid trouble by reading both the overt and the hidden curriculum, including teachers' moods, values, and behaviors, but not necessarily to see pedagogy's relationship to theory. Waller (1932) argues that these images of teacher held consciously and unconsciously take on greater power precisely because they are laced with issues of dominance and control from teachers' own childhoods in schools. Our students attested to this in their descriptions of previous teachers who had influenced them to become teachers and in their descriptions of what they believed teachers do and who teachers should be in classrooms. These were teachers whose authority our students believed in—teachers with whom they had entered into some transferential relationship.

The relationship with former teachers is further complicated for many students because they come from families in which a parent or close relative is a teacher. Anne, one of the students in our study, said:

> My dad is a teacher, my aunt is a teacher, and education has always been important in my family. From first grade on, I used to play teacher down in my basement, and my dad would get these skill books, and I'd fill them out and lay them out on some desks my dad brought home, and I'd pretend that my students had filled them out, and that I'd pick them up and grade them. From seeing my dad and my teachers, I remember thinking, "I want to do that."

Anne's words suggest that students' lengthy accidental apprenticeships have provided them with a vision of the life they want to lead. Many of our students suggest that teaching is a way of life that fits the identity in which they picture themselves as persons and as teachers. Teaching represents for them a career and a life that are geographically and philosophically close to the life they have known, to their parents and their parents' lives, and to the familiar context to which they're accustomed. In fact, when we ask students where they imagine themselves being in five years, many of them say that they will still be in Nebraska, either close to their hometowns or in the Lincoln-Omaha area where they've lived as college students. This need for familiarity also suggests to us that for many of our students, teaching represents a profession in which they are not just in familiar territory geographically, economically, and stylistically, but also intellectually—a territory that will not require them to unsettle their conceptions of who they are or how the world operates. Indeed, their very motivations for becoming teachers may be based on their desire for this accustomed life. Thus, when their deliberate apprenticeships suggest that there are other ways of thinking about teaching, learning, and literacy—and that these conceptions might require a different role for the teacher—more than a familiar pedagogy is being placed at risk; students' very conceptions of the kind of life they want to live and their most basic reasons for entering teaching are unsettled.

As well as providing an image of a familiar life, students' accidental apprenticeships also provide them with familiar pedagogies. Anne went on to say that the image of teacher she carried with her from her parents and family and from her own precollege education remained foremost in her mind as she entered the teacher education program:

> When I first started as a freshman I envisioned that I'd teach like I had been taught. You know, I always thought about standing up there teaching grammar and spelling. I'm angry now that they taught that way. I wrote a lot when I was in elementary school, but then I pretty much stopped writing. I mostly remember grammar and literature courses, but I did write a couple of research papers in high school.

Anne reminds us that students' accidental apprenticeship provides them with powerful images of the pedagogies that will characterize their behavior as teachers. Like Anne, many students, when asked to talk about their most important teacher, described teaching practices centered in a tradition of order and control. It became clear as we listened to students that the classrooms they had experienced shared some common features that influenced their conceptions of the role of the teacher and the nature of English. Students described classrooms in which teachers stood at the front lecturing and giving directions, rules, interpretations, and information. In these classrooms, students sat in rows of desks and were expected to listen to and absorb what teachers said, then were tested and graded on their performance.

Victoria's description of the script she envisioned for herself as teacher supports this pattern:

> I'm going into English teaching and I'm probably mainly going to be in mechanics type of stuff, teaching the different sentences and

word usage, and I was talking to my dad and saying that it worried me, and my dad said, "Well, you'll have the answers in the books, so you won't have anything to worry about."

Victoria seemed only partially satisfied with this image of the teacher, dependent for her authority on the answer key. Such an image reduces the teacher to a pseudo-authority figure who possesses information (or answers in a teacher's edition) that she passes on to others. She initiates learning when she presents students with information and tasks, and she acts as mediator between students and knowledge or texts that are inaccessible to them without her intercession. Because of her authority, another vital part of her function is to evaluate students' performance on the tasks she sets. But, perhaps, her primary role is to keep order and maintain standards.

Other issues of authority and control emerged as some preservice teachers described as their most influential teacher one we would consider an authoritarian or even dysfunctional teacher—someone who belittled, embarrassed, or even terrorized them. But from that experience they had constructed an idealized interpretation. That these abusive relationships with teachers have been reconstructed as positive is particularly troubling when one considers that students may have internalized these abusive conceptions of authority and may perpetuate that abuse. For example, students told stories of their best teachers—of one who had an "idiot row" where he publicly exiled students or of another who wrote "bullshit" in big letters all over papers that fell beneath her high standards. In both of these cases, these preservice teachers had apparently never seriously examined their experiences in these classrooms beyond the assertion that the experience had been good for them, had challenged them. And in both of these cases our students had not been directly victimized by the teacher—had not been exiled to the idiot row or had "bullshit" scrawled across a paper—nor had they imagined the teacher from the perspective of one of their classmates who had been so victimized, and thus, perhaps, they were able to idealize the experience, to persuade themselves that it had been good for them and their classmates. Without an opportunity to reflect further on or critique these experiences, these education students remained convinced that "good" teachers exerted their authority in these ways—and they imagined themselves doing the same.

Other students were aware of the damage teachers had done and wanted to correct their negative influence. Janelle said:

I had a teacher who accused me of cheating, copying. My friends and I were so enthralled with the book we were reading, you know, we talked about the book outside of class. So when we wrote our papers there were similarities . . . [and] we were pulled into her room and accused of cheating. I was in tears . . . I learned that any sort of collaboration is cheating. At that point I never talked about books that we were reading for class to other students again . . . even though we learned all sorts of stuff about the books from talking. I think that brought all of us into college incapable of classroom discussion . . . I want to change that.

Janelle's most important teacher, then, provided for her a negative model. She knew that she had been hurt and that her opportunities for learning had been limited by this teacher, but without further reflection or critique, she too was left with only one-dimensional conceptions of teaching, knowledge, and literacy.

These narratives of teaching that our students were constructing from their own experience often rest on a belief that knowledge is objective, that knowing is a linear, progressive process that can be easily measured and quantified. In language education, such an epistemology manifests itself in the belief that reading and writing arise from conscious linear processes; that they are silent, solitary activities, given to definite forms and best taught in steps. This kind of epistemology assumes that learning to read and write is a matter of mastering a body of information or skills, like decoding skills; that form and correctness are paramount; and that they can be measured and evaluated objectively. The teacher's job, then, is to dispense those skills and then judge whether the student has acquired them.

From their experiences in traditional classrooms, students often constructed caricatures of reading, writing, and learning. Victoria revealed her limited vision of English when she described in an early interview the most important thing an English teacher needs to know:

They need to know mechanics, because once you learn the mechanics of English and word usage and things like that, you can understand things a little bit better. I mean, you can't really go into reading and not be able to pick out the different parts of a sentence.

This narrow, atomistic understanding of English and teaching was not surprising, given what we heard from Victoria and many of the other future English teachers that their time in classrooms had been spent in grammar drills, vocabulary study, taking notes, and answering the questions at the end of stories.

Writing played only a small part in most students' precollege classrooms, and the writing they did was often limited to five-paragraph themes and conventional research papers. What attracted many students, like Margie, to English was their enjoyment of reading:

> I have crates and crates of books at home. I've always liked to read and was never real fond of writing. They never really made us write in high school until my senior year when we had a research paper to do, but I've always enjoyed reading.

But literature study, as students like Sandy described it, is also based in traditional practices:

> The teaching that I experienced in junior high and high school . . . everyone reads the same books and we answer the little worksheet. They were the same worksheets that my sister and my brother before me had answered . . . That was your understanding of the book.

Such traditional practices, however, are not limited to their elementary and secondary education. Tim described a literature class he took during a recent semester:

> We take notes during his lectures, . . . but during the discussion, it's like he's really only interested in what two or three people think, and they're the students who follow his interpretation . . . He says we can write about anything we want, but it's pretty obvious that only certain topics or approaches will fly.

How these students were taught—and what they were taught—has influenced their beliefs about English instruction. In general, they described literature classes focused exclusively on canonical literature and centered on genre, theme, history, and literary elements—plot, theme, character, point of view. John, for example, said, "I think there's a body of literature out there that deserves to be read. I'd say, the classics from *The Iliad* on." Regarding the teacher's role in literature study, John also said:

> The teacher has to impart to the student a thematic area like Fitzgerald writing about the lost generation . . . A teacher has to supply

a certain amount of biographical information about the author . . . explaining where does this work fit in the history of American literature.

Students' lengthy apprenticeships in these traditional classrooms contribute to the development of reductionist caricatures of reading and writing as they are practiced in schools; they also keep students from experiencing language in schools as little more than a set of rules, skills, and information to be mastered. Students seldom have an opportunity within schools to experience the power of language to help them make sense of their lived lives and to carry on a dialogue with others, to create community, and to act and prompt action in the world. Instead, their reading and writing practices in school reduce these complex processes to mere acts of decoding and transcription. Most of the writing students do does not encourage "composition" or genuine construction of meaning; it requires only transcription or filling in blanks. And similarly, most of the students' reading does not require the construction of meaning in interaction with a text; instead it asks for a recall of plot and character and a search for hidden meaning. These pedagogies limit the range of students' experience with language and therefore limit their understanding of the potential that language holds to reflect, rename, recreate, and therefore to construct meaning anew.

These approaches also limit students' opportunities to reflect on issues of power in conceptions of content and pedagogy. Nowhere in their accidental apprenticeships was the status quo of schooling—curricular departmentalization, seven- or eight-period days—or conceptions of teaching as dispensing knowledge and of language arts or literacy as "skills" ever called into question. Never were these students asked to consider who was privileged by such conceptions of schools, teaching, learning, and literacy, nor whose voices and perspectives were excluded.

As we acknowledged earlier, our tidy dichotomies don't always hold. And despite this dreary picture, students also described classrooms that were not so limiting, that suggested a more expansive view of reading and writing, of learning and teaching. Janelle described elementary, secondary, and college classes that have allowed her to develop as a writer:

> I wrote stories, lots of letters to friends here and about, and when I was in junior high I started a book-of-the-month club for my friends and charged 'em for books. They were really funny, . . . just little papers stapled up, . . . and one of my friends still has them all. Before that my friend and I said, "Let's write a play." And so we wrote a play and [the teacher] let us perform it before the whole

fifth and sixth grade. But I never really got the idea that I was any good, so to speak, until in high school, a student teacher commented how she loved to read my journal entries because they were so funny, and then I had a fiction class here at the university, and the teacher really commented on how he liked my satire, and he wrote that I should consider working these out and submitting them. It was a real open class.

Janelle had begun this interview by repeating the cliché that writing is important because it is a way of communicating. As she reflected on her early experiences, she began to see beneath the cliché, to see that writing has much more profound implications. It was more than a way of satisfying the requirements of teachers and institutions or of demonstrating mastery of skills or form. As Janelle was able to retrieve this experience through our interview prompts and to reflect on it in light of her current experiences in her deliberate apprenticeship, it became a useful lens through which she could begin to question and imagine alternatives to the assumptions underlying positivist notions of literacy learning and teaching.

DELIBERATE APPRENTICESHIPS: NARRATIVES OF PRESERVICE TEACHERS' EXPERIENCE IN NONTRADITIONAL CLASSROOMS

While there have always been important countertrends to positivist conceptions of literacy and learning, most recently they have arisen from several sources—cognitive psychology, poststructuralist and critical theory, feminist and cultural studies, and American pragmatism. In English education, more specifically, reader-response approaches to teaching literature and "new rhetoric," "writing process," and whole language approaches to teaching writing have promoted a different set of assumptions about literacy and learning. These perspectives assume that reading and writing are creative processes of immense perceptual, linguistic, and psychological complexity, always situated within and contingent upon social and political contexts. Individuals construct meanings through active and continued interchange among writers or readers with unfolding texts. These perspectives value reading and writing for their heuristic function as much as for their communicative function; they assume that humans possess natural competence to organize their experience symbolically and that they will mature in that competence given supportive environments that take into account the personal and interpersonal contexts of the learner. The role of the teacher in these conceptions of teaching, learning, and literacy is also in striking contrast to that played by teachers in more traditional paradigms. The teacher does not preside as an authority figure, a purveyor of information and truth, but is instead guide, facilitator, and a model of a more experienced writer and reader, one who continues to learn.

The deliberate apprenticeship we had hoped to provide for our students included key courses in education such as Linguistics for the Classroom Teacher, Adolescent Literature, and English Methods. In English, it included Composition Theory and Practice and Approaches to Literature—as well as work with specific instructors who, regardless of the names of their courses, were known for teaching from the epistemological and pedagogical perspectives we were attempting to promote. And, in addition, the deliberate apprenticeship included field experiences with local English teachers—often teachers who had done graduate work with us—who were known for teaching within these progressive paradigms. We want to acknowledge the difficulty of labeling these teachers, their beliefs, and their practices. And as we said earlier, we do realize that within these alternative paradigms, there are a variety of epistemologies and pedagogies.

When students described their most important experiences as readers and writers, they often described classrooms and teachers that seemed to promote these progressive perspectives. They spoke about situations in which reading and writing became intensely personal and interpersonal processes, allowing them to make sense of their lives. Equally important, reading and writing in those situations allowed them to engage in dialogue with someone who seemed to care about them and allowed them to participate in a wider community of readers or writers.

Carol described a college class—one course in her deliberate apprenticeship—that allowed her to articulate what she had begun to understand about writing and its purposes:

> Throughout my education, I felt myself becoming more and more rigid. I see now, looking back, that I was losing my voice and losing the feeling that I had something to say. It became more and more difficult. Free writing was the lightbulb that went on in my head. I had learned about free-writing just before I started my comp theory class, and I wrote a tremendous amount for that class, and it was just like all these things were pouring out of me and all the confusions, contradictions, stresses, and tensions I was experiencing worked out in the journal. I kept two journals, one for the instructor, about what was going on with the class, and one about what was happening to me outside of class, and that was a tremen-

dous freeing up for me of a lot of thinking processes that I'd felt were going on in my head, but there was just no getting a handle on it, because there was no outlet for it to put in an understandable form. It was so important to have that class where the emphasis was on self-directed learning, and the teacher was a writer/learner in the class.

Carol's experience of learning to write had little to do with skills or rules or formulas for writing. It centered on her sense of taking control over her ideas and her words, and of using language to make sense of her life and gain control of her thinking and learning. It involved genuine composition—the construction of meaning—and not simply transcription or encoding. In addition, it connected her own development as a person to her development as a teacher, bringing together the personal and the professional in ways that enhance the development of each.

Katrin made a similar discovery about reading:

It was a Renaissance lit class of 60 people . . . that's where I sort of learned that literature is personal . . . The professor asked all of us to write a response journal for every class and he'd hand them back the next class. With responses on every one . . . and I was totally awed . . . every class. I'd always written other people's ideas, research papers or essays like that . . . I saw reading as being very personal, connected to me and my thoughts, not to what the professor wants . . . To know literature isn't to know what the author wanted, but for you to be able to attach some personal meaning to it . . . [This professor] said, "These poems are yours to enjoy and to interpret as you want, and once you feel like you have a grasp on them, they belong to you." I really liked that, and I intend to carry some of those feelings with me when I teach.

The role the professor assumed in this class and his conceptions of literature and reading combined to make this class stand apart from others for Katrin. The professor managed to give Katrin a sense that she had carried on a dialogue with him through her writing and his responses. In addition, Katrin felt that her own interpretation was important, that she had been given ownership of the literature she was reading, that reading literature involved connecting herself personally to reading.

As Sandy described one of her high school English teachers, she began to articulate an alternative role for herself as teacher:

> She really cared what we thought about the novels, and she encour-
> aged us to come in and talk about them, not just during class, so it
> wasn't like a usual class, it was more like we shared a close, continu-
> ing conversation that year.

Sandy has touched on a crucial factor. As she and other students reflected
on their experiences in nontraditional classrooms, they began to highlight
alternatives to the roles teachers have traditionally played. Teachers in
this alternative paradigm, by resisting the role of mediator and lawgiver,
can allow students to teach themselves, but the teacher is still an important part of the process, either overtly as a fellow reader or working writer
in the class, or implicitly as the supportive, caring partner in a tacit or
real continuing conversation.

Janelle had also begun to recognize that when a teacher takes on a
new role, she permits her students to take on new roles as well. Janelle
began to understand the importance of the personal and interpersonal
dynamics of learning as she described the composition theory class she
was then taking:

> I've really learned in this class that writing is a helpful way to
> work through your own thoughts . . . to come back around and
> then look at them again . . . whether it's a paper for a class or a
> problem in your own life, or something that's really troubling you
> at the society level . . . At first I saw no reasons to read my writing
> to my group. I just didn't want to do that. I thought I knew what I
> wanted to say and if they didn't like it or couldn't understand it, so
> what, . . . but then it dawned on me as I heard us talk about our
> writing that I could learn a lot from them and we ended up being
> so close . . . They helped me a lot.

Janelle's class allowed her to see the generative and heuristic function
of writing, the internal dialogue it enabled her to engage in. She also
began to appreciate the possibilities for wider dialogue and relationships
that writing can produce. She began to value responsive readers and a
supportive social context where her peers were as important as the
teacher in providing a supportive audience. Furthermore, Janelle was beginning to see that writing had implications beyond self-exploration and
affirmation. It could allow her to reexamine and revise her experience
and ideas and, in short, to engage in exploratory, critical thinking in order
to solve personal and public problems.

The alternative narratives about teaching that Carol, Katrin, and Janelle were composing assumed that learning is rich, untidy, and compli-

cated. Writing and reading are not merely skills that allow students to operate as functionaries in schools or workplaces; they are connected to the most fundamental processes of human personal, social, and intellectual development.

NARRATIVES AND "THE PERSONAL" IN TEACHER APPRENTICESHIPS

Just as media images and representations of teaching construct students' accidental apprenticeships, so does their sense of interpersonal relationships in the classroom. It becomes a part of the accidental and deliberate apprenticeships of preservice teachers. As we listened to students in our study, we found it particularly important to explore what students meant by a key phrase they all used in describing transformative learning experiences: "It was personal." Students had a strong sense that learning occurs within meaningful interpersonal relationships, but they had not examined this intuitive understanding critically. We found that the personal influences students' decisions to become teachers, their descriptions of "good" teaching, and their conceptions of literacy. In general, students found these experiences "personal" and thus transformative because the experiences joined literacy learning to the meaningful work of negotiating both personal and professional identities.

When students described their most important experiences as readers and writers, they spoke about situations in which reading and writing provided an opportunity to construct interpretive narratives of their own lived experience. Describing her semester in Composition Theory and Practice, Janelle said, "I've really learned in this class that writing is a helpful way to work through your own thoughts." She went on to say that she recognized that she wasn't just learning methods. "Writing and reading and how to teach them became an intensely personal matter." In this case "personal" denoted the self-constructive and self-interpretative nature of learning, especially as it related to literacy and to Janelle's development as a reader, writer, and teacher.

A second meaning of personal as students used it suggests that important learning occurs in relational, transactional environments—in personal relationships. The personal experiences students described in literature, writing, or methods classes occurred in a climate of caring, or mutual concern and conversation among students and teachers. Students were recognizing, without necessarily understanding, the importance of language learning within a social/classroom context in which their writing and reading were part of a meaningful ongoing conversation or relationship with others. Janelle—like many others—said that in her Composition Theory class she had come to value the interaction with her small group, although she had at first dismissed its relevance to her writing. She said that she began to feel "close" to her group, and as she shared her writing with them, they helped her to see new possibilities in her writing. The experience Janelle described suggests that her personal reflection and the exploration of selfhood were supported and encouraged in a mutually caring social climate that not only encouraged and validated her perspective, but also created the potential for dialogue with alternative or multiple perspectives. Dialogue in the small group provoked and affirmed critical reinterpretation and revision.

Without necessarily understanding what they were naming in these "personal" experiences, students were defining important ways in which language functions to clarify and critique experience. Because the courses in their deliberate apprenticeship allowed them to choose the topics about which they would write and to engage in reader response to literature, much of these students' writing took the form of narrative. These experiences allowed them to begin to see that by its very nature, the act of composing is both a personal and a socially mediated process. Although language arises from and is shaped in social/political contexts, genuine composing requires the writer to take a stance, to bring together disparate elements, to make choices about what to include or emphasize, and to convey a particular perspective; it is personal. As Katrin, Janelle, especially Carol, and other students also noted, constructing narratives is personal because it assumes and creates connection between the teller and the listener/reader, and this relationship, in the best instances, leaves both transformed.

The written and spoken narratives students were constructing also felt personal and transformative because they were composed in *social* contexts that allowed them to engage in dialogue with others with whom they felt some mutual concern. Learning in these situations is not solitary or individual. Janelle and Carol found added meaning when they were able to place their own personal meanings in dialogue with others. These are personal in the sense that this dialogue allowed them to undertake the important work of identity development, and as they heard the responses others made in dialogue, their own sense of identity was refined and revised. This process seemed transformative also because in it, personal and professional development were not cut off from one another. Instead these students joined literacy learning to the meaningful work of personal and professional development.

As we listened to students talk about the "personal" in their deliberate apprenticeships, we had hoped these relationships would allow some of them to construct narratives of teaching far more complex than those caricature narratives of the popular culture. Teaching and learning consist of more complex patterns of interaction than occur within the narrow boundaries of formal, didactic, authoritarian models of teaching and learning. From these more personal relationships, we had hoped they would be able to imagine teaching and learning as a more complex set of interpersonal relationships. While it would be naïve to assume that this image of teacher identity is not also bound to themes of authority and power, as Waller (1932) and Lightfoot (1983) suggest, students were at least beginning to recognize and value in their learning reciprocal dialogue, human connection, and caring, rather than the impersonal transfer or presentation of information or methodologies.

TRANSFORMATION—PARTIAL AND INCOMPLETE

We believed we could see this alternative conception of teachers' roles emerging as a result of their experience in nontraditional classrooms. The caricatures of teacher developed from their years in traditional classrooms and from popular culture no longer seemed to dominate their images of themselves. Students described teachers as giving ownership and creating possibilities. They spoke of the teacher as guide, as someone who was also engaged in reading, writing, and learning, and who encouraged students in an ongoing exploration. Instead of foregrounding "control" or "structure" in the class, teachers—they began to claim—needed to create an atmosphere that allowed students to articulate their ideas and responses and to feel invested in reading and writing.

Students' apprenticeships in these classes seemed to hold at least the promise of an expanded vision of what their goals might be in teaching. The traditional script suggests that the purpose of school is to prepare people for future education and jobs, and that thus it seeks to help them conform to established standards. It also seeks to preserve and pass on a defined set of traditions and values. As such, this traditional paradigm promotes a narrowly public conception of language. In progressive, student-centered, feminist, or critical paradigms, students generally value education because it has become personal. Rather than only serving a public need to conform, to fit in, it helps them continue their ongoing self-definition; it offers them a sense of agency that is usually denied students in traditional school reading and writing.

We also recognized that these same qualities that made the narratives students were composing and the contexts in which they were composing them seem so transformative could also restrict their development as critical teachers. In postmodern discussions of subjectivity and in current debates about process and critical pedagogies, the personal has been under scrutiny as a humanistic, naïve, and potentially dangerous notion because it masks the power of cultural forces in shaping subjectivity.

We, too, are concerned about students' conceptions of the personal. Although our students' understanding of the nature of the personal in language and learning seemed to mark a significant shift away from the traditional caricatures of learning in which they have been well schooled, it also seemed incomplete—perhaps even dangerous. One danger is that students continued to believe in an autonomous, unified self. Another is their unquestioning valorizing of personal narratives of experience without understanding the ways in which such narratives are socially and historically constructed. And a third is that students did not fully recognize the complex dialectic of personal, political, and social in which learning and knowledge are constructed. We often heard students proclaiming the importance of exploring their personal connection to the literature they were reading or of the personal essays and literacy histories they were writing, but we worried that they were not challenged to also acknowledge that their experience and even their reading or writing of a text are also shaped by their histories in particular social and political contexts, by their race, gender, and social class. Without the opportunity to examine and challenge their personal experience and their response to the personal in teaching and learning, we worried, students could simply erase the socially situated dynamics of language use. We also wanted students to see that literacy and learning are continually shaped within a social and thus historical and political frame of reference, and that our personal growth is dependent upon the social transactions that allow for personal development.

But we also see dangers in dismissing the importance of the personal and interpersonal in learning, and thereby creating again a false division between the personal and the social. Any of these reductionist stances leaves prospective teachers with a simplistic understanding of the complexity of language learning and the role teacher–student relationships play in that learning, and thus leaves them without the critical authority they need to challenge such reductionist notions of teaching.

One of our students, in particular, suggested an expanded conception of the social and political functions of language and education that we hoped for in all of our students. For example, with regard to writing, John said:

> It's important because otherwise you end up with people who are
> desensitized, . . . overwhelmed with a succession of images that
> are being spewed at them from television sets, and movie theaters

. . . If you can't make sense of it yourself, if you can't shore up your own thinking and come to terms with it in an individual way, then you're going to be lost . . . I'm not a philosopher. What's important is confronting what's in front of me now, and right now that's the mess. The fact is that whether or not it's a mess, I don't think you can get close to that order, or you can feel like you've actually reached an order within yourself, and sort of a communion between yourself and the society that's around you, unless you can express yourself. And I think that's best done through the act of writing.

John seems to understand the social and political implications of language. He is concerned about the power of language to serve the various social and political ideologies that surround us and thus define us. But John is also aware of the power individuals can wield when they use language to reflect critically on their lives. John finds a similar power in literature:

The reader's interest is what's going to lead a person. I mean, you can argue for days on end that Chaucer's *Canterbury Tales* are the greatest literature work ever, and that everyone must read those, but to a lot of people it's not . . . Literature is emotive stuff, and it evokes reactions and experiences . . . A person such as a Caucasian middle-class male is never going to experience *Native Son* like Richard Wright did, but if you submit yourself to that experience and allow yourself to read it, you're going to somehow reach a closer bond between yourself and the human condition that you otherwise wouldn't have reached . . . That means we need to incorporate a really vast array of literature, and we need to allow students to read a lot of stuff . . . not just mainstream stuff that confirms our ideas, but also stuff that shocks us.

When asked what led him to believe this about writing and reading, he pointed to his own experience with a high school English teacher:

I saw what she did for me, and I thought it'd be such a vital thing to be able to bring that sort of experience to somebody. For that one hour of the day . . . I felt like the world made sense, even at one small level . . . that it's not just a blind human race out there going nowhere, but that people do experience a lot of the same emotions . . . I think there's some Wordsworth poem that says something about that, a commonality of feeling of a populace . . . She made that come alive . . . There's a lot of fear in schools, a lot of caution, and that causes people to be careful about what people can read and think . . . and teachers have to decide whether they'll take that risk or not . . . She wasn't restrictive . . . The ideal literature teacher [is] willing to experiment.

Through reflecting on his own experience, John had begun to claim that both writing and reading are intensely personal and interpersonal processes with implications for social dialogue, critical thinking, and citizenship. He also understood that reading and writing are always located within a political and historical context and that his own personal identity—as a middle-class white male—had been socially constructed. Furthermore, John was beginning to realize that teaching is very much a political activity and that teachers can be active, intelligent agents for change within schools and classrooms.

We looked for reasons why more of our students had not begun to construct such complicated theories of teaching, learning, and literacy. We think several factors in their accidental and deliberate apprenticeships account for this. Many of our students' formal educations had been devoid of successful mutual, collaborative, "conversational" learning. In addition, these students had been given few—generally no—opportunities to reflect on and question their educations or the status quo of their lives. Without ongoing critical dialogues between their old and new assumptions about teaching, learning, and literacy, their new assumptions could not become fully transformative. Genuinely transformative knowledge, as Patti Lather (1986) argues, highlights "the contradictions hidden or distorted by everyday understandings, and in doing so it directs attention to the possibilities for social transformation inherent in the present configuration of social processes" (p. 259). In other words, genuinely transformative knowledge would be critical and reflexive about what seemed "given" and natural in our students' experience as well as about what they considered personal and transformative. While our students seemed to be moving away from one caricature-like narrative of reading and writing, we worried that many were moving toward another fragile and equally narrow script, one that might eventually undermine their own good intentions or collapse under the weight of the status quo in schools.

3

Untheorized Experience: Crisis of Authority

The greatest asset in the student's possession—the greatest, moreover that will ever be in his possession—[is] his own direct and personal experience. Failure to bring to bear their experiences reinforces their intellectual subserviency.
—John Dewey, *The Relation of Theory to Practice in Education*

We believed that the perspective our students were gaining on their own experiences through their writing and reading in their deliberate apprenticeships would be the vital asset to learning that Dewey suggests. We hoped that students would be able to use their experiences in their deliberate apprenticeships to author their own experiences rather than to be authored by them. We soon saw that our optimism was naïve. As we gained a more complete view of the complexity of students' apprenticeships within contradictory epistemologies, we saw that traditional assumptions based on positivist conceptions have shaped and continue to dominate the institutions that in turn determine students' understandings of teaching, learning, and literacy. These assumptions also continue to exert an influence on these preservice teachers as they move from the university into secondary classrooms. As we followed our students into their schools and classrooms, we saw even more clearly the normative force of educational discourses in the classrooms and communities our students entered as teachers. Curriculum guides, administrative dictates, experienced teachers' advice and attitudes, and even their students' behaviors shouted or whispered powerful values and assumptions to new teachers, often undermining the sense of authority and the knowledge of their discipline and of themselves that they had developed in their teacher preparation program.

Several factors in their preservice education account for the difficulty new teachers had in facing the challenges of new classrooms and institutions. Britzman (1991) describes four types of fragmentation that are kept in place by the discourses of educational culture: "compartmentalization of knowledge; the separation of content from pedagogy; the separation of knowledge from interests; and the separation of theory and practice" (p. 33). To these we would add the invisibility of students' identities and experiences from preservice education. All of these forms of fragmentation arise in part from the vexed relationship between theory and experience—experience of pedagogy and in one's personal life. We see them in overlapping patterns among our own students and in the deliberate and accidental apprenticeships in which they were immersed.

Rather than revising their understandings of teaching, learning, and literacy, our students were often merely adding on new, alternative notions to their existing, and often unexamined, assumptions, and they did so with little apparent sense of tension or conflict. Students who did recognize some tension only did so selectively. Most of our students' views about theory and pedagogy in English were so compartmentalized and depersonalized that they were unable to recognize how many of their beliefs were in tension with their own newly articulated histories as readers and writers. In addition, their own experience could not yet be the asset Dewey suggests because it was only partially examined and had not actually been used to engage in dialogue with or to critique more traditional assumptions about language and learning. They knew, for example, that classrooms that allowed them to explore their personal connections to reading and writing felt transformative, but they did not yet understand why that might be the case or what the limitations of such learning might be. Their deliberate apprenticeship did not provoke them to bring conflicting epistemologies and beliefs into dialogue or to historicize them in relation to their own experiences. As a result, our students often were left thinking in binaries that, for example, separated personal from socially governed forms of thinking and learning. Ultimately, in many cases, their own experience and the authority they might derive from critically examined experience were often subverted or erased by far more powerful traditional narratives of teaching, learning, and literacy.

In this chapter we explore some of the forces that limit the effectiveness of teacher education and limit our efforts at teacher change. First, we examine and problematize the status of experience as a source of knowledge and the difficult relationship between theory and pedagogy that contributes to undervaluing and trivializing each at different moments in teacher development. Then, in two sections, we further explore the selective nature of preservice teachers' recognition of conflict or tension among various theoretical and pedagogical perspectives which they encounter—and how the fragmentary nature of their education fails to promote a climate of dialogue among conflicting theories of learning and literacy and undermines their fragile authority. Finally, in the last two sections—using the experiences of two of our students as examples—we explore how incomplete conceptions can leave new teachers vulnerable to crises of authority as they face the powerful socializing forces of their new schools and communities.

EXPERIENCE AS A PROBLEMATIC SOURCE OF KNOWLEDGE

The stories we tell in this chapter underscore the problematic status of experience as a source of knowledge for our students as they move into teaching. Throughout our study, as we interviewed students about their histories in classrooms, their experience became an increasingly important narrative in their teacher preparation. It also became clear that preservice teachers imbue experience with authority in a seemingly capricious way. Their experience—or rather their constructions of it—counted in some circumstances to support new conceptions of their role as student and teacher, but in other circumstances it held no authority against existing dominant ideologies.

Several conflicting assumptions about the nature of experience and the relationship of theory to practice account for the deeply ambivalent status of experience as a source of authoritative knowledge in educational culture. As we pointed out earlier, positivist assumptions about teaching, learning, and literacy are so pervasive that they are invisible. Discourses of "the normal" in educational contexts discipline teachers and students into conformity with established rituals of the classroom and educational culture. These assumptions are "the way it is" and are often unquestioned. This is what feminists, for example, have called "the God trick," a claim to absolute, objective, transcendent certainty (Haraway, 1988). This position can never recognize contradictory views outside the foundational perspective. As we will see in Toni Siedel's chapter, in her first years of teaching, the systematic protocol for the five-paragraph essay, which had become an intricate set of procedures, rules, and sequenced steps in her school, became an authoritative discourse for teaching writing that was impervious to any questions or alternative practices. Teachers at that school had years of their own experience invested in that paradigm and used their experience, and the traditional theoretical perspective from which it was derived, to block Toni's questions and to undermine the authority of her preservice education as she sought to bring those alternative paradigms for teaching writing into her classroom. Other examples can be found in education more generally; Benjamin Bloom's (1956) "scientifically" derived taxonomy of levels of thinking, or the current schemas about "learning styles," take on the status of objective, impartial "knowledge," and teachers often do not have enough grasp of the wider narratives circulating in the educational culture to recognize from what partial perspectives this knowledge might have been derived.

The common culture of education mitigates against the authority of experience. Knowledge generated from individual historically situated experience, as feminist Sandra Harding (1991) and other philosophers argue, also has ambivalent authority. Often, experiential claims, especially those generated by people whose experience has always been marginalized, conflict with dominant forms of knowledge. These experiential claims do not count as knowledge because they do not coincide with the dominant perspective, which is assumed to be objective and universal in its perspective. In educational culture, quantification is generally still privileged over ethnographic narrative as data. Teacher "lore" is devalued as a source of theory. Yet lore also is used by teachers to discount theories or perspectives that might require them to change their practice ("I tried peer response groups, and my students couldn't do it"). For some teachers, theory is another top-down mandate for teacher or curriculum development. Theory is often abstract and detached from teachers' immediate contexts, and used to impede rather than support teacher initiative.

The movement in teacher education and educational research to value teachers' stories, to invite teachers to reclaim their experience and to use it to consider their pedagogy, subverts more top-down approaches to teacher development. Still, standpoint theorists caution that there are dangers in reliance on "the spontaneous consciousness of individual experience" (Harding, 1991, p. 141). These experiences, unexamined, can also distort by virtue of their parochialism. Put more simply, the stories we construct of our experience may also lie to us, because they are often part of our larger misrecognitions of ourselves within ideology. As Scott (1992) argues, experience should be the catalyst for questioning the ideologies and contexts that have constructed that experience.

COMPARTMENTALIZATION AND FRAGMENTATION

One of the main sources of fragmentation in our students' teacher preparation was the lack of opportunity to bring the conflicts between those competing ideologies and experiences into the open. Britzman (1991) says: "Compartmentalized knowledge is . . . self referential; it seems to hold no other context beyond its immediate presentation" (p. 36). Competing assumptions about learning are often stripped of their historical or situational contexts. Students may not be assisted in understanding, for example, that cognitive psychology and linguistics may theorize some aspects of language learning differently or that ethnographic studies have highlighted the role of difference—gender, race, class, sexual orientation—in language learning. This lack of dialogue among conflicting educational theories promotes the view that theory and pedagogy are politically neutral, that all that matters is whether or not "it works in my class." Thus, for example, when a teacher claims that "small groups just don't work for me," the underlying assumptions about student ownership and wider questions about student learning and the classroom climate necessary to help students develop effective peer response groups may be ignored. In addition, the view that our pedagogical choices are a matter of personal choice, style, or student comfort often erases the importance of students' gender, ethnicity, or social class in pedagogical decisions. They ignore that learning to read and write are not simply matters of personal development, but are always implicated in wider issues of social power and access. Such concerns often remain unaddressed in pedagogical discussions when we fail to bring into dialogue competing theoretical assumptions that shape our practices in language instruction.

Progressive philosophies in English education have long argued for the reciprocal relationship between theory and practice. But the inability to sustain a dialogue between the two fosters further ambivalence toward experience and theory and compounds the confusion for preservice teachers. On the one hand, education, and the public more generally, often underconceptualize and thus trivialize pedagogy as a set of techniques anyone can master; pedagogy is encapsulated in a three-ring binder with nicely sequenced activities, ready-made questions, and an answer key. Britzman (1991) and others point out that the position of students in their accidental apprenticeships reinforces this notion of pedagogy as a set of activities. The result is teacher-proof curricula that strip teachers of the authority that comes from an alternative and much more complex definition of pedagogy as the production of knowledge in teaching. When teaching is conceived as the active development of knowledge, as the ongoing development of careful observation, reflection, analysis, and assessment of students and classrooms—not as a bag of tricks and methods—teachers can see that theory lives in practice and practice is generative of theory (Salvatori, 1994).

It is not surprising, then, given the multiple sites of fragmentation, the contradictory way that experience functions in educational culture, and the vexed relationship between theory and practice, that preservice teachers are also confused about the relevance and authority of their own experience when it contradicts dominant theories of learning and literacy. Katrin, one of our students, provides us with an example of students' inability to sort out the sources of knowledge about teaching. More specifically, Katrin demonstrates that she has had few opportunities to explore the tensions among contradictory beliefs. She speaks of reading literature as more than decoding and "understanding what the author or teacher intends; it's finding some personal meaning in it." But at the same time, Katrin defines writing as if it were only encoding rather than the creation of "personal meaning." The fact that Katrin's only writing instruction has been in journalism classes may contribute to her valuing surface features. Thus, she also said that in order to write, "you have to know grammar, mechanics . . . literacy is more than just being able to read. If they can't spell, I really wonder if they can understand words." Katrin's repeated focus on surface features of language and writing in our interviews with her and in classroom discussions suggests an overly simplistic or atomistic view of language learning that fails to understand both the public, communicative function of language and its personal, heuristic functions. Yet she seems to understand that literature can be personal and heuristic. Katrin is working from a binary and contradictory conception of language that she has not been led to examine or challenge.

Margie, another student, recognizes contradiction, but only selectively. One day she arrived in our office for an interview asking if we had seen Robert Brooke, her professor from Composition Theory the previous semester:

> I need to talk with him. I'm in this class and there's something wrong. The professor is talking about standardized reading tests and dividing students into ability groups and readability levels, and I know something's not right about what she's saying, but all the graduate students in the class, who are teachers, support what she's saying, and I'm not sure how to think about it, but it goes against everything I believe, and I need to talk it through with him.

That earlier course with Robert had given Margie an important experiential and theoretical lens through which to critique other learning experiences. In Composition Theory, a course modeled after the writing project, Margie had been asked to become a writer, and then to step back and—in the company of authors such as Atwell (1987), Calkins (1983), Rose (1989), and Smith (1986)—to consider the implications of her experience as a writer for her future role as a teacher of writing. Her new class, a class in reading methods, conflicted with the fragile conception of language development she had begun constructing in Robert's class. A further source of conflict and confusion for Margie is that experienced teachers were the ones contradicting what she had learned about language learning in her university composition theory and methods classes.

Margie was clearly trying to construct a theory of language development based on holistic conceptions of language and its function. Yet despite her strong critical reaction to what she felt were faulty assertions about language learning in her summer reading methods class, the next semester Margie was unaware of similarly disjunctive assumptions in an educational psychology class in which she was enrolled. This class attempted to present students with a broad array of learning theories, but it was conducted as a set of lectures taken almost directly from a textbook on which students were given multiple-choice tests. The course did not seem to practice any of the theories it promoted and contradicted much of what Margie had found valuable in her composition theory class. For example, it suggested that reading teachers should break reading apart and focus on one "domain" of reading at a time—decoding, vocabulary development, or comprehension. It urged teachers to teach students to recognize and define story structures in advance of reading. This atomistic perspective was contrary to the more holistic theories of language learning on which Margie's composition theory and practice course had been based, but Margie found nothing discontinuous in it and even reported feeling that the course had clarified some of her questions about teaching. "Even though the class is taught as a lecture class and the professor basically goes over what's in the textbook and then tests us with multiple-choice tests . . . it's helped me a lot."

We can only speculate why Margie, in the second case, was unable to see the contradictory messages, why she didn't rush off again to her composition theory professor to discuss the tensions she might well have felt in this class. One of her classmates also described this educational psychology course as being consonant with the other courses such as composition theory and English methods. When we asked him to explain this to us, he cited the teacher's use of anecdotes from her own prior high school teaching experience in her lectures as evidence of the personal and student-centered perspective she was advocating. It is almost as though the anecdotes made palatable the atomistic approaches on which the course was operating. Those narratives seemed to bring students within sight of the classrooms within which they were imagining themselves teaching. Because of this, they granted the teacher a kind of authority that seemed to blind them to the contradictions and tensions within the format and content of this textbook- and lecture-based course.

But something else may have been operating here as well. Because these anecdotes gave Margie and Jim a sense that they were personally connected with the speaker—the teacher—they felt that this course was the equivalent of their Renaissance literature course, where they insisted they had been in a personal dialogue with the professor and the texts, or the same as their composition theory class, in which they relished the opportunity to write their own meaningful narratives and to engage in dialogue with others about them. They didn't see that in their educational psychology class it was only the teacher telling stories. There was no dialogue; it was only a monologue with no opportunity to examine or bring the teacher's stories into conversation and potential critique with other perspectives.

This illustrated again for us the lack of dialogue between theory and practice in the educational culture that surrounded students. It also highlighted again how students' notions about the personal and about narrative could be seductive and limiting. The "false" personal can give the illusion of dialogue with others, but it may simply be window dressing for monologic authoritarian teaching practices. In this case there seemed to be no way to expose for our students the contradictions in their experiences in educational psychology and composition theory, or between the way this educational psychology class was taught and the theories of learning the teacher was trying to teach, and there was no mechanism for helping Margie and Jim reflect on and analyze the nature of the stories the instructor was telling. Their education had not taught them to be critical consumers who might ask: For what purpose are personal narratives being used? How do these stories function in a given context? What is its intended effect on listeners or readers? Without the regular habit of analyzing such stories, Margie and Jim were colonized by them.

This situation suggested that students also might not have thoroughly understood the assumptions on which the courses in their deliberate apprenticeship were based. They seemed to know only that a course felt personal or affirming or different than many of their other courses. Most of their learning in schools had been remote, disconnected from who they believed they were as people. And on the occasions when they felt personally affirmed or addressed in their classrooms, they had little theoretical explanation to rely on. It was as though they were using a gross sieve to make distinctions, to sort one kind of course from another based on their sense of a felt personal connection to the teacher, often perhaps where none really existed. We were hoping that students would be able to make more carefully examined distinctions and build learning theories and pedagogies based on close, critical examination and dialogue between competing assumptions about learning.

In fact, our students were probably theorizing from their experiences—but perhaps building learning/teaching theories that suggested that all one needed to do was add personal experience or a process overlay to the atomistic and behaviorist pedagogies that had pervaded their own educations. One could render a lecture palatable by adding anecdote—or the five-paragraph essay by providing opportunities on Monday to prewrite and on Wednesday to revise. As we suggested at the end of the previous chapter, this seems dangerous and incomplete. It may, however, be a necessary step in a movement toward a transformation or a shift from one paradigm to another. Perhaps such a shift is likely to involve the dressing up of old ideas before one is able to reconstruct them.

UNDERMINING FRAGILE AUTHORITY

After two and three semesters of prompts to compose and reflect on stories of their own literacy and learning, many of our students were beginning to examine and understand their own writing and reading processes and the assumptions about language learning these implied. But as they moved into practicum and student teaching, there was strong competition among their emerging beliefs, the beliefs in which their most sustained apprenticeship in schools had steeped them, and the assumptions they found present in the schools they entered as preservice teachers. Many students were therefore finding it difficult to sustain the fragile connections they had constructed between their understandings of themselves as writers and readers and their images of the teachers they hoped to become. Katrin, for example, wrote in her journal:

> Now as I'm approaching an actual teaching experience, I'm terrified. Where does my straight A record get me without a creative mind? Sure I've read Atwell, yet I still seem to cling to the conservative approach in which I was taught. Is there hope for me or am I doomed?

This crisis of authority Katrin and many of her classmates were beginning to feel emerged from the tensions they were experiencing between their identities as students and their projected identities as teachers. These tensions came also from students' real understanding of the disciplining power of pervasive school cultures. Katrin wondered, for example, whether her identity as a "good student," developed in positivist classroom settings, would be of any use to her as a teacher. She had partially assimilated the ideas of Linda Rief (1992), Nancie Atwell (1987), and others, but she herself was aware of the normalizing power more traditional conceptions of teaching still asserted on her and wasn't sure she had the creativity or strength to move beyond them, especially as she entered the schools where traditional conceptions of teaching still governed the roles teachers might assume.

Carol also articulated the tension she felt as she began to think about her transition from student to teacher: "I've been thinking about writing from my own position as a writer and from what the needs of student writers seem to be. Now I feel I need to start thinking about writing as a teacher." Carol had learned a great deal about writing and about herself as a writer, but the prospect of moving into the classroom made her uncertain about whether that knowledge was good enough or whether it would allow her to help students with their writing.

These symptoms of fragmentation, of incomplete understanding, and of students' fragile new sense of authority are understandable given the shift in position students were engaged in as they moved from student role to teacher role. The causes of their uncertainty do not lie in them or reflect a lack of intelligence or maturity. They lie in the nature of their long-term apprenticeships and in the ways their experiences in traditional behaviorist classrooms and in progressive, feminist, or student-centered classrooms interacted to create competing and contradictory narratives that remained unexamined. Although from our perspective these classrooms were based on competing assumptions, for our students this often was not the case.

The power of these traditional narratives of teaching can be seen in how they interact with new or competing ideas. It seemed to us that alternative, progressive, or feminist pedagogical theories of teaching and learning were swallowed up or merely seen as added on and were in that way effectively neutralized. Thus a teacher might hold one set of beliefs about teaching writing and another about teaching literature. Or one might have a nine-week unit on discrete grammar instruction and a nine-week writing workshop instead of using the students' writings as a context for identifying and helping them develop the skills each of them needs. In this case, two very different conceptions of language learning could exist side by side without ever appearing to conflict. And positivist assumptions—because, in part, of their atomistic nature—expand their borders to suck in and neutralize alternative beliefs. We have seen that happen generally in English education, for example, with "new rhetoric" or "writing process" approaches to composition. The "writing process" has become, in many venues, yet another lockstep, linear formula like so many schemes that have gone before it, without real attention to the needs and abilities of individual students. Textbooks merely change (or add to) the section on outlining to include prewriting, brainstorming, and mapping techniques, and proofreading sections become "revision."

Conservative pedagogical assumptions also remain powerful for pre-service teachers because they are supported by the most basic intellectual habits of our society, which value objectivity, quantification, and generalization. Because of this, we have a system of education that values products rather than processes, certainty over speculation, and abstractions or clichés over personal understanding. This view of knowledge and authority also shores up an incapacitating separation of public and personal knowledge. As a result, our students may privilege the language of outside authority over the knowledge of their own internally persuasive experience—or they may do the opposite by failing to bring conflicting pedagogical stances into dialogue.

Sandy, for example, said, "I got hooked on reading and writing with this one high school English teacher. Reading and writing became enjoyable, like an ongoing exciting conversation." But Sandy's rich interactive view of English seemed to go underground when we asked her, a few minutes later, to talk about what teachers should do to promote reading among students: "They have to do things like have vocabulary tests."

Sandy, other students, practicing teachers, and we ourselves, hold contradictory assumptions without being jolted by conflict. We do so because of another of our society's most basic intellectual habits: our liberal pluralistic stance toward diverse points of view, which often results in a bland "melting pot" approach toward education. Students say, for example:

> There are different styles of teaching and different learning styles; some things work better with some students than with others. You have to find what works best with your style as a teacher. It doesn't matter exactly how you teach as long as you can give a rationale for what you're doing.

Instead of promoting a tolerant but rigorous dialogue among plural philosophies, a more common result is a relativistic stance that forecloses dialogue and debate, an "anything is right if it works for you" way of thinking that, in fact, constitutes a failure to critically examine assumptions and beliefs—to investigate what we mean when we say, "It works."

But where in students' experience is there a place for dialogue between competing assumptions and beliefs about education or for discussions about what counts as knowledge in education? Indeed, where is there time or place for simply reflecting on the education they have endured? Gerald Graff (1987) points out that little dialogue exists even among those shaping the curriculum of university English departments today. The apprenticeships of our students—accidental and deliberate—fail to encourage them to undertake a rigorous examination of the fundamental assumptions on which their education has been based and the implications they hold for teaching, learning, and literacy, much less helping them reflect on, articulate, and bring into critical perspective what is currently happening to them in their classes.

Victoria, for example, in her last semester before student teaching, described two literature classes in which she was then enrolled. She believed one was more effective than another, but little in her education would allow her to understand why that might be so.

> It's important to have a kind of personal investment in your read-
> ing . . . I have two literature courses this semester, and just from
> having the two very opposite-end teachers, it's really made me real-
> ize what literature study is about and what form I would rather
> take . . . In one course, we're tested over, you know, the themes and
> things like that, and that's all. In my other course, the twentieth-
> century women writers course, we learn about the literature
> through group discussions, and everybody can say what they feel,
> and also we write journals on the literature and discover the
> themes on our own, and then maybe she writes back a comment,
> "Well, you know this is what direction I saw the author taking."
> And so I prefer the one-on-one type of relationships with the
> teacher. There's a real big difference there I think, and so I'd like to
> have an emphasis on group discussion and critical thinking so that
> it was teacher/student, student/teacher feedback and not just
> teacher to student feedback.

Unless we can help Victoria understand more fully why one approach to teaching literature might be more effective and valuable than another, she may not be able to sustain her belief about reading instruction, nor engage in a critical examination of competing practices and beliefs.

We saw dramatic evidence of the consequences of this fragmentation and incomplete understanding—of this failure to place competing assumptions into dialogue—as our students moved from the university into classrooms. We also began to understand the powerful pull of socialization, of the ways in which the culture of school and community can undermine even well-crafted and examined beliefs.

TEACHERS' STORIES AS A SOURCE OF SOCIALIZATION

As our students moved into the schools in their practicum experiences, they found their emerging dialogic conceptions of teaching, learning, and literacy challenged at every turn by the rigid authority structures of schools, and also by the entrenched assumptions of many practicing teachers. Once again we recognized the very conservative power of stories of teaching that schools themselves overtly and covertly tell students. Students often came to methods class, for example, telling of having spoken with a former teacher or an aunt or cousin who teaches. Those teachers often told stories of classrooms and students that contradicted many of the conceptions of learning the students had been developing in their university apprenticeship.

After a conversation about "idealism" and "realism" in Dave's methods class, Dave suggested in a further conversation that idealism in teachers is not a bad thing and is not the opposite of realism. One of his students sent the following e-mail message:

> I have been told before that my idea of the classroom is too ideal. One time I was told to "face reality because the classroom just isn't like that." This was in response to my assertion that it is possible to help all of my students learn. I believe that for my own sake and to maintain my positive outlook on teaching I need to be "ideal." It seems wrong to go into the classroom thinking that "Okay, some of these students aren't going to learn."

But preservice teachers often have more trouble sustaining their idealism when they enter the school culture. The messages they hear— "Students need more structure . . . That might work in university classes or in urban high schools, but we'd never get our students to write that much"—are too powerful to resist. Because experienced teachers—former teachers, sisters, or fathers—work in the very real contexts that students are about to enter, they often hold more authority for students than either their university professors or their own examined histories as learners. Those stories from others call into question the very theories and practices in which students are engaged and that seem so transformative to them. The stories experienced teachers tell often reflect their own colonization by the narratives of schooling and their misrecognition of themselves in the ideologies of education. They construct stories that erase their own authority.

A further source of power, in experienced teachers' stories, is inherent in the socializing force of stories. Stories create a sense of belonging;

teachers' stories represent insider knowledge and insider membership. "A story is constitutive; it makes for collective identification," says Susan Rosenholtz (1991). Rosenholtz goes on to argue:

> Within a school culture, teachers tell stories because they bond us together; and they also make us feel good, feel that problems aren't our fault. "It's those inattentive parents' fault." Stories are conservative in nature, reinforcing and reproducing the status quo of schools. (p. 125)

Recently in a on-campus seminar, a cohort of new student teachers talked about hearing words like "young" and idealistic" as accusations. "I am young and idealistic," one student said, "but it's like I'm supposed to feel bad about that." Others talked about how the experienced teachers in their buildings talked of "what works" and doesn't work, suggesting that these student teachers will soon come to their senses and learn that small groups, writing workshops, and reader response just "don't work." Indeed, in some circumstances these student teachers acknowledge that what they're trying isn't working. Sara spoke of attempting peer-response groups and having it fail miserably. Her cooperating teacher said afterward, "I didn't want to stop you, but I knew it wouldn't work." Still, Sara said, as she looks into the classroom of a woman who graduated from our program five years ago, she sees this teacher enjoying apparent success with peer-response groups. "I can't make it work yet," Sara said, "but the fact that she can gives me hope."

In the course of this seminar, these student teachers came to resist the conservative insider stories that Rosenholtz (1991) suggests help teachers maintain the status quo of schools. They did this in part by constructing their own collective narrative and identity as young, idealistic teachers, in opposition to the status quo of their English departments. As they told their stories, Dave prompted them to examine them and see how their youth, inexperience, and idealism were being used against them. Students began to reclaim these terms, viewing them as assets rather than deficits. "You need your idealism," Dave asserted. "It will carry you through student teaching and your first few years as a teacher. It will make you Xena, Warrior Teacher."

In this seminar, then, students told stories that illuminated the normalizing narratives of their new schools, critiqued those stories and the assumptions on which they rested, and then began to compose their own new narratives of teaching and identity, reclaiming and unpacking terms like "it works" or "that doesn't work." In this instance, these student teachers began to see that "it works" was code for any practice that lulled students into complacency and passivity and "it doesn't work" implied a practice that resulted in noise, movement, or disruption. This resistance and revision was enabled by these student teachers' strong sense of community, their history together as a cohort, and the forum this on-campus seminar gave them for telling and examining their stories.

Much has been written, often critically, about the power of teacher lore. While we don't agree with those who denigrate teachers' use of experience as a source of evidence for theory-building, we also recognize, as Freire (1986) and others point out, that it is when experience is theorized and scrutinized that it can become an important source of knowledge about teaching. We realized that preservice teachers often lacked a space in which to challenge and scrutinize more experienced teachers' stories and the assumptions behind them. Without this opportunity to examine and challenge the conservative narratives of schools, preservice teachers' authority to articulate alternative narratives was often severely undermined. Margie's story is one example of the consequences.

THE DISCIPLINING NARRATIVES OF SCHOOL AND COMMUNITY

We had not intended for our study to go beyond students' preservice education. But we continued to observe our students as they graduated and in most cases left Lincoln and the surrounding area. Some of them kept calling or writing to us throughout their first year. Margie was one of those students. As we noted earlier, Margie had begun to examine the assumptions about language and learning in her own deliberate and accidental apprenticeships, and she had developed some sense of authority in her ability to question and critique the teaching practices and assumptions from which her courses were taught. She did, for example, question the experienced teachers in her reading methods class. Margie graduated from our program idealistic, committed, and seemingly sure of the philosophy of teaching and language learning she had been constructing. But that sense of authority was severely tested in her first year as a teacher.

Margie had returned to a town near her hometown to teach. As the new unmarried, attractive teacher in the school, she had to contend with the sexism, jealousy, community politics, and power plays of her colleagues, administrators, students, and parents. She had to deal with the tests of stamina her students put every outsider through, including attempts to weave her life into their own social and sexual struggles, and she had to deal with the realities of small-town life, where her every move was under scrutiny. She was the women's track coach and directed the speech and drama club, and as a result went home exhausted every night and had little time for reading, writing, reflection, or class preparation. And she had no colleagues with whom to discuss the dilemmas she was facing.

During her first semester of teaching, we had several long-distance calls from Margie as she once again sought someone to talk with about the dissonance she was experiencing in the small high school near the South Dakota border where she had taken a position. In her first call, she told us how one of the older teachers had discounted the importance of the journals Margie was asking her students to write and had urged Margie to "structure" her students' learning using the grammar book in order to prepare them for this other teacher's class the following year. Margie said the principal had "yelled" at her because the librarian had complained to him that Margie was sending too many students to the library to select their own books for reading rather than giving them assignments from the anthology. One of the older male teachers who taught in the same wing of the building called her "sweetie" and "cutie" when they monitored the hall between class periods. Such experiences heightened Margie's sense of isolation, exhausted her, and began to destabilize her sense of confidence, competence, and the authority that had grown in large measure from her well-articulated beliefs.

In the second call we received from Margie, she told us how the department chair had condemned her and reported her to the principal for asking students to actually perform the plays they were studying in her drama class and to give speeches in her speech class. This teacher insisted that the curriculum required only the writing of speeches and the reading of plays.

Margie said, "We're just supposed to read the plays, study the history of the theater, and not perform them??? What sense does this make? That's like studying about writing rather than *doing* writing."

At times during the first semester Margie considered quitting, because of the pressure she felt to conform. After a long-distance conference with Dave in January in which they talked about how to cope with the pressure she felt to conform and compromise her beliefs about language learning and teaching, we didn't hear from Margie for several weeks.

As part of our study, we decided to visit Margie near the end of the spring semester. When we arrived, making our way into her classroom, a converted outdated science lab located in the oldest part of the building, Margie seemed as energetic as the student we'd worked with off and on for the past three years, with all the enthusiasm we'd seen in our interviews on campus. But after talking with her for an hour or two and observing three of her classes, we realized that in some ways she was not the same person who had left Lincoln the previous summer.

Margie had been through a powerful initiation into the culture of schools, an initiation that had begun to subvert the beliefs she had developed in her preservice program. She reminded us of a young person who had finally made it through boot camp and now identified herself unquestioningly as a Marine or of a college student who after a semester of hazing, now writes about the wonderful benefits of being in a fraternity.

"Things are great," Margie said to us that afternoon. "I like the principal and the teachers and the kids I teach." But the stories she told us of her hazing and the somber look on her face made us wonder how she was able to say this. The principal yelled at her frequently, though she had learned to ward off his anger. She said she had had to modify what she called her "overly idealistic ideas" about how much writing she could ask students to do. She had made friends with the department chair who had originally criticized and "told on" her for having students give speeches and act out plays, and they were now planning some new English units for next year. She said her teaching philosophy had not really changed, but she had become more "pragmatic." When she talked about her students, she used many of the stock phrases one hears from teachers about not trying to be a "friend" to students and "being tough on them so they will respect you."

All of this suggests the power of socialization. A woman who had left the university with such clear, emerging, and well-articulated beliefs seems to have had them hazed out of her. In order to become a member of the community and faculty, Margie had slowly surrendered or was in the process of surrendering many of those thoughtfully crafted beliefs. The price of membership in this community was extremely high for Margie. If they had blatantly said, "These are the rules for membership in this community; follow them or be left on the outside," Margie would likely have told them to forget it. But such socialization happens much more subtly than that.

And Margie did have a strong need to be a member of a community. She had known what it meant to be an outsider, having come pregnant as a freshman to the university, where she was verbally and physically harassed by others in her dorm, who called her "slut" and "whore" as they pushed her around. During the remaining three years of college she had been a single parent, pushing herself hard to finish her degree and certification in four years, and at the same time to be a good parent. In Robert's class she had written often about the prejudice she'd felt as an unmarried pregnant college student and as a single parent. When she moved to this new community with her child, she didn't want to be an "outsider" any longer. Margie had begun to seriously date a local man and imagined the possibility of marrying him. She now wanted to belong. Given these desires, how could she not compromise and pay the price of membership? Hannah Arendt argues that the disciplining force of dominant discourses "normalizes" people because "behavior has replaced action as the foremost mode of human relationships" (quoted in Britzman, 1991, p. 29). It seemed that Margie could do little to intervene or author her own life as teacher; she could only conform.

Of course, this is only one construction of Margie's experience. We don't really know to what extent Margie has compromised or surrendered the beliefs with which she left our deliberate apprenticeship. There are other ways to interpret what has happened to Margie. Perhaps what seems to have been a capitulation to local culture has been a negotiation in which Margie claimed some power for her own beliefs and perspectives. Her cooperative planning of new units with the department chair who had opposed her was a strategic response to a situation that might otherwise oppress her. She has married a man from the community, has had another child, and has become an active participant in both the school and surrounding community. In a recent e-mail message to us, Margie said:

> I have thought about you and your class often. We really thought
> we knew it all! Little did I know that my learning process was just
> beginning. Now I'm much more confident; I feel good about what
> I'm teaching; I think I've found a happy medium between: "the
> old school philosophy and my own philosophy." I teach grammar
> mini-lessons and I work on vocabulary and spelling; we also have
> sustained silent reading and writing lab after writing lab. Some
> of my students astound me; they're wonderful writers.

Margie's letter suggests an alternative to our earlier narrative of her experience, which suggested that she was completely overpowered by the local educational culture. We know that identity is never determined by a single socializing ideology; we are constituted by multiple, often conflicting discourses. The intersections of these discourses are often sites for critical reflection, resistance, and continued development. Margie has clearly created a workable personal and professional life at the intersection of several competing discourses, and she is continuing her development as a teacher as she works on a master's degree in English education at a nearby state college. Like the teachers who write their own chapters in this book, she is no doubt continuing to negotiate the relationships between her personal and professional lives.

Margie's isn't the only story of socialization we have heard. John, Toni, and Carol all have stories from their first year of teaching of episodes similar to those Margie told us. Recently we received a letter from Anne, one of the students in our original cohort. In contrast to Margie's story of socialization, Anne's story is evidence of the ways beginning teachers often get caught in a web of school politics and workload exploitation that leaves new teachers without any reserves for reflection on the intellectual work of teaching, much less on their personal lives. No one seemed to be attempting to "discipline" Anne into the community. As an innocent bystander, she simply became the victim of community and school political intrigue around her. She was hired to replace a popular teacher who, she says,

> was fired in the midst of great controversy. This was not intimidating to me, because I just wanted to teach. It didn't occur to me that because of the circumstances parents and students might not want me there.

In mid-September the principal responsible for having fired the popular teacher and for hiring Anne was charged with sexual harassment and resigned. Anne originally had six classes, but the only other English teacher, a veteran of 28 years, decided the ninth grade class was more than she could handle. So the class was turned over to Anne, who then had seven different preparations (in three subject areas: PE, psychology, and English) in an eight-period day, in addition to coaching volleyball, basketball, and the speech team. Meanwhile, at the end of the semester, a third principal was hired. Anne comments that all of this "led to nights of tears, exhaustion, and a three-month battle with ear infections and strep throat and finally my regretless resignation." After leaving the small Kansas town, she returned to Nebraska to marry and resumed her teaching career in a large urban setting. She substituted for two years, then taught for a year, and now, after having a child, has decided that substitute teaching affords her the professional engagement in the classroom that she wants, but with strong enough boundaries so that she is left with the time and energy to have the personal life with her son and husband that she also wants.

Margie's and Anne's stories emphatically foreground the importance of teachers' own identities, the force that their own personal lives, histories, and school/community contexts play in their development as teachers. Although we do believe that it is important to bring theory and experience into dialogue in teacher preparation, to help students contextualize competing theories and practices and to see that pedagogy and theory are not separate but are both generative in producing knowledge, these alone are not enough to help teachers resist the disciplining force of educational and community cultures. An equally powerful factor is the interaction of those multiple narratives of education with students' own personal issues of selfhood. Margie's identity as a 22-year-old single mother shaped how she negotiated with the normalizing narratives of the new school and community. The fragmented and emerging understandings about teaching and learning and the struggle that occurs as students negotiate their own developing identities as teachers—indeed, their developing identities as people—puts teachers at risk when they face the inevitable socializing and political processes that greet all new teachers as they enter schools.

What Margie and Anne lacked, which we felt powerless to supply them at such long distance, was an ongoing supportive community of fellow teachers with whom they might continue to compose, interpret, and scrutinize narratives of teaching and of personal identity. In this way the full range of examined experience—pedagogical, theoretical, and personal—as a source of knowledge might be brought to bear on their lives as teachers.

4

Reclaiming and Revising Personal
and Professional Identities

> When our lived experience of theorizing is fundamentally linked to processes of self-recovery, of collective liberation, no gap exists between theory and practice. Indeed, what such experience makes more evident is the bond between the two—that ultimately reciprocal process wherein one enables the other.
>
> —bell hooks, *Teaching to Transgress*

We believe that teacher educators have not fully recognized how teachers' identities and histories are always part of the conscious or unconscious development of theories of teaching. As Margie's story in the previous chapter suggests, the convergence of personal and professional development is complicated, unpredictable, and certainly not subject to the control of Margie's teachers at the university. Margie lacked in her school environment what she had had, at least partially, in her university environment—the opportunity to engage in ongoing theorizing of both her personal and professional lives. At the university, she could seek out someone with whom she might engage in dialogue about the conflicts she encountered. In her first year of teaching, she attempted to do this for a while by long distance. But an ongoing structure in which to name, interpret, and critique the powerful socializing forces she was experiencing, a supportive structure from which to negotiate her beliefs, practices, and identity, was not available to Margie.

Other stories in our research affirm more fully the possibility for teachers to resist conservative socialization into school cultures, to continue to compose and examine stories of their own and of their students' learning and to use them to examine the dominant cultural narratives of teaching and learning. We find support for bell hooks's (1994) argument that theorizing, when linked to self-recovery and the ongoing exploration of selfhood, can provide a powerful tool for resisting dominant narratives and for bringing together theory and practice.

Although we think our representation of Margie's experience in the previous chapter is in many ways accurate, it is also foreshortened. Her story does not allow us to see that becoming a teacher involves an *ongoing* process of negotiation and struggle among various narratives—narratives composed as scripts from teachers' histories in gender, social class, and racial, ethnic, and family groups; multiple and often conflicting conceptions of teaching and education in our popular culture; and the stories surrounding teaching and learning that preservice teachers have composed from years of experience in educational institutions. All of these constructions continue to shape their understandings of teaching and to shape them as people within and outside educational institutions.

We began to see that our research methodology was also a powerful pedagogy. As we watched and listened to prospective and new teachers compose and revise their stories in interviews, conversations, and writing, we discovered that their storytelling, when accompanied by opportunities to examine critically those stories in dialogue with others, helped them resist other stories that would narrow and constrain their identities and their notions of language and learning. As preservice teachers composed, reflected on, and critiqued their learning and literacy stories, some of them began to place their stories in dialogue with the stories of teaching and learning told in their English and education classes, practica, and schools they entered as beginning teachers.

The convergence of these narratives highlighted for some students the conflicts and tensions among competing narratives. Those students were then able to begin to critique and revise their assumptions about writing and reading, reexamine their earlier learnings, and continually reflect, reinterpret, and reevaluate their experiences and understandings. They recognized, often for the first time, resisted, and at times broke the hold of the narratives murmured and shouted to them across their long apprenticeships in English and education. They were able to examine and at times revise the identities they had claimed or that had claimed them.

This process of naming, resistance, and revision was best illustrated in the work of Carol MacDaniels, a student who was a key participant and participant-observer in our study from the outset. In this chapter, using Carol as an example, we examine the ways in which teachers' personal and professional development are interdependent. In our retelling of Carol's story, we foreground the crucial processes in Carol's development: her emergence from silent, passive outsider in her early education and marriage to authoritative insider in the graduate work and research that prompted her to tell her stories, and her ongoing resistance and revision of her own beliefs and practices and those of the institutions in which she worked as she moved into teaching. Finally, in a third section, we describe and theorize from Carol's experience how narrative can become a critical instrument for resistance and revision of personal and professional identities.

FROM SILENT OUTSIDER TO AUTHORITATIVE INSIDER

In early interviews we asked Carol to reflect on childhood experiences at home and in school that had—to her mind—shaped her understandings of and attitudes toward literacy. Carol told us that she grew up in a large family and attended a small rural Nebraska school through the elementary grades. It was a shock for her to move from that school setting in which she and her family played central roles to a larger, more distant junior high in a neighboring town. It was at that time that Carol began to think of herself as an outsider.

> I was really different when I was a kid. I don't know if I can talk
> about it. It's still very painful. I guess I was a rebel, but as a defense
> mechanism for being different; different because I never quite fit in
> with the other kids, was always dressed differently, didn't have the
> money to do things, either. We lived far out of town; we were never
> able to join [activities, clubs], and we couldn't afford to join.

After graduating from high school, Carol attended a local private college, where she met and married a young man from the East Coast. Interrupting her college studies, she moved east with her new husband, where their life was dominated by his patriarchal Eastern European family, quite different culturally and religiously from Carol's own family. Still, then, Carol remained an outsider.

> While I had a great interest in seeing and learning about other
> things rather than playing sports or finding entertainment through
> movies and television, I always felt uncomfortable about my inter-
> ests in learning about anything and everything because they were
> rarely shared by the people around me. I came to regard myself
> as . . . different and began to hide my desires to know more.

Carol completed her baccalaureate, both satisfying and provoking her desires to know more. It was, in part, this coursework—particularly a sociology class—that raised the possibility to Carol that the life she was living was not inevitable.

After 17 years of marriage, Carol and her husband divorced. She then returned to Nebraska, where she felt she could better afford to raise two children independently. Soon after, she decided to pursue a teaching certificate. Carol believes this decision marked another significant turning point in her story.

> The first couple of years I was here it was pretty much what I expected. Everything was cut-and-dried, and I had an answer for everything, took my ed psych courses, learned how to read skills tests and intelligence tests, and how to give these tests—how many nonsense syllables you could remember, and felt that . . . this is hardly to do with education, but it didn't really mean anything for me yet.
>
> Then I had a couple classes with Larry Andrews, a professor in Curriculum and Instruction, and I credit him with getting me started. He saw something in me that I had never seen, and encouraged me and got me in touch with Dave [Wilson]. People started talking to me as if they saw something in me that I didn't know was there yet. I really didn't. I felt totally inadequate. I didn't know how to think. . . . It's because I was never allowed to think for myself. I was never encouraged to think for myself, in school or in my marriage, because I was always feeding back what other people wanted to hear, either on a test or in a paper, or to other people. My ideas were unimportant. What was important was what other people wanted to hear. Larry would look at me as if I knew what he was talking about, or would say something like, "Well, Carol knows." And I would sit there and say, "Carol doesn't have any idea." And I think that discomfort level was that transition. . . . So it was through that insistence by others that I do have thoughts in my head, that they do want to hear what I have to say, that I became more aware of what was going on in my head rather than just becoming a mirror to what other people would ask.

It was, then, in a Content Area Reading course that Carol first recognized herself as being treated like someone who knew something. The professor's respect for Carol led him to recommend her to us as we searched for someone to help us with interviews we were conducting in that first semester of our study. Carol became our research assistant. The following semester, because Carol was a member of the cohort we were studying, we asked her to serve as a participant-observer in a Composition Theory and Practice course in which several participants in our study were enrolled. Carol's role as researcher placed her in a different relationship with the course and with the professor than she might have had otherwise. Rick Evans was teaching this class for the first time and was therefore particularly receptive to dialogue with Carol, who needed—as he did—to make sense of what was happening in the class. Carol consistently cites Rick's class as a significant turning point for her—as a writer, as a researcher, as an authoritative insider, as a valued member of a community of teachers and scholars.

Earlier Larry Andrews had made voice and authority an issue for Carol by insisting that she could speak authoritatively, although she believed otherwise. Rick Evans made writing an issue by insisting that Carol could be a writer despite experience that led her to think the contrary.

> Looking back . . . from my current perspective as a writer, I feel a great deal of anger and resentment toward those who, while well meaning, made me despise putting words on paper to such an extent that I dreaded the prospect of having to write for most of my adult life—until I was reborn as a writer in my . . . [teacher preparation courses].
>
> . . . I remember facts, drills, worksheets, boredom, tedium, resignation, and then, later, looking at school with dread, loathing, and hate. School offered me no joy or solace in the painfulness of my adolescence. Rather, education was a trial I bore with little grace or heroism. Ironically, I did well in my academics and was admired for my compliance and ability to succeed by most of my teachers.

Carol reflected on her own precollege education and then described the composition theory class that allowed her to articulate what she had begun to understand about writing and its purposes:

> Throughout my education, I felt myself becoming more and more rigid . . . [Writing] became more and more difficult . . . I would put it off until absolutely the last minute, then I would start thinking seriously about what I was going to write—the right ideas. I would sit down and write three or four sentences—write, revise, edit. One paragraph then would be done, and I would put it away because I couldn't do more than that. To face writing for an hour was just too massive . . . So I was writing these little chunks, trying to tie them together, and it would take a long time . . . It was tightly edited—

no excess words . . . In early adolescence I did poetry and some short stories. Most were associated with class assignments, though. I don't remember doing anything outside of class. In high school I never did any writing.

In Comp Theory, free-writing was the lightbulb that went on in my head. It was so important to have that class where the emphasis was on self-directed learning, and the teacher was a writer/learner in the class. I had learned about free-writing just before I started that class, and I wrote a tremendous amount for that class, and it was just like all these things were pouring out of me and all the confusions, contradictions, stresses, and tensions I was experiencing worked out in the journal. I kept two journals, one for the instructor about what was going on with the class, and one about what was happening to me outside of class, and that was a tremendous freeing up for me of a lot of thinking processes that I'd felt were going on in my head, but there was just no getting a handle on it, because there was no outlet to put it in an understandable form.

Carol's experience of learning to write highlights the active use of language as a tool for making sense of her life and gaining control of her thinking and learning. Her sense of authority and voice influenced her understanding of the nature of written language use. Carol's growing sense of herself as writer cannot be traced merely to innovative teaching methods. Her teachers provided an invitation, a safe space, the expectation that she was intelligent, that she could and would write, and supportive response.

Carol's beliefs about writing also emerged within the context of new close and caring relationships with the professors with whom she was working. In speaking about her relationships with her teachers, Carol said:

Rick and Larry [the Composition Theory and the Content Reading professors] were probably the first I came in contact with. With them it was a significant interaction. I was always afraid to admit that because it seemed like it was wrong. You can't have that intimate a relationship with a teacher because it is not acceptable, but it was a very intimate, personal relationship. I don't think learning would have happened without it. It ties back to my whole experience as a married woman, and where I have been. I found myself resisting and probably not getting the full benefit of what I could have had out of those two men because I was afraid to seek a closer relationship. I find that going on from there, losing that [relationship], even graduating is a parting, and it's painful. I don't want to lose that contact.

That nurturing environment has been extremely important to me. I'm not sure whether this [coming into my voice] would have happened without that closeness . . . Listening to you [Joy and Dave] talk to me and accepting me as a person. It's all tied up with my marriage and coming out as an individual as opposed to a wife. That was all part of it. I was just becoming an individual finally after forty years of being someone else's idea of a person.

We had affirmed our confidence in Carol when we offered her the role of researcher, a role in which she came to understand the power of observation, reflection, and questioning not merely for her job as participant-observer, but for her role as teacher.

[These] last few years . . . I have learned how to reflect on what is happening to me and around me . . . Ever since I have become a participant-observer, I have never been able to withdraw from that again. And it's added depth and richness to everything I have done. I look at what is happening in my classes differently. As I asked other students questions [as part of my researcher role] I could see my own processes of thinking better. That started me reflecting on my own experience—becoming more aware of what was happening to me.

As Carol asked her classmates to compose their learning and literacy stories, she found herself provoked to compose, recompose, and examine her own. She began to internalize the questions. Research of others' lives supported her "re-search" and ultimately her "re-vision" of her own.

Always before then, I hadn't really understood the process of questioning . . . how to revel in the complexity of the whole thing. Always before that I had looked for an answer, and I finally understood somewhere in that semester that there is no answer. It's only more and more complex, and I finally accepted that complexity . . . I feel I am someone who's very committed to looking for the complexities and looking for the underlying nuances . . . In schools, it seems to me that they're looking for that answer. They're looking for very straightforward ways to approach very specific things. They're trying to diminish the complexity. As a reflective teacher/

observer I stop looking at things as problems that require solutions. I am more accepting of this group of students, in this situation, in this setting, in this school, at this time of their lives . . . I am more accepting of the students for what they are.

Carol's graduate coursework and her relationships with Larry and Rick helped her develop a sense of her own authority and voice; her work as a participant-observer and co-researcher with us helped her develop a sense of the power of observation, questioning, and reflection. This, along with her ongoing prompts to articulate and reflect on her own stories and her own internalization of the questions, allowed her to begin to name and then to resist the restrictive narratives through which educational culture positions students as problems requiring solutions. Instead, Carol began to embrace the questions and complexities these students raised for her, composing her own, more complicated narratives of students' lives.

MOVING INTO TEACHING: RESISTING AND REVISING BELIEFS AND PRACTICES

Carol graduated from our program full of confidence and ready to put into practice the principles that had been so important in her own development. But her first months as a teacher were not easy. She told us that for a few weeks after she began teaching, she worried about how other teachers and administrators in her small K–8 district would react to the obvious noise and chaos in her workshop classroom. She told about the day when the students were performing plays they had written. It was an exciting and noisy class. The principal walked into her room unannounced, fidgeted with the thermostat, looked around disapprovingly, and left. As the newcomer to the school and community, she knew that everyone was scrutinizing her work. She was angry about the principal's intrusion and found that it made her begin to discount the positive aspects of the work her students were doing. She—like Margie—began to doubt herself and her students, focusing on the noise and apparent lack of control. As a result, she spent every night for the next three weeks frantically designing worksheets and study guides to keep them quiet and under control. But as she began to relax, observe, and think again about how they were spending their time, she decided they weren't learning as much as they had under her previous practices. She moved them back to the workshop format.

> I made a conscious decision that I was going to be true to what I ac-
> tually believed in and not worry about expectations of others. I've
> established a routine of reading and writing each morning. Now I
> think my students are ready to do more work with each of those.
> My expectations are probably too high, so I'll need to look at
> what's happening with each of them, to focus on specific things
> with each of them, and keep them looking at their own learning.

Carol's stance as an ethnographer/researcher had become a habit, a
way of standing back and observing her students. This, along with the
examination of her own and others' learning narratives and her sense
of her own authority, gave her the insight, strategies, and confidence to
eventually resist her principal's critique and implied prescription for her
teaching and move her practices back to align more closely with her beliefs and her students' observed needs. Unlike Margie, Carol had extended practice in questioning and observing. And also unlike Margie,
Carol had continued to live in Lincoln, maintaining her membership in
the professional community she had joined in her teacher preparation
program, continuing to talk with us and others about her teaching.

When we asked Carol to characterize her relationship with students,
she described it in the same terms she used to describe her relationship
with her professors. She said she was establishing a close, caring, dialogic
relationship, attempting to help students believe in their own authority
as learners as she corresponded and conferred with each of them.

> I encourage them to write to me whenever they have questions or a
> problem. I find letters on my desk all the time. Then I can give the
> letter one hundred percent of my attention. I see it more as lines
> running between them and me through our writing. That relation-
> ship or dialogue through writing is the best. They're seeing that
> writing is absolutely connected to their lives. Some of their writing
> has been so sterile, but when they write to me it's never boring. I
> want them to understand that doing English is talking and writing
> about their concerns; it is being able to say, "This is what I want to
> happen to my learning."

Carol had put into practice a conception of learning and teaching that
had been modeled for her in her deliberate apprenticeship (in courses
with Rick and Larry) and that had emerged out of observation and close
reflection on and critique of her own and others' literacy and learning

stories. She was committed to providing her students with the same op-portunities for connecting their school learning with their lived lives and for claiming their own voice and authority within caring relationships.

NARRATIVES AS CRITICAL INSTRUMENTS IN PERSONAL AND PROFESSIONAL DEVELOPMENT

Carol had described herself as a person who for a long time had no way of articulating or giving voice to who she was. She had remained silent, hearing only the stories—the murmurings—of others. She accepted the identity that her family, her school, her culture articulated for her—a woman, a wife, a mother. She was often uncomfortable with these pre-scribed roles and identities, but she had no words, no vehicle for uttering to herself the "otherness" she sensed about herself, the voice that might have resisted and said, "No, that's not who I am," the voice that might have articulated an alternative or contradictory sense of her being.

Carol's story persuades us that telling our stories can be, as de Lauretis (1984) says, an "original, critical instrument" (p. 186) for articu-lating and thus resisting and revising the constraints placed on our social roles and identities. In Carol's case, the storytelling that provoked and aided her resistance occurred as she wrote her journals, composed her story for us over a period of three years, and invited, listened to, and wrote the stories of her peers. But what was the difference between Car-ol's experience and Margie's or that of other students who had experi-enced much the same deliberate apprenticeship as Carol? Beyond the on-going opportunity to engage in dialogue with supportive peers, we believe several key experiences in Carol's life converged to help her con-tinue to compose and revise narratives about herself as woman and teacher.

Claiming Marginality as a Space of Resistance

First, Carol's life experiences and her writing and reading enabled her to recognize and claim her own marginality, or otherness. Recognizing and naming her status as an outsider provided Carol with what bell hooks (1990), following Freire (1986), has described as a "site of radical possibil-ity, a space of resistance" (p. 151). In this space Carol was able to identify the power relationships that defined her identity. And having named them, she could also begin to resist the oppressive roles she had been assigned. Listening to her own voice rather than listening only to the external scripts of others, she had come to critique others' expectations for her rather than always accommodating them. Sandra Harding (1991) and other feminist theorists have further explained the importance of theorizing from one's location on the margin.

Theorizing from the position of the margin or of otherness offers both the one marginalized and those at the center an expanded and less partial account of history or reality. Looking at life in the Middle Ages or at junior high from the vantage point of women's or girls' lives enables the historian or the educator to provide a much different account of either context. Even more important, to encourage the junior high school girl or the woman teacher to tell her own story allows each to define and reclaim the historical reality of her life and thereby revise an identity that was constructed for her. Illustrating this concept further, poet and writer Minnie Bruce Pratt (1984) begins her analysis of her white Southern racist history from her identity as a white lesbian. Using her adult marginal position as a lesbian, she critiques and revises the identity and perspective that her Southern culture tried to construct for her. In doing so, she understands herself better, she constructs a new identity for herself, and she gains a new perspective on racism.

Although Carol is not an African-American woman or part of a group marginalized because of her race or ethnicity, she had identified herself as an "outsider" because of her gender, her social and economic situations, and the tense family relationships in her life. Like Minnie Bruce Pratt, Carol seems to have used that experience as one critical standpoint from which she considered her own development. bell hooks (1994) says, "It is not easy to name our pain, to theorize from that location" (p. 74). hooks goes on to talk about the importance of formulating theory from lived experience, of making the pain of exclusion a starting place for action and change. We'll see later in Carol's own chapter how she continues to use this pain and her outsider status for her own personal and professional development.

The continuity between Carol's personal and professional self-reflection, her emerging public writing and speaking (in professional journals and at conferences), and the accompanying change in her sense of authority has been described by the authors of *Women's Ways of Knowing* (Belenky et al., 1986) as the "hallmark of women's emergent sense of agency and control" (p. 68). This process has allowed Carol to define and redefine herself as teacher—a process that enables her to resist the definitions of teacher implicit in stories of schooling in our society, in much of her own schooling, in her school system, and in the teaching profession.

Relationships of Care and Love

Although she had been able to name and theorize from her marginal position, Carol had also found a place where she was not on the outside. In her professional preparation she developed mutually caring and respectful professional relationships that created a sense of belonging. While teacher educators have seldom theorized the significance of love or caring in learning, Carol attributed her emerging capacity to claim her own authority and voice to those caring professional relationships. In those relationships, she moved from the margin to a "center" in which her authority was examined but also reaffirmed and valued.

The caring relationships Carol described occurred in classes that encouraged students to become invested in composing what was meaningful to them, classes in which these narratives were shared and responded to by peers and teacher. Composing and telling stories both engenders and requires a mutual relationship between the teller and the listener, an empathetic and mutual concern. Madeline Grumet (1991) says, "A story requires giving oneself away" (p. 70). The stories Carol was composing and giving away involved all of us concerned in an array of complicated relationships. This social atmosphere was one of trust and of risk-taking, of giving and of receiving. Carol's developing professional and personal identities were both contextualized and historicized in her lived experience. But most important, they were also part of an ongoing social dialogue.

The personal and interpersonal relationships Carol experienced in literacy learning and teacher education contradict conventional assumptions that place reason in conflict with emotion and view learning as a technical/rational process that is undermined by emotion or love. These caring relationships suggest, instead, that learning occurs in complex self–other relationships, not in formal, bureaucratically defined or authorized relationships. Nel Noddings (1984) asserts the important distinction between legalistic relationships of authority and responsibility and relationships based on an "ethic of care." In *Teaching to Transgress* (1994), bell hooks describes how such relationships in her own education in all-Black schools in the South enabled her to thrive. Her teachers knew the students, their life circumstances, and their families. Their caring relationships with students inspired and supported learning in the face of the racist culture around them. hooks (1994) argues that relationships, pleasure, excitement, and even love must not be feared or banned from classrooms but must be recognized as vital to learning. She says that "To teach in a manner that respects and cares for the souls of our students is essential if we are to provide the necessary conditions where learning can most deeply and intimately begin" (p. 13).

We think it's important to emphasize, especially in light of recent critiques of personal narrative in "process pedagogies," that "feeling good" about herself, reclaiming her experience, and having her writing validated are not what are most important in Carol's experience. Instead, the potential for critique and revision made possible in those learning experiences is what is most central. As hooks (1994) argues: "A feeling of community creates a sense that there is commitment and a common good that binds us" (p. 40). hooks suggests that this sense of community can also lead to a sense of individual and community agency and thus to action. Carol's caring relationships were part of a fragile but nevertheless important sense of community that enabled her, for example, to act, resisting the intimidation of her principal and teaching from her own beliefs about teaching and learning.

Of course, caring relationships within educational settings do pose risks, as Carol herself earlier acknowledged. Carol was wary because close relationships between teacher and students are highly suspect and even potentially dangerous. As Noddings's critics point out (see, for example, Hoagland, 1991), even these caring relationships can become paternalistic and condescending, especially across gender differences and differences in authority, with the caring participant patronizing or exploiting the less powerful member of the relationship. Some readers may indeed feel that Carol's relationships with male professors were merely another example of paternalism, of male professors manipulating the novice female and determining her course yet again. We cannot speak to this issue for Carol; we'll instead let her address it in her own chapter. But we do affirm that despite the risks, these complex interpersonal relationships are important to personal and professional development. Teachers, male and female, must not abandon them, but neither can they afford to be blind to the potential misuse of power.

Revising Theory and Practice Through Narrative

A third important feature of Carol's history of personal and professional development is that her examined stories became a lens through which to examine her own classroom, to reflect on the experiences of her students and her ongoing attempts to resist and revise the conservative socializing narratives she encountered in her first teaching job. Composing her stories was not merely self-affirming and clarifying. It was not merely a precursor to action and change. As hooks (1994) and Freire (1986) claim, it constituted in itself a form of language in action that bridged the gap between theory and practice.

As she moved into teaching, Carol used her examined experience to challenge standard practices and conceptions of teaching and learning.

> I kept finding myself saying: "No, school doesn't have to work this way." I think because I was so new at becoming a writer myself, because I was a student who had gone through a tremendous change in my life, that I knew that it didn't have to be that way. I had had other learning experiences that worked . . . Reflecting on my own experience I knew that sitting in rows, handing in homework assignments, working off worksheets, bowing to the teacher's authority . . . there are other ways. Especially in student teaching there were some great things that students wrote that were so rewarding and that came from nontraditional expectations.

Carol's own storytelling allowed her to bring together reflection and critique of her personal life and her professional life. Rather than being locked into the murmured stories and scripts that constrained her personal and professional identities, Carol used her examined experience to resist and rewrite earlier scripts and stories that had defined her, thus redefining herself.

We want to consider what in this process of storytelling opens this possibility for resistance and revision. Jerome Bruner (1986) says that narrative, unlike "logico-scientific language, inhabits a realm of potential, of possibility, of uncertainty, contradictions and silences" (p. 11). Narratives, like those that Carol composed and recomposed, create multiple potential meanings and even contradictions, and therefore create spaces for rethinking and resisting old interpretations. In the process, Carol came to understand that "there are other ways," that there is no single answer.

Freire (1986) emphasizes the importance of these contradictions in the process of claiming agency. The scripting power of ideology is never unified or absolute. Individual identity is never singular. We are, for example, men, fathers, partners, teachers, brothers, employees, colleagues—all at once. In addition, each of us resides in multiple locations by virtue of our gender, religion, ethnicity, race, sexual orientation, and physical characteristics—all of which place us in different, sometimes competing, roles. In the gaps, contradictions, and tensions among competing identities, the potential for resistance and revision arises. And exposure of these gaps, Freire (1986) points out, becomes possible in the moment when the individual begins to name her own experience, to interpret it in relationship to wider cultural/political narratives. This process makes possible the recognition that cultural narratives about who one ought to be and how one might live are not monolithic or homogeneous. When individuals begin to see the multiple and often conflicting nature of those narratives, it becomes possible to hold them up to scrutiny, to resist them, and to break their hold over us.

In writing and rewriting her stories, Carol articulated and exposed the tensions and contradictions among converging narratives of self-hood—self as writer in high school, self as writer in a teacher preparation program, woman as writer, mother, daughter, and teacher. In the convergence of these narratives she found new understandings and the possibility of resisting and revising old narratives. Carol is able to continue to assert the authority of her lived and examined experience, rewriting herself as woman and as teacher.

As we have noted, conceptions of teacher education and development arbitrarily compartmentalize knowledge of content and knowledge of pedagogy and theory. But more important, these conceptions of teacher education, because they exclude the lived experience of our students, are literally disembodied. Common academic conceptions of teacher education—and therefore our programs—are depersonalized and disconnected from students' lives and their gendered, racial, ethnic, and social class identities. Carol's story demonstrates how professional knowledge and personal location are in fact inseparable.

Carol used these narrative explorations to bring theory and practice together. She and other preservice teachers were composing, interpreting, and revising their lived experiences in a few of their English and education classes. In addition, they were also self-consciously beginning to study theories of writing and reading. At the same time, two or even three times a semester, we were conducting interviews with students in our research cohort in which we asked them to compose their literacy and learning histories—and in so doing to reflect on, analyze, and articulate emerging understandings of English and teaching. The convergence of these narrative experiences highlighted for many students the inextricable connections between language learning and their development as people—and between their personal and professional identities.

Instead of taking on what Bakhtin (1981) calls "authoritative discourse," accommodating themselves to the critical perspectives of authoritative critics, theorists, or university professors or teachers, students were being asked to set their own "internally persuasive" narratives in dialogue with theoretical narratives of teaching and learning. As we watched this occur, we began to see more clearly that the *convergence* of narrative experiences had the potential of providing preservice and practicing teachers with ongoing opportunities for critical reflection that could help them resist and revise confining narratives of teaching and learning. Theory and practice were not decontextualized abstractions; students were enacting and critiquing them in tandem. They were practicing their developing theories of literacy alongside interpretation of their life experiences and their sense of selfhood. Paulo Freire describes this as "verifying in praxis what we know in consciousness" (cited in hooks, 1994, pp. 47–48). Simply "having theories" is not enough. Nor is blind action useful. What is necessary is reflection *and* action. Carol, Toni, Ruth, John, and other teachers with whom we have worked continue to resist and revise the limiting, caricature-like images of teaching and learning that surround them. They do so with narrative as a critical practice linking reflection and action in the communities that they help to sustain through their participation.

5

Renaming as an Act of Resistance

Carol MacDaniels

My silences had not protected me. Your silence will not protect you . . .
What are the words you do not yet have? What do you need to say? What
are the tyrannies you swallow day by day and attempt to make your own,
until you will sicken and die of them still in silence? And of course I am
afraid, because the transformation of silence into language and action is
an act of self-revelation, and that always seems fraught with danger.
— Audre Lorde, "The Transformation of Silence
into Language and Action"

I legally changed my name last summer, finally dropping my married
name and adopting the surname of a great-grandmother. Hearing about
what I did, a few people accuse me of being a "feminist." Others congrat-
ulate me on getting remarried. The office staff at my daughter's school
can't seem to get it straight that she and I have different surnames. My
mother gives an embarrassed laugh when she introduces me to her
friends, explaining that "she changed her name." Then she'll look at me
to give a fuller explanation, which I always do. Now that most people are
used to MacDaniels, I simply mention "dropping my married name" if
my old name appears to confuse anyone. When salespeople call on the
phone, I simply say, "She doesn't live here anymore."

I had been wanting to rename myself for a long time and played
around with different possibilities for years, wanting a new name to reflect the current me rather than a label connected with wife or, in taking
back my maiden name, daughter. I know my great-grandmother got Mac-
Daniels from her father, but he was a "wandering man," my grandmother
said, and no one ever knew him well because he kept moving on. I can

live with that. Besides, the name is me, is mine. I swore to it in front of a judge. There were only three of us in the courtroom last August 27th, the judge in somber black robes, the clerk in a bright lime-green silk suit, and me. And in less than three minutes, swearing that I wasn't attempting to defraud anyone, I became someone else.

Perhaps I finally became myself, finally and totally my own person, leaving behind the labels that others had placed on me or that I had placed on myself. There's an old cliché from the 1970s of people going out and "finding themselves." As corny as it sounds, I think I have. Working with Dave and Joy in graduate courses, in the preservice teacher research study, and in writing drafts of this chapter, I've pulled together my thoughts and experiences from the past 12 years, reflecting on my teaching, looking back at my struggles as a divorced single mother, my struggles with school systems, and what it means to be a student. I've learned a lot about how and how much I've grown and changed.

I've learned that I can't separate out the teacher I am from the person I am. I've learned that telling stories and making sense of those stories helped shape my life and my thinking. I've learned that the discovery of my own voice changed what I say as well as deepened what I think. I've learned that certain structures and strategies contribute to continued personal and professional growth. And I've learned that I want and need to maintain relationships with caring colleagues who push me, challenge me, and see things in me that I can't always see for myself.

The past 12 years have transformed me. I've changed from being a person who let others dictate what I think and how I act to someone who is critically aware of the choices and possibilities in my life. I no longer regard events in life as "given," blindly accepting what others say. I know that thoughts and actions are socially constructed, controlled by dominant ideologies and discourses. For a good portion of my life, I failed to question why things are the way they are. I've learned to ask questions.

Like Joy, my options as a girl and young woman in the 1960s were limited, yet I never recognized or questioned those limits. Only after a divorce threw my life into chaos did I begin to look at the world differently. Fortunately, in trying to find new directions for myself, I accidentally stumbled into a program at the university where I was able to begin making sense of my past, my present, and my future. Participating in the research study on teacher development, along with my graduate coursework in teacher preparation, provided the structure for telling my own stories, for developing my voice, and for working with caring colleagues.

Now I try to replicate, for my students, the conditions that led to my growth as a learner. For me, teaching writing provides the perfect setting for telling stories, for examining those stories, and for discovering what those stories have to say about how the world works and how we as individuals are shaped by that larger context. Writing becomes the lens that helps us, students and teacher alike, see the world more clearly, one frame at a time, so that we can look closely at the details and think about, talk about, and ask questions about that picture. My transformation began 12 years ago and remains an ongoing process. I meet with students for one 15-week semester, perhaps two. What I try to do during those few weeks is invite them into a process of discovery, of constructing meaning for and about themselves. Students generally enter my classroom unaware of how they have been shaped by their stories. I want to help them recognize the complex interweaving of history, ideologies and experiences that make up their identities so that they leave my classroom as reflective, self-aware learners.

Throughout this chapter I attempt to sort out the elements of the learning process that serve me so well. I tell my own stories about how I see myself both personally and professionally, trying to pull apart the transformative experience into component parts, helping me understand better how I've evolved from being timid, passive, and acquiescent to being critical, resistant, and more in control.

BEING SILENCED

When I was six or seven years old, I remember sitting on the floor in the living room behind my father's recliner. We were all watching television and although I didn't realize it, my bare foot rested on the chair's wooden leg. As my father put the chair into the reclining position, my foot got caught between the base and the reclining mechanism. Although it hurt terribly, I didn't cry out or make a sound, fearful of my father's anger. So I sat there for what seemed like an eternity, until my mother noticed what had happened.

I'd learned early in life that drawing attention to myself meant punishment, so I made myself as unobtrusive as possible, growing up shy and withdrawn. In my family, children were to be seen and not heard, and women played a secondary role to their husbands. The greatest safety lay in being quiet and quick to obey my father's commands.

School only reinforced my belief that obedience to authority was the secret to getting through life unscathed. Up through seventh grade, I attended a one-room country school where I learned three rules: sit still, be quiet, and wait your turn. Student desks were arranged in rows, youngest in front, older students in back, facing the teacher's desk at the south end of the room. Lessons consisted of filling in lots of worksheets to keep us busy while the teacher worked with students in other grades, but I was a good student because I had learned at home the importance of keeping quiet and following instructions.

School at District 61 seemed like an extension of home in more positive ways, too. Six of the 13 students attending were either siblings or cousins of mine. I enjoyed activities like hikes through the neighbors' pasture for picnics twice a year, making a communal vegetable soup in the winter with each student contributing a potato, carrot, or onion, singing around the piano every morning after standing together to say the Pledge of Allegiance, performing skits and songs in a Christmas pageant every year for our parents, and lots of games at recess every day.

Unfortunately, my enjoyment of school ended abruptly when I entered eighth grade, when the country school closed and my brothers, sisters, cousins, and I rode the bus 20 miles each way to town school. Although this new school was still relatively small (49 in my graduating class), a sharp class distinction and strong prejudice existed against "country kids." Here is where I really began hating school and everything to do with education.

It might have been different if I had come into the school a year later as a freshman when other country kids came to the local high school, but I entered as the only new student in the class, and I didn't fit in. Not only didn't I fit in, but I found myself alternately taunted and ignored by cliques that had been long established before I arrived. Whenever I spoke up or tried to make friends with someone, I'd be made fun of, so eventually I gave up and became even more silent and withdrawn.

My success as a student afforded me some satisfaction in school. Teachers liked me because I always did my assignments, always did what I was told, and never gave them any trouble. Once again, as they had in elementary school, lessons consisted of the familiar worksheets, rote memorization, and listening to the teacher as authority. I never had to think about anything, only parrot back what someone else had decided was important. No one ever asked my opinion, and every question had a right or wrong answer. As at home, I blindly accepted that someone else should rightfully tell me what to think and how to act.

I'm convinced that the only thing that brought me through the severe depression of those five years of junior high and high school was my interest in reading. Books became my escape and my sole source of pleasure. Every afternoon, I'd lose myself in a book until time for feeding the chickens, gathering eggs, setting the table for dinner, or doing homework.

At night, to help myself get to sleep, I'd make up stories based on my favorite fictional characters, and for a time I could ignore the misery of what I had to face every day at school.

Books also gave me my first clue that there was something else in the world beyond the limits of my own unhappy experience. While living vicariously through reading, I also began to imagine myself in that other world where people spoke up for themselves and earned liking and respect from others. I began plotting my escape for real. The minute I graduated, I promised myself, I was taking off and leaving my old world behind.

Unfortunately, as badly as I wanted to escape, to go somewhere far away and reinvent myself, as if location were the primary problem with my life, I still found myself restricted by obedience to my parents. And my parents wanted me to accept a four-year, full-tuition scholarship to a local college. Instead of going off to the romantic, idealized locations of my books, I ended up at a small college less than an hour away from home. But I did get to live in the dorms, which helped. Here, for the first time since seventh grade, I found myself accepted into a peer group, and school didn't seem quite so terrible anymore.

However, I was still the epitome of the good student. I remember being called upon in an English class to tell the rest of the students how Mark Anthony's wife had died (she killed herself—suffocated by putting live coals into her mouth). The instructor had asked all the students to look up this fact, which later appeared as a question on a test. As it turned out I was the only student who had actually done so. I could always be counted upon to do what was asked of me.

Going to college during the height of the Vietnam War opened my eyes just the tiniest bit into thinking on my own. I had a woman teacher for an American literature class, and we were studying Thoreau's *Walden* (1854). I remember our small class sitting in a circle of desks (that itself a radical concept for me), and this teacher asked us what symbolism we could find in the passage about the frozen pond. I picture that moment clearly. "Wow," I thought to myself, "she wants to know what I think." But I didn't have the faintest idea what I thought. No one had ever asked me a question like that before. I also remember the war protester who was a fellow student in my history class. He had long hair and a beard, a bandanna around his forehead, and wore army fatigues over a wildly colored Hawaiian shirt. Although he argued a lot with the teacher, I remember most the fact that I was scared of him. I had never seen anyone who argued with a teacher before, let alone protested the actions of the government.

Although these unsettling memories stayed with me, I clung to my "good girl, good student" roles and sailed through courses, easily maintaining my grades and knowing full well what others expected of me. At the end of three years, rather than finishing my degree, I married, ready to take on the new role of obedient wife, still believing that others could and should make decisions for me. My husband and I got along well enough for years, acting out the traditional family structures of husband as head of the family and wife as helpmate and keeper of the home. We moved to New York, 60 miles outside the city, which I thought finally fulfilled my fantasies of living in an exciting, exotic location where meaningful and important things would happen.

By now feminism had followed the Vietnam War and protests had taken on a different tone. Still a voracious reader, I read over a wide range of topics and authors, not realizing that I was informally continuing my education—or maybe even beginning my real education. I couldn't help but pay attention to the rhetoric and apply what I read and heard to my own life. I worked full-time, but still had full responsibility for our home. Although I had finished my college degree shortly after getting married, I had always wanted to go back to school for graduate work, but my husband dismissed my interest as a foolish waste of time and money. We began to struggle more and more with the changing roles in our relationship, and as I became more independent, questioning, and outspoken about our marriage, my husband grew more angry and frustrated that I wasn't the same person he had married years before.

By now we had been married 17 years and had two children under the age of six. Despite my growing awareness of the unbalanced partnership in our marriage, I still regarded myself as a wife and mother first and foremost, realizing that by raising questions, by talking about what I wanted and needed, by refusing to remain passive and silent, I was bringing about the end of my marriage. I kept thinking, "If only I were good enough, this terrible thing, this embarrassment of divorce, wouldn't be happening to me." But it did happen.

BREAKING THE SILENCE

I remember standing in the foyer of my split-level suburban house one gray April morning. Nothing had been said, but I knew, absolutely and finally at that moment that my marriage was over. I stood there with my right hand on the wooden railing, letting the realization wash over me. Nothing in my life would ever be the same again.

At first, I necessarily concentrated all my energies on simply surviving. Confused and frightened to be on my own for the first time in my life, I floundered from kids and home to work to home again wondering how I'd come to be in the position in which I now found myself—a single parent of two small children, fearful of what the future might hold for the three of us. I had no experience in making decisions or even thinking for myself, having moved from my parents' home to college to marriage. Certainly I had been competent and held considerable responsibility and authority in my different jobs, but this was different. This was personal; this contradicted all that I believed about relationships, about identity, about what made sense. My life experience offered me no models for what single mothers were supposed to do. What were the rules? How did I act around my friends? Would people see me as a stereotype? How did I tell people I was no longer married? What would my grandparents say?

I moved from my home and friends in New York back to Nebraska to be closer to family, knowing that I would need their support with getting started on my own. Although they did help, every single moment in every single day now represented something new and unknown, requiring some response from me. My previous definitions of wife, woman, daughter, and mother no longer fit. I would have to redefine my identity within the parameters of my new life.

I'd been on my own for about a year when I realized that there was no way I could support the three of us on the salary I was making. I needed to change jobs. So I sat down at my kitchen table one evening and started making lists: what was I good at, what were my skills, what did I want for myself, what practical considerations did I need to take into account. Much to my disgust, I kept coming back to teaching. On the positive side, I liked working with kids, I loved learning, and a teacher's schedule somewhat matched her kids' routine. Summers off, right? On the negative side, I kept remembering how horrible my own experience had been in junior high and high school. I hated worksheets and answering problems at the end of each chapter, and I harbored deep anger and resentment toward my former teachers, who allowed a troubled student like I had been to be so profoundly lonely and depressed through five years of school while no one noticed.

I took an afternoon off from work and went to the teachers' college office. Since it was late June, flowers bloomed across the manicured lawns of the university campus, and summer sessions meant no parking problems. Excited to be there, I felt I had made the right decision. By good fortunate I ended up talking to Maggie Sievers, a college advisor, who made everything happen for me. She was welcoming, encouraging, and enthusiastic about my becoming a teacher, helping me fill out papers and explaining what I would need to do to get started. Two months later, for the first time in 15 years, I found myself seated in a college classroom.

That fall semester began a journey that, so far, has lasted 12 years and has brought me teaching certification, a master's degree, and (soon) a Ph.D. But more than the degrees and certificates, the journey has brought me to a different way of looking at the world, a new knowledge of my position in that world, and an ability to both stand up and speak up for myself. My traditional images of wife and woman had shifted unalterably with my divorce. Now my traditional images of teaching and learning would shift and enable me to resist the model of teaching that I had experienced in my own education.

Larry Andrews taught my first graduate course that fall, and I have no idea how it came about, but Larry saw something in me, some potential that I never realized existed. Over the course of the semester, he drew me into classroom dialogue. He turned to me, saying, "Carol will know," when someone asked a question, and he praised and encouraged my work. Larry knew me as a person and treated me as an equal. I remember walking across campus one winter afternoon, meeting Larry heading the other direction. He stopped and invited me to sit with him on a bench adjacent to the bus stop. He'd heard of a part-time instructor's position opening up at a small local college, he told me, and had recommended me for the position. Before I could respond, he raised a hand to stop my words. "I know what you're going to say," he said. "You don't think you can do it." He was right, I didn't, but Larry went on to describe what I'd have to do, my qualifications, and why challenging myself in this way would be a good thing. I took the position, my first teaching job ever, and learned a lot about myself and teaching.

Larry is also the one who recommended me to Dave Wilson and Joy Ritchie as a research assistant on a study of preservice English teachers. Knowing that tuition remission would help put me through school, I eagerly agreed to accept the position. My job included interviewing students in the English education program, participating in the study myself, and conducting participant observation in a composition class.

As a research assistant, I gathered a variety of stories from other preservice teachers—good experiences, bad experiences, teachers they loved, teachers they hated, humiliating things teachers did to students in the classroom, books they read, writing for school, writing outside of school. Their stories prompted me to question my own past, my experiences with school and teachers, something I had never thought to do before. As students talked, I composed and compared my stories to theirs. In addition, Joy and Dave asked me these same questions in their interviews with me. Over time, I internalized this process of questioning.

At the same time, as part of the study and my teacher preparation program, I enrolled in a Composition Theory and Practice class with Rick Evans, where he introduced us to process-oriented theories and pedagogies, including free-writing and writing my own stories. As part of the research and as a requirement for the composition class, I needed to tell my own stories.

Talking and writing about my experiences proved incredibly difficult at first. My life had been so chaotic since my divorce that I had trouble organizing my thinking. The frenetic pace of my days seemed to make me both incoherent and inarticulate. But what a fantastic moment in my life. Three college instructors, people with status, people whom I liked and respected, were inviting me to talk about myself and to tell my own stories. No teacher from my past had ever wanted to hear what I thought. None had trusted me to make choices in my own education, and none had encouraged me to tell my own stories.

Through my research assistantship, I ended up spending a lot of time with Dave, Joy, and Rick, so I came to better understand their beliefs, teaching strategies, and genuine caring for students. I remember meeting with Joy in her office one winter morning, and we sat and drank tea together and amidst her interview questions talked about feminism, feminist theory, and the choices women have to make for themselves and their families. Joy said something to the effect that, "I can't imagine what this must be like for you," referring to my being a single parent, working full-time, and going to graduate school. That simple statement validated me.

I learned from moments like these that conversations between colleagues make a difference, not only in offering support and caring, which sustain me as an individual, but also in affirming the significance of our work as professionals. Knowing that Joy accepted me as a person and acknowledged my struggle changed my politics. Because I mattered, I no longer had to be silent. And by refusing to be silent, I entered the political arena, a move that few outside education understood.

When I had decided to go back to college, my family and friends offered lukewarm support at best. My mother sighed, "Oh, Carol," as if she couldn't believe I didn't have better sense. One sister asked how I'd have time for dating. My father worried about money. No one said, "Go for it," but I did find affirmation in two places: from my professors at the university, and from my son and daughter. My children were seven and three when I started my coursework, but as they grew up with my studies as a constant in their lives, they realized how important graduate school was to me and have always encouraged and supported my decision.

As difficult as it was to keep going, I loved going to school, and gradually began speaking up more in class, always welcomed by instructors who accepted and encouraged my participation. As my confidence grew, I had more to say: in class discussions, in talking about the research study, and on paper as I began journaling and writing down my stories.

A dam had burst inside me, and 36 years of stored-up words and stories came pouring out.

FINDING VOICE AND RESISTING EASY ANSWERS

I have drawers full of writing now, journals, papers from class assignments, stories I've written, classroom observations, some published articles, lots and lots of drafts of work in progress, and a few letters to newspaper editors. However, the writing is only part of my story. Working closely with Joy and Dave also challenged me to pull apart my stories, to ask why things happened the way they did, and to identify the constructs that shaped and orchestrated my life. With my students, I call this looking beneath the surface. Stories have multiple layers, beginning with the visible, readily apparent details: I got divorced, I went to graduate school. However, underneath those two facts lies the complex webbing of forces and impulses that brought me to that point in my life. Telling my stories was hard enough, but understanding them became even harder.

It surprises me now that my first two pieces of writing for sharing in composition class were both fiction. One story fictionalized an experience my sister had when someone tried to break into her house. In the other, an old woman plots to kill the teenage girl who lives next door. I can see that I was playing it safe, nothing personal, nothing about me. My early journal writings consisted of my thinking about the class and my writing, but I appreciated that Rick Evans, the instructor, always wrote back to me, affirming my right to speak and proving to me that he was listening. However, he also, through his responses, invited me to go back to my entries and look at them again to see what I could discover about the forces at work in my life. In addition, my role as participant observer in the class, pushed me to further reflection and analysis of my past experiences and my writing.

Dave and Joy encouraged me to reflect on my stories, too, inviting me to probe deeper, pushing me to look beneath the surface, and to try and understand why I had hated school so much. I finally had a chance to talk about and examine the negative feelings I'd harbored for so long toward my previous school experiences. Telling these stories about feeling the outsider at school, about how much I disliked worksheets and textbooks, and about how I grew to hate writing proved to be the seeds of a philosophy about schooling, students, teaching, and learning that still continues to evolve.

I poured onto paper the anger and frustration I'd held inside for so many years. And as I put these stories and feelings onto paper, I learned another important lesson about the power of telling stories: writing functions as therapy. Once transferred to paper, my feelings diminished in intensity. Also, by being articulated, resentment and anger emerged as tangible experiences rather than confused tangles of emotion, allowing me to examine what had happened and why I felt the way I did. By writing about my memories, I was able to make sense of what I felt, and with this new understanding, I was able to let go of the emotional baggage I carried.

However, growing as a learner also brought new frustrations and setbacks. As time went on and I became more adept at analyzing my own thinking and exploring multiple perspectives, I began to struggle with the contradiction that the more I thought about things, the more complex and confusing they became. Even though I relished the expansion of my thinking, at times I still wanted simple, concrete answers. Life had seemed simpler when others told me what to think and do.

I also didn't always get the kind of response I thought I wanted or needed. After about three years of graduate school, I finally started writing about my divorce and what it meant to be a single parent. I trusted that this new writing instructor would respond in affirmative, supportive ways. Meg read my portfolio, and while I can't remember specific comments, the gist of her response was that I'd "get over it." Her response shocked me. I'd invested so much emotion in that writing, confessing my fears and anger to an outsider's eyes, but her response dismissed and trivialized everything I had written. That piece of writing got put away, and I've never gone back to it since.

I realize now that I failed to tell Meg what kind of response I wanted, and I now know that instructors also bring their histories and experiences to their readings. Meg had been divorced and lately remarried at the time we met in class. I suspect she responded to the pain she found expressed in my paper. She told me what she thought I might want and need to hear: The pain will go away. You will heal. Someday I'll go back to that writing because it was so important to me.

The sound of my voice literally turned out to be a problem, too. Wanting to remain in the background all my life, not having opportunities to express myself, and letting others speak for me, I had developed a soft voice that came across as passive and shy, rarely rising above a whisper. During teacher education classes, my instructors and cooperating teachers shook their heads at me. "I don't know how you're going to teach with such a quiet voice," they'd say. I shared their concern and worked hard to develop a "teacher voice" that carries both volume and authority.

Through internalizing these lessons about teaching, my authority and agency in personal concerns changed as well, partly of necessity and partly because I could contextualize and analyze situations. I felt more in control of circumstances and became more confident in making decisions. By using the lessons I'd learned in my coursework about asking questions and reflecting on my experiences, I didn't let things just happen anymore, I acted and responded thoughtfully and with deliberation.

Being in a graduate program and a single parent at the same time led to some interesting conflicts for me. One of the ongoing litanies I heard from experienced public school teachers, popular media, and some university instructors blamed single-parent families for most if not all the problems in schools. This idea directly contradicted the evidence of my own eyes. My family was fixed, not broken. We were all three healthier than we had ever been as a nuclear family. Despite that, I watched the school system treat us with indifference and insult: my seven-year-old son being asked to stand up with all the other "free lunch" students the first day of school so the teacher would know who they were; my having to announce that I needed an application for reduced lunches in front of a group of secretaries and office personnel because the receptionist wouldn't cross the room to speak to me privately; waiting in line 45 minutes to talk to a counselor at parent–teacher conferences only to have her get up and walk away without apology when it came to my turn. "Oh, she had a meeting to go to," another counselor told me.

Another conflict involved the teaching of spelling. All through second grade, Becky struggled with spelling and brought home relatively low grades. Then she began not wanting to go to school on Fridays because of spelling tests. I finally got her to tell me that she hated spelling because the teacher said students had to study the words at home with their parents, and she couldn't ask me to help her because I was too busy all the time. Our family time together meant too much to all of us to spend it studying spelling lists, so I pulled together all the research I could find on how kids learn to spell and the ineffectiveness of most direct spelling instruction and brought it to the attention of the teacher, the principal, and the district curriculum specialist in order to have Becky removed from spelling instruction and tests.

During my son's third grade year, I couldn't believe how many worksheets he brought home on a daily basis. So I began collecting them with the idea that at the end of the year, I would haul a box down to the district office and have a little talk with them about killing trees along with killing my son's interest in learning. By the end of the year, we had a full carton of paper, but I never visited the school office. I knew my son had to spend another three years in that school and worried that my gesture might not be well received.

For three or four years, I put away the kids' report cards without looking at them, trying to emphasize to Matt and Becky that grades didn't have anything to do with learning. Secondary teachers thwarted me, though. They couldn't seem to talk about my children without pointing to a grade in the grade book first. I haven't opened my own grading slips from the registrar at the university for over 10 years.

Along with advocating for my children, I have also become an advocate for democratic principles in education, student-centered classrooms, and teacher autonomy. As state and federal governments move to control more and more of what goes on in the classroom, I am taking a strong interest in the politics of education. Although my involvement so far consists of only a few letters to the editor and campaigning for local candidates for political office, I am not finished yet.

Having learned to resist cultural notions of family, women, and schooling, I don't think that anyone who knows me now would describe me as passive and quiet anymore.

EVOLVING AS A TEACHER

When I registered for classes at the university 12 years ago, I had an image of teachers as all-knowing, poised, confident authority figures dispensing knowledge from the front of the classroom. I didn't exactly see myself in that role, but fortunately that stereotypical image didn't last even into my second semester at the university. It seemed then that education had changed a lot since I had last been in school. As I took more courses and worked with different instructors, my views on schooling moved away from thinking I would end up duplicating my own experience, and I began imagining other possibilities for what teaching and learning might look like. Much of my early thinking about teaching consisted of promises I made to myself: I won't depend on worksheets; the classroom will be student-centered; lessons will be relevant and meaningful; I will never assign the questions at the end of the chapter; students will have a choice about what they learn and how they learn; I will be an advocate for students.

Fortunately, learning to reflect on my school and home experiences complicated my thinking about what it meant to be a teacher, about what it meant to be the parent of a student, about how the personal and professional merge, and about how we all are fundamentally shaped by the world around us. As my thinking became more critical, I became more adamant about what should and shouldn't happen in a classroom. What shouldn't happen is what had happened to me in junior high and high school, where learners sat passively while meaningless facts were thrown our way. What should happen is that students become active participants in their own education.

My own experience as a student taught me that instruction was often limited to traditional, meaningless curricula handed down from some mystical, long-dead higher authority. My high school teachers valued canonic content and allowed only narrow, "correct" interpretations of the text. They rarely, if ever, gave students the opportunity to explore their own ideas. Students were discouraged from thinking because divergent thinking challenged official knowledge. Having formed an alternative vision of education through the content and pedagogy of my courses at the university, I knew the kind of teacher I wanted to be.

When I left campus to get my first teaching job, I was hopelessly naïve. I can't quite believe it of myself now, but I actually thought that all schools and administrators wanted to improve instruction in their districts and buildings. Although I went on lots of interviews in both large and small schools, I didn't get hired. Only years later, after meeting a lot more administrators, did I finally realize that while I spoke enthusiastically about giving students choice, about constructing knowledge, and about improving education, the administrator would be sitting on the other side of his (they were all male that first year) desk wondering if I would upset his nice little applecart of a school and what was wrong with lecturing and giving multiple-choice tests anyway.

Finally in mid-August I did find a job in a great K–8 school, with a supportive staff, interested parents, and a fair amount of teacher autonomy. My classroom included seventh and eighth grade blocks of language arts and social studies, for me a dream combination. What I didn't realize, though, is that the students and the schedule both revolved around worksheets, reading chapters from the textbook, publisher-generated activities and tests, vocabulary and spelling lists, and every other traditional assignment from my past that I had tried so hard to forget.

By the end of the first week of school, I was struggling. By the end of the first month, I knew I was in trouble. The students resisted my attempts to give them choices. They didn't talk when I gave them opportunities to express their opinions. They didn't want to write in journals. They wanted to know why they weren't reading chapters in their social studies books, and they wanted to know why I had put the grammar books on the top shelf in the cupboard. In addition, I was trying to work within the framework of the school schedule, which had students changing classes every thirty minutes all afternoon.

I don't know whether I doubted everything I thought I had learned at the university, but I certainly realized I had to do something if I was going to survive. So I took down the grammar texts, assigned chapters in the social studies books, brought back the vocabulary and spelling tests, and photocopied worksheets by the dozens. Things went fine for a while, but then I found myself in a different kind of hell, trying to get all that paperwork graded.

Besides, I knew I had made a mistake. Nothing the students produced with this blizzard of paper had any value or meaning to them. I remember sitting at my desk at the end of each afternoon staring at piles of newsprint worksheets and ragged papers torn from spiral notebooks, knowing that I would have to read and grade each sheet before collecting the next day's assignments. Although my students were familiar with this kind of work, not one word on any single sheet remotely connected with anybody in this little village of 300 set in the loess hills of eastern Nebraska where kids played softball in the summers and rode their sleds down Main Street during the winter. How could a manufacturer's worksheet designed to apply equally to hundreds of thousands of students across the United States have the slightest meaning to a single one of my students?

These assignments served only to keep students busy and out of trouble (like the good, docile student I had been) and had no connection to real learning. I resisted being that kind of teacher. Falling back on the processes that had helped me so well during my graduate program, I started journaling and reflecting on what I saw happening and not happening in my classroom, analyzing what needed to be done. I concluded that I needed to help students learn how to function in a student-centered classroom. I needed to teach them how to speak up in the same way I had been taught to give voice to my thoughts and ideas. And I needed to give them time to learn and develop. After all, it had taken me years to resist school's role for me as a student and become a more active learner.

We made some compromises. First, I approached the administration and received permission to lengthen class periods for seventh and eighth graders. We kept the grammar books, but we worked through the assignments together, or the students taught the lesson. For vocabulary and spelling, students generated their own word lists. Instead of reading every chapter from the social studies text, I'd outline the unit objectives with options for reaching those objectives, and the students decided collectively how we would proceed. I provided journal topics as well as instructions about when and how much students would write, gradually reducing my input while offering more choices.

Although the classroom schedule and activities changed a number of times that first year, the students had been well schooled. None of them questioned me, as the teacher and authority, as to why we were always doing something different. Giving up grading all those worksheets proved to be a tremendous relief to me because I had discovered that I hated grading worksheets almost as much as I hated filling them out as a kid. How much my classroom had changed came home to me one day about midway through the fourth quarter that year. Parent conferences were coming up the next week, and when I opened my grade book, I saw a totally blank page for Language Arts. The students had been working hard with reading and writing, I had responded to their work, we had discussed our books and stories, and we had found ways to connect our lessons to our own lives. We just hadn't graded anything.

After I got over my initial panic, I realized that real learning is not measured by numbers or letters. Because of the work we had done together, I could talk at length about each student's abilities, strengths, and interests. However, I also realized that parents and administrators would expect a grade, so in later quarters I made sure my grade book had numbers in it. When it came time for conferences, the students and I did a twofold presentation. I had invited students to reflect on what they perceived to be their interests and strengths as students as well as some personal goals for the rest of the year. Then I asked the students to come to the conferences with their parents and talk through what they had written. I joined the conversation with some of my observations and stories about the student, and then, and only then, would I pull out a list of grades.

That first year taught me some invaluable lessons about teaching. When I have problems in the classroom, I write and reflect on what's gone wrong and what needs to happen to fix things. I also ask the students for help. Once they discover that a teacher really does want to hear their opinions and really does value their answers on how the classroom operates, students can offer powerful and responsible insights and advice.

Jennifer reinforced the lesson about learning from students. She had come into my classroom the first day of school telling me, "I've never read a book all the way through," as if she were daring me. When I abandoned the traditional for a more student-centered classroom, I allowed students to choose the novels they wanted to read. A group of four students decided they wanted to read Tolkien's *The Hobbit* (1988). I read along with them, and we had wonderful discussions and activities based on the book, like making maps, drawing pictures, doing skits, and comparing the characters to other heroic figures from literature. Our community of readers pulled Jennifer in to join us, and before the end of the year, she had not only read *The Hobbit* (1988), but two of Tolkien's sequels as well. I'm convinced that if I had stuck with the worksheets and text-book assignments, with a single novel assigned to all students, Jennifer would have maintained her record of never having read an entire book.

Another lesson I learned that year was that my administrator pre-ferred traditional classrooms. I could tell right away that putting desks into a circle or groups instead of straight rows seemed suspicious to him. He also didn't like the noise coming from my room, assuming that stu-dents only learn when sitting quietly. Even though the students and I held a wonderfully natural and engaging discussion during his first formal evaluation of my teaching, he gave me a low score because students did not raise their hands before joining the conversation. After that, the stu-dents and I agreed that whenever he dropped by, they would raise their hands, and they always did. He took to barging into the classroom unan-nounced, swinging open the door (I'd covered the glass window with student artwork), glaring around the room or fiddling with the thermo-stat. I got the message: He didn't like what I was doing, and although I might not have crossed the line yet, I was on notice. He was watching me.

He retired the next year, and we were fortunate to find a new princi-pal who valued student-centered classrooms, which could be as noisy as necessary to get students interested and involved. My classroom in that little school still seems like the perfect teaching job to me—small class sizes, flexible scheduling, teacher autonomy, a staff that supported one another without any bickering, and a progressive administrator who trusted teachers. Unfortunately, teacher salaries in the district ranked among the lowest in a state that ranked among the lowest in the nation. I could not stay there and support my family.

Since that first job, I have worked in other schools with other admin-istrators, and I'm surprised to admit that I do not always get along well with them, a startling admission for someone who grew up thinking that obedience to authority was the right and safe thing to do. Administrators intimidate me, but only to a point, because I'm not willing to inflict mean-ingless tasks on students. I've met many outstanding administrators who respect the people they work with and genuinely care about students. However, I have also met administrators who are all about image and control and not making waves. If students are quiet and out of sight, it doesn't matter whether or not they are learning anything.

I have also worked with a variety of teachers, many of whom I re-spect and admire, but again there are some who clearly should not be working with students, some who are downright dangerous. I'll never forget my shock on hearing one veteran female teacher describe a student as a "waste of human flesh." In addition, some teachers exerted subtle pressure on me to change how I taught, asking pointed questions about my not using textbooks or saying that my students would not fit into so-and-so's class next year, suggesting that a certain group of students would do better "with more structure," or that "this group can't do the kinds of things you do in your room." I see these comments now as attempts to normalize me back toward traditional teacherly roles. I wish more of my colleagues would ask me *why* I do things the way I do, but it seems we cannot talk about improving teaching. I have learned that there is an acceptable form of silence in schools, and that silence is a way to stop us from asking the hard questions.

REFINING MY CLASSROOM

Currently I teach composition part-time at a small state college while working on my doctorate. Incorporating the same processes and principles I learned during my own coursework, I help students improve their writing, develop their voices, and become critical thinkers. Admittedly, students are limited in gaining from a one- or two-semester course what has taken me 12 years to understand. And my understanding of how the world works is still imperfect and evolving.

In my classroom, writing stories is an essential first step in a *process* of constructing meaning from our lived experiences. I want students to leave my class appreciating the value of telling stories and reflecting upon those stories, so I invite them to write about their hometowns, their families, and their school experiences. Then we share our stories, and through talk and written response, I encourage students to reflect: Why did they pick this story? What does this story say about who they are and why they think, feel, and act the way they do? (What is the larger context? What stories are left out?) What beliefs and social discourses shape their thinking and their stories?

Writing stories helps establish a strong sense of community in the classroom, and sharing information about ourselves establishes a degree of intimacy that brings students and instructor closer together. Personal knowledge also prompts greater reflection on how to make sense of what people are writing. In addition to peer response, students receive written response from me, as reader and as teacher, so that I can push them to think critically about their writing. In the same way I once accepted that others could and should control my life, I see students accepting circumstances as somehow predetermined or inevitable, so I challenge them to recognize and examine the forces that shape their thinking.

While I believe in the value of developing writing ability by asking students to write on topics meaningful to them, I also struggle with the ethics of encouraging students to share personal stories in the classroom. Even though I caution students about going public with private information, many seem to appreciate the opportunity to share intimate and privileged information. The bottom line for me comes from my own experience and desire to tell the stories I had kept bottled up for so long. I told my stories in order to make sense of difficult experiences. Students need and deserve that same chance in a supportive environment where they know that what they say will be accepted, validated, and held in confidence. Then, as I learned to do, I encourage students to probe their stories for meaning and understanding.

I'm always amazed when I read students' writings about their experiences. They'll talk about traumatic childhoods, about tragedies in their families, about being raped, about living with crippling diseases, and about the intensely immediate struggles of being young college students. None of them arrives in my classroom with their stories fully articulated and examined, yet those stories have shaped who they are, who we all are. If I can help them find joy in writing, develop their abilities as writers, and glimpse the complex stories that make up their identities, then I'm satisfied.

Being an adjunct instructor isolates me from the rest of the faculty at this small college because my time on campus is so limited, and when I am there, I am busy. Although I no longer have a disapproving administrator or colleagues questioning my teaching, I find that I have to resist imposing parameters on my teaching from what I suppose or imagine other faculty or administrators *might* be thinking. For no apparent reason, I sometimes find myself second-guessing my teaching based on totally imaginary criticism from outsiders. Because I have little contact with colleagues, for support I turn to students and share my doubts and hesitations with them. Or I write in my journal and try to analyze my uneasiness. Talking with students and writing reflectively helps me work through these periods of second-guessing myself.

DEVELOPING CARING PROFESSIONAL RELATIONSHIPS

I try to establish close, mutually respectful, and caring relationships with students through journals, through writing stories, and through class discussions where we talk about ourselves and where we are from. I also bring students into the discussion of course objectives and invite them to tell me when lessons and activities are not working, even though I sometimes hear things I would rather not know. Getting to know students and really listening to them talk about themselves and about the classroom provides me with powerful insights into my teaching.

When I returned to school after 15 years, it seemed strange to have instructors paying so much attention to me. Although I imagine that some of my former elementary, high school, and college teachers must have cared about students, none demonstrated any real interest in me as a person. Curriculum and content took precedence over students. Responsibility for any failure to learn rested with the student. School didn't allow for or welcome student input. We were receptacles for information, incapable of learning on our own.

Caring instructors like Larry Andrews, Rick Evans, Joy, and Dave made all the difference for me. They modeled what good teaching is all about, challenging me to become someone other than the person I had always been and encouraging me to think critically about my life. The teacher love, the caring, unquestioning acceptance of me as an individual, created an atmosphere where I felt confident to take risks, to tentatively articulate my thinking, and to learn from my own mistakes. For someone who had defined herself by fulfilling others' expectations and who had let others control her life, this looking within for meaning, knowledge, and awareness seemed radical indeed. In such an environment I finally could be myself. I finally belonged.

From that set of caring relationships, I have moved on to establish others. My personal and professional lives now merge in associations with teachers, college instructors, and different organizations across the state and the nation. Especially important is my writing group, which meets weekly at a local coffeehouse. Although the participants have changed somewhat over the five years since we started, the camaraderie, warmth, and response we share sustain themselves through these transitions. This group keeps me writing. There are always other things that need doing, but knowing that my colleagues will be waiting on Thursday nights with their writing, ready to respond to what I wrote, prompts me to get words down on paper.

Another association that has significantly contributed to my personal and professional growth has been the Nebraska Writing Project. During my first summer in the project, I barely understood the implications of what I experienced in those five weeks as I immersed myself in writing, becoming part of a community of writers and learning about teaching writing from other teachers. After that first summer, I became a teacher consultant to the Writing Project, facilitating institutes first at the university, and now in rural areas of the state. I serve on the Writing Project's Advisory Board, have represented Nebraska at national conferences, and serve as state coordinator for a Rural Voices, Country Schools research team focusing on good teaching in rural schools.

The Nebraska English Language Arts Council (NELAC) also supports my professional growth. As the state affiliate of the National Council of Teachers of English, NELAC is the window through which I've observed national adoption of standards in reading and language arts and now the state's struggle to implement and assess standards in all curricular areas. Through my association with NELAC, I've presented papers at state, regional, and national conferences as well as holding a number of positions on the executive board and serving as editor of the *Nebraska English Journal* for two years.

Along with establishing a network of teachers and organizations, I enjoy the work I do for my doctoral program. Being in a structured setting where I can read, talk, share, argue, write, and think about issues relevant to education stimulates and challenges me. I doubt that I'd maintain the discipline of professional development if I abandoned this degree program. Continuing to learn was one of my primary goals in going back to school 12 years ago, so I am where I need to be.

WHERE AM I NOW?

As I know myself better, I realize just how pervasive the forces are that still pull me toward complying with authority, whether I agree with them or not. I continually struggle to overcome the need to have everyone like me, even if making someone else happy means making personal sacrifices or poor choices. However, I'm now able to recognize this tendency in myself and try to think through decisions before I make them, knowing that acting with conviction and moral integrity may make people upset with me.

As my voice is stronger, so too is my ability to act independently, to resist forces that would mold me into what image-conscious school systems want teachers to be. I'm proud of the fact that I stand by my principles, but at the same time, I worry about what others think of me. Although I speak up more as I continue my education, I still sometimes suffer anxiety attacks when confronting authority figures. I cringe as I send off letters to the editor responding to attacks on schools. I stutter from nervousness when I speak up in classrooms or at meetings, and I constantly second-guess myself. Part of me wants to return to the security of being dutiful and obedient again so that no one gets mad at me. I resist, instead doing what I believe is right for me, for schools, and for students.

Like all good teachers, I'm incredibly busy, and my family life suffers because of my professional involvement. I don't know how to balance teaching with a personal life, but then I also don't know how to separate who I am as a teacher from who I am as a parent, a woman, a financial provider, an individual. Over these past 12 years, I've fundamentally changed from the person I was in my "first life." I've learned that the more I've grown as a teacher and learner, the better my personal life has been. I know myself so much better because the processes I've developed for professional growth have proved equally valuable to me personally. Telling stories and reflecting on those stories helped me make sense of the circumstances in which I've found myself. Likewise, the more I learn about feminist theory, dominant discourses, social constructs, ethnographic research, the politics of education, and a wealth of other ideas and possibilities, the more connections I make to my own life, enriching me personally and helping me identify, resist, and revise others' scripts for me.

Right now, I'm close to finishing my coursework for my doctorate. Although I began this latest graduate program hesitantly, consciously keeping open the option of quitting at any time, I've not regretted one minute of my work. Much of what I know about teaching really seems to be coming together now, and I love that feeling that comes when I can make a connection between past and current understanding or find that I recognize obscure references to educators, theories, or philosophers.

In my personal life, too, I'm finding that the struggles aren't quite so overwhelming anymore. I'm sure the fact that Matt and Becky are now older and relatively independent has a lot to do with this newfound sense of relief. Although we've had some difficult times as a family, I appreciate that we've done as well as we have, and I'm grateful that both my son and daughter have unwaveringly supported my work as both teacher and student.

My children are different people because I have changed so profoundly from the woman I was when they were born. I know they are stronger and more independent because I've shared my own learning and philosophies with them. I model my processes of reflection with them as we analyze experiences and try to understand why things happen the way they do. I am proud that they both learned to resist the dominant discourses early in their lives, although this resistance has not made things easy for them, as there are consequences for standing up or speaking out against tradition. Matt and Becky represent my greatest success as a teacher.

When I talk about metaphors with my students, one example I use equates my life as a single parent and teacher over the past 12 years to the fate of Sisyphus, forever having to push a boulder up a hill. I feel as if I've been experiencing a similar struggle for 12 years. Every time I thought things were smoothing out for me, something would roll over me, and I would have to start all over again.

I sense a maturing of my learning and teaching, where instead of pushing so hard to move continually upward, I can begin to see the top of that hill, and there, over the crest, waits a measure of confidence and understanding. Not that I will ever stop growing and learning. This change I see in myself is a reconciliation of identities—me the learner and me the person, blended, growing, confident in my ability to continue to be both. The turbulence of the transition years is smoothing out, and I am finally getting that damned rock over the top of the hill. I like who I am and where I am going now.

Perhaps the weight got lighter when I renamed myself last fall, shedding some of the baggage of my past. Perhaps my name change was the ultimate act of resistance; even my name isn't a "given" anymore. I can resist and revise. I like that. And I like thinking about my future that way. Nothing is inevitable.

6

Claiming Authority: Learning to Trust My Questions

Toni Siedel

> We have been socialized to respect fear more than our own needs for language and definition, and while we wait in silence for that final luxury of fearlessness, the weight of that silence will choke us. The fact that we are here and that I speak these words is an attempt to break that silence and bridge some of those differences between us, for it is not difference which immobilizes us, but silence. And there are so many silences to be broken.
> —Audre Lorde, "The Transformation of Silence into Language and Action"

Journal entry—February 8th, 1990 [second semester, first year of teaching]. I'm feeling really crappy today. I don't feel like I'm a part of the English department, and Paul is frustrated with my students from last semester's Accelerated Composition. I know he blames it on me. I'm going to talk to him about it—if I get up enough nerve. Ellen said I could come talk to her about it. I feel really insecure about what I know as a teacher.

In one sense, this entry now seems far removed, written a long time ago. It's a glimpse of the young, uncertain beginning teacher I used to be. Yet I could have written the phrase, "I feel really insecure" on any given day during my teaching career. Insecurity is a feeling I've become very familiar with over the last nine years, but it hasn't grown comfortable. It's been a catalyst, causing me to pursue the nagging questions that I face. If anything, the questions have become increasingly complex—finding answers has led to asking new questions. But the questions and insecurities are more comfortable and less threatening. I expect the insecurities, and now I'm even fearful that I won't have time to ask, recognize, or pursue the important questions that continue to arise as my life as a woman and a teacher becomes more complicated.

In the first part of my teaching career, I was looking for validation or authority from external authorities, but now I've begun to trust my questions, and they guide my practice. I've come to this position through reading the theories I found in my graduate courses, through continual reflection in nine years of teaching, and within the collaborative communities of teacher-learners with which I've surrounded myself. Through posing and pursing these questions, I've come to trust my own authority to explore questions, and I can now claim a kind of internal authority.

I remember vividly why I wrote those words in that first-year journal entry. I had a great group of students in my Accelerated Comp class that first year; they were bright, witty, and a lot of fun to teach. I was only five years older than they, and we quickly grew very close as a class. Second semester came, and these students went to the next class, taught by a veteran teacher, Paul, who didn't like the "touchy-feely" way I approached writing. To him, writing instruction was a very precise science, definitely something that was either done "right" or "wrong."

A few weeks after the start of second semester, I ran into Brenda, a student from my first-semester class. I asked her how English was, noticing she wouldn't look me in the eye. She told me she wasn't having as much fun as first semester, made a few disparaging remarks about Paul, and then, finally looking up at me said, "Mrs. Siedel, he told us we didn't learn anything first semester!" I didn't know what to say, and I was panicked because Brenda was looking to me to come up with something in retaliation. I don't remember what I did say or how I reacted. But I do remember those words stung me to the core, and at least at some level, I wondered if he were right. Had I really taught them anything?

As a new composition teacher, I was very insecure. I remember that when teaching writing was mentioned in my interview for the job at Northeast, I swallowed hard the panic I felt rising in my throat and gave very convincing, confident answers to the questions that followed. When September arrived, I tried to make my writing class student-centered; I allowed students to find their topics, experiment with form. I remember saying in answer to students' questions, "I don't know," and then searching for answers with them. My practices as a writing teacher had come from my experiences in undergraduate writing classes, but I hadn't yet really reflected on my beliefs about writing, nor did I have theories to support them. I had a kind of dual personality in the classroom; while trying my own ideas about writing, I also spent that first year copying what other writing teachers in the department were doing in their classrooms. I remember the worksheets that accompanied almost everything, and trying to figure out how to teach the "character development essay" using X, Y and Z as a form. And I remember, despite being able to connect and relate well to the students, how wrong my teaching felt. I didn't know why I was teaching the way I was, except that others around me were teaching in similar ways.

One day I was typing alongside some students in the computer lab. I don't know if they realized I was a teacher (I was often mistaken for a student in those first years of teaching), but if they did, it didn't soften their criticism of the Northeast English department. In particular, the young woman sitting next to me was upset about the composition classes, how hard it was to figure out the writing structures imposed, and how hard it was to move from teacher to teacher at the end of the semester. "It makes no sense to me!" she complained. "Popham wants it one way, and Schulz wants it another! I don't know what they want, and I don't care!" Like this student, I—as a writer or a teacher—couldn't make sense of the way composition was being taught. It wasn't connected to students' needs and interests, and it wasn't coming from a coherent set of theories. Once again, that pesky question resurfaced: "Why am I teaching the way I am?" I needed some answers but wasn't sure where to get them.

That spring I went to a teacher inservice, hoping it would be an opportunity to get some of my questions answered. The inservice involved the teachers in reader-response and writing process pedagogies. I felt validated because it modeled many of the strategies that I was trying in my classes and that Paul had called "touchy-feely." For the first time, I had confidence that although I didn't know why I was teaching the way I was, maybe some of it was "right." Meanwhile, Paul was sitting across the table from me looking uncomfortable and complaining under his breath. Feeling a little smug, I stood up and boldly spoke in front of all the teachers in the room about the importance of modeling writing for our students. "It's really important for them to see you write too," I said. But as I looked back across the table at Paul, my confidence disappeared. Sitting down quickly, I added, "But I'm only a first-year teacher." I felt foolish at having spoken up when I really didn't know anything. On my way out of the inservice, I met Dave Wilson, who complimented me on what I had said and told me not to apologize for my inexperience. A few months later, while flipping through the summer schedule of courses at the university, I noticed that Dave and another professor with whom I'd studied as an undergraduate were teaching a graduate course on literature. I enrolled in my first graduate class.

"SO WHAT THE HELL AM I DOING?"
LOOKING FOR ANSWERS IN GRAD SCHOOL

When I went back for graduate school, it most certainly wasn't to get the theory I was lacking to understand my practice better. I was looking to theory to help alleviate my painful sense of inadequacy. I felt like bell hooks, who says, "I came to theory because I was hurting. . . . I came to theory desperate, wanting to comprehend—to grasp what was happening around and within me" (hooks, 1994, p. 59). I was looking for answers, for prescriptions to "fix" my classes or more importantly, fix/heal the way I felt about my classes and pedagogy. I felt insecure and incompetent; I didn't know why I was teaching the way I was, and I didn't like not knowing. I believed there were answers out there that I didn't have, but that Paul did. In our planning conversations, he would spew out book titles by the dozen. He spoke of writing in such absolutes. For him it was all about prescriptive forms. I was scared, fearful of criticism, fearful of being a fraud. And that was painful. But Paul's answers really didn't hold a satisfying authority for me either; instead, they intimidated and oppressed me. I felt bullied by Paul, but I also saw him bully students and my colleagues in department meetings, where he often silenced others. He also reminded me of one of the worst teachers I'd had, who would put people down with his arrogance. I never trusted him, either. I guess I didn't trust teachers who had a kind of absolute certainty about the way the world worked, and who at the same time were disrespectful of others' ideas.

Despite my resistance to a pedagogy of absolutes, I had convinced myself that there were some definite answers to resolve the tensions I felt in my classroom. Initially, graduate school frustrated me because I wasn't offered any answers; in fact, I began to realize that there were no answers! How different this was from my previous educational experiences, where I mostly memorized the answers and was successful because I did what the teacher wanted. So theory was something I happened upon only after I learned to trust the nagging questions in my mind. And that took a while.

My first graduate course was Literary Response in the Secondary Schools. I had never been so engaged in my own learning, never been so moved by discussions (people breaking down and crying in class, for heaven's sake), and never been so connected to pieces of literature. But the professors didn't tell me how to accomplish this in my own class. I didn't know how or why this experience had been so powerfully different from any other class I had ever taken up to that point. The experience was confusing, complicated, complex. And from it I realized that learning could be intensely personal, not just a body of information to memorize. The community in the class, and not the teacher's authority, was crucial to my learning and vital to what worked about the class.

The following summer, I participated in another class that helped me compose my authority as a teacher. It was a seminar on writing across the curriculm in which I wrote an "I-search" paper that explored what I believed about writing and why. I read and digested Applebee, Atwell, Elbow, Britton, Rosenblatt, and others. These voices echoed and affirmed my beliefs about writing, reading, teaching, and learning, beliefs that had not been supported in my first two years of teaching at Northeast, beliefs that I hadn't developed the "whys" to back them. This theoretical background was crucial for me to begin to construct a writing classroom that made sense to me. Armed with the "whys" for my beliefs, as the new school year began, I felt confident enough to break from the established curriculum. My classroom became even more student-centered; the students began choosing their topics and their reading. On the surface, they seemed more engaged, and I felt good about the changes.

But in the midst of it all, I was still the teacher and they were the students. I hadn't allowed them to see me as a learner or allowed them to see me struggle with writing. I had only just begun to fight against my own educational experience and the traditional teacherly roles. My teachers hadn't been learners; they were the "experts" who filled my head with knowledge. I never felt as if my teachers were learning alongside me, and my first experiences of not being the "teacher as expert" in my own classroom were disconcerting, especially when it came to writing. If I wasn't the authority, who was I?

I took another graduate course the next summer, the Nebraska Writing Project (NWP), which helped me focus on seeing—for the first time— myself as a writer. In my experience, school writing wasn't a tool for making sense or exploring new ideas, although on my own, I used writing in this way by keeping a journal. School writing was about writing the way your teacher wanted you to, "the way you would need to for college." But in NWP, for the first time I got to concentrate on how I write—my quirks, habits, procrastination techniques. Finally, I was participating in the process of writing and thinking about the process, which is sometimes painful and time-consuming, and which I asked my kids to undertake daily without ever participating in it with them.

In *Teaching to Transgress*, bell hooks (1994) writes of the importance of using one's own experience:

> Personal testimony, personal experience, is such fertile ground for the production of liberatory feminist theory because it usually forms the base of

our theory making. While we work to resolve those issues that are most pressing in our daily life . . . we engage in a critical process of theorizing that enables and empowers. (p. 70)

After NWP, I found a theory for my practice for the first time, because I was given a chance to live the theory, given the chance to view myself as a writer. I had never thought about and lived the process of writing, and up to this point, teaching writing had kept me on the fringes of the process because I was the "assignment-giver." In the writing project I learned to look at myself as a writer and to use that experience to look at my students as writers. This important connection allowed me to develop an internal authority as a writer rather than only looking to outside authorities for how to teach writing. In fact, I didn't so much find a theory as construct one from the reflections on my experiences as a writer. For the first time, teaching was not an act outside my being; it felt connected to who I was.

This marked an important shift in my pedagogy and helped me revise my vision of "teacher as expert." I no longer thought of teacher experts as possessing absolute certainty. I realized more about why I didn't trust Paul; his authority didn't rest on lived experience, but more important, it was never open to change and revision. I began to see the teacher expert as a person who drew on and trusted her own and her students' experiences with literacy. And it made me realize that I should trust the questions that nagged me in the classroom and followed me home at night. I began to understand that those questions were the key to composing my own pedagogy and to resisting the traditional absolutes handed to me by others—and there were so many absolutes to resist.

Since those first three summers of graduate courses, several nagging questions have guided my ongoing exploration as a teacher: How do I, as a privileged, heterosexual, middle-class, white teacher understand, work with, and even support gay, lesbian, and bisexual students? How do feminist theory and pedagogy help me think about my own life and the lives of others who have been marginalized? How do I work with school policies about diversity that seem limiting? How do I create and nurture supportive communities of colleagues who are necessary to my ongoing growth? How do I reconcile all the competing components in my own life: as a teacher, mother, wife, daughter, student-learner?

"WHAT IF A STUDENT CAME OUT TO ME?"

His name was Ben, and he stood out from the very first day of class. He was a small young man, very soft-spoken and effeminate. The other kids, while not mean to him, didn't interact with him much. Ben would often hang around after class to talk or pop into my room at different times of the day for a chat. Then one day Ben asked me to hang a P-FLAG (Parents and Friends of Lesbians and Gays) poster in my room announcing a dance. I wasn't sure what to say. What would the administration think? What would other students say? What would other teachers say? Uneasily, I took the poster from him but never hung it.

I'm not sure where my fear of this simple poster came from, but it was certainly reinforced. In my first graduate course, I read gay literature for what I thought was the first time. But as we talked in class, I realized I had read lots of gay authors throughout my education, although their sexual orientation and the way it shaped their writing had never been addressed. I excitedly discussed the literature with a social studies colleague of mine and about how I planned on incorporating it into my own classroom. He cautioned me and asked questions like, "What if a student comes out to you and her parents accuse you of encouraging her homosexuality?" I didn't know how to answer. His comments worried me, and remembering back to my graduate course, the two gay professors teaching it had initially dodged any discussion about the gay literature we read. Maybe I should, too.

But my memory of Ben never faded. In the years that followed, when I thought about him, I had many regrets: betraying the trust Ben felt in me, not being more aware that he was outing himself to me, not being a teacher who clearly supported all students, including gay and lesbian youth. And by this point in my teaching career, I had begun to trust my inner naggings. My classroom needed to change.

A few years after I had Ben in class, I took a lesbian literature course and read Audre Lorde's (1984a) "The Transformation of Silence into Language and Action." This piece helped me think about the silences that were taking place in my own life and in my classroom. I became aware of how I was participating in a system that worked against Ben, worked to keep him silent and in the closet. And I became aware of how dangerous that was to gay and lesbian youth. When I had Ben in class, I wasn't brave or aware enough to challenge these silencing factors or to realize that for the most part, my fears were invented out of ignorance. For most of my life, homosexuality had been such a taboo subject. Even within my own family, we remain silent about (and with) a close relative who still has not come out to us or talked openly about his long-term live-in partner and their relationship. This silence seems deafening at times. As I write this chapter, I know that silence remains an issue for me even now. I can only partially break the silence. I can't yet speak the name or the relationship of the one involved. But this isn't my silence to break. From Lorde's essay and personal reflections about the silences in my own life,

I realize that I can prevent these silences from entering my children's lives. And I can also work against those silences in my classroom. Knowing this, I reentered my classroom a very different person and with a different perspective. To date, it has created the most radical, life-changing events for my teacherly and personal lives.

Claire was the next student who came out to me. I had Claire as a sophomore and encouraged her to take Advanced Placement Comp from me her junior year, the same year I was taking a graduate course in lesbian literature. I noticed that the second I was done with a novel from my course, which I talked about with my students, Claire would check the novel out and read it quickly. I was ready this time when Claire shared her sorrow and pain at having broken up with her girlfriend. I treated her with the respect and understanding she deserved. We talked throughout the year, and I discussed with her my heterosexual privilege. She helped me to really grow and reminded me why I must break the silences in my classroom. She helped me understand even more fully Lorde's (1984a) words:

> I have come to believe over and over again that what is most important to me must be spoken, made verbal and shared, even at the risk of having it bruised or misunderstood. That the speaking profits me, beyond any other effect. (p. 40).

The next year, two lesbian students approached my colleague, David, expressing a need for a group for gay/lesbian/bisexual youth at Northeast. David knew of my interest in supporting gay youth and invited me to help organize this group. Another high school in Lincoln had a group, and with approval from our administration, we began. The furor surrounding our group initially was overwhelming, and I remember days when I would leave Northeast exhausted at the attention it received. This young teacher had started to get "political," and other teachers in the building weren't quite sure what to think of me or the club. "Why are you suddenly interested in this topic?" they'd ask. "What's a straight woman doing supporting gay/lesbian issues?" A group of students began to gather names on a petition against our group. But after the first club day, when we had more kids show up than names on the petition, the student council found the petition easy to ignore.

Our GLBSA (Gay, Lesbian, Bi-sexual, Straight Alliance) was a pretty radical thing for Northeast High School. Our students are from a working-class background, and the Northeast community is fairly tight-knit, with a big dose of "good old boy" sentimentality. Although resisted by some staff and students, I was pleasantly surprised at the ease with which our club was accepted by administration and parents; parents actually called in support of the club, and our administration not only fielded phone calls but attended our first meeting to say, "This is a great thing."

But resistance lurks around the corner almost on a daily basis, at every level. A secretary in the office who typed the announcements would censor the words "gay and lesbian" out of the GLBSA announcements. Only when we approached the principal and talked with him did she stop. While our administration has mostly been very supportive of our GLBSA, one incident with an administrator was unforgettable. A colleague and I had a poster hanging in our room titled "How to Be a Fabulous Feminist." Some students, not our own, who were working in the room in which one of our posters was hung took offense to parts of the poster, wrote down the text with "offensive" lines highlighted, and gave it to the administration. We were called in to talk to an administrator. Obviously nervous, he explained that he felt the poster "promoted homosexuality." I was waiting for him to quote the line "support lesbians," but instead he said, "like the line, 'visualize perfect birth control.'" I was confused. What the hell did birth control have to do with homosexuality? He went on to explain that "the only perfect birth control was between gay partners." My head began to reel.

Unbelievably, it got worse. He explained that he had gay friends. He even went out for drinks with them! And he told the story of gay teachers he knew in Texas and how nice they were. "But," he said, "I can't accept their lifestyle because of the boys I worked with at Boys Town who'd been sexually assaulted." My face turned red, and I became visibly angry as I tried to explain that pedophiles were about assaulting children, not about being gay, and that pedophiles almost always are heterosexual. He backpedaled. Ultimately, the only thing that resonated with him was that I had had the poster in my room for over four years and no students had ever objected. He seemed "okay" with that rationale, and even though he told us to take down the posters "for a while" while things cooled off, I didn't.

My struggles with these issues continue with other members of the faculty and staff. More often than not, while teachers recognize and confront racist and sexist comments, when it comes to homophobic comments, they say nothing. Currently, a phrase I hear too often is "that's so gay," and teachers are letting it slide. Kids tell me that blatant comments like "you fag" are being ignored, too. One of our GLBSA students had a gay rights sticker on her backpack and was being harassed by some males in her class. When she approached her teacher, she got blamed for the "attention" she was receiving. Not only did the teacher let the harassment go untouched, she threatened to refer the student for discipline when she stood her ground against the teacher's obvious bias.

One of my biggest challenges is that becoming a sponsor of GLBSA has changed the way people view me as a teacher. During the year we started GLBSA, I had Alan in class. Alan was a great student—funny, hard-working, friendly, and easy to like. We got along wonderfully, and I enjoyed the fact that Alan would often hang around after class to just talk. At our open house that fall, his father came in to meet me and complimented me on how excited Alan was about his English class that semester. But after the start of our club, my relationship with Alan's father changed quickly, and he called to tell me that he was "very disappointed" that I was "involved with it." Alan felt torn, too, and my support of gay youth clashed head on with the messages he was receiving at home. Clearly, in his father's mind, I was no longer a good teacher. My relationship with Alan was never the same.

On a personal level, I have faced challenges, too. One of my close friends, Tim, wondered where my "sudden interest" came in g/l/b/t issues. I tried to explain how it linked with my feminist perspective, but the conversation must have grown too "heavy" for him, as he quickly changed the subject. Usually when I talk with him, he makes a point to tell a gay joke, "all in the name of fun" and "because I like to piss you off," but I explained to him that these jokes reflected his homophobia, an idea that he clearly rejected. But the ironies of the world exist for a reason. Recently his brother came out to his mother and father, but not to him. When I asked him why he thinks his brother hasn't told him and suggested that maybe it was because he sensed his attitude, he rejected this idea.

Despite our having a loved one who is gay, my husband has also had a hard time understanding my "interest," as if being interested in gay issues is a hobby. He politely declines my invitations to attend speakers, poets, authors, or movies with me if the main theme is gay/lesbian/ bisexual/transgendered. Even at home, where the issue most concretely affects us, the silences around this topic continue.

"WHY ARE YOU TRYING TO RUIN OUR FUN?"
BECOMING A FEMINIST TEACHER

I began to own feminism because it made connections to other marginalized people, to the "others" in the world, and gave me a way to come to understand racism, classism, and heterosexism. Immersing myself in feminist theory also allowed me to see women as another silenced group. Graduate school was the first place that offered me a chance to hear the voices that had been absent in my education, voices that reflect my own, voices that give me insight at times, voices that reinforce who I am. I wanted to give students a chance to hear these voices earlier than I had, so I began Women's Literature at Northeast High School. I hoped to give my students the understanding and validation of their own experiences that I didn't get as a young woman. I wanted them to know that we are socialized as women as sexual objects, as bodies, and that we need a way to understand that so that we can resist. I wanted my students to have a women-centered community in the classroom so that their life experiences could be examined.

Women's Lit has been such a powerful class to teach and is well received by students. It is offered to seniors, most of whom are at the point where it's easy to reflect back on themselves as they grew up and to begin to question the ways in which they were socialized. For most, the idea that they *were* socialized is a new concept. Men are an important part of the classes, and ironically, some are less resistant to feminist ideas than the females in the class. Feminism makes sense to students once they get past the longstanding notion that it is about male-bashing. Unfortunately, the notion that Women's Lit is just for women still persists, and this may prevent many young men from registering. Another notion is that because we read some things by lesbians and because we discuss issues that affect lesbians, Women's Lit is lesbian lit. In fact, one student who was considering registering for the course asked me if the women taking it were mostly lesbians. I'm sure this issue is closely connected to my sponsoring GLBSA.

Because the initial offering of Women's Literature coincided with the organizing of GLBSA, I quickly became known as the "radical feminist." The year before the rumors around school were that I was sleeping with an attractive male colleague. That next year I became the "wannabe lesbian." These stories about my identity were perpetuated when I went up against a Northeast tradition, the Star Studders, a group of boys who dress up in the drill team's uniforms and perform a routine. They had performed their routine at a drill team show that was a fundraiser, and the next day I heard the kids talking about "how funny it was" and about the "props" the boys used: wigs, makeup, and, of course, stuffed bras.

In an effort to get more kids to attend our poorly attended pep rallies, one of the administrators thought it'd be great to have the Star Studders perform for the whole school. I wasn't the only teacher incensed at this idea, and many of us took our concerns to the administration. An audience who paid to see the Studders was one thing, a captive audience another. I, however, was the one who took a lot of flak for "trying to ruin their fun," and while walking by some of the boys' lockers, I heard one of them shout, "Get a life, Siedel!" While I had no regrets challenging the administration on a tradition that obviously poked fun at females and female traits (the bigger the boobs, the bigger the laugh), the familiar sting that accompanied criticism was there.

I didn't like the label that was attached to me as a teacher, and that year for the first time, students walked into my classroom thinking they had me pegged, thinking they knew what I was about. But I also knew that I contradicted their image of a radical feminist and that it was to my advantage to play with their construction of me. Given my appearance, students probably see a pretty, energetic young woman, wearing fashionable clothes from the same stores where they shop. I can talk to them about popular culture, like the latest edition of *Loveline* on MTV or which is the best tattoo parlor in town. I've heard students say, "She doesn't seem like a mom; she's more like a cool big sister." They think of radical feminists as looking butch, being angry and aggressive, and I don't fit this image.

My experience with Jason illustrates my developing sense of confidence to work with students' resistance about issues of gender and sexual orientation and other highly political issues. I worked to help Jason examine his assumptions about terms like *feminist* and *woman* and to complicate his conception of those terms. Because I contradicted his stereotypic ideas about feminists and femininity, I unsettled his certainty that he knew the way the world was. And my success in working with him helped me gain more confidence in working with other students on similar issues.

Jason was the president of a conservative youth group and thought Rush Limbaugh was god. He was staunchly conservative and would try to get me into debates about issues. As a student, he believed in traditional conceptions of teacher authority, especially about how English should be taught, and had traditional and narrow conceptions of women's roles. And he continually challenged my authority as a teacher and my feminist perspective. But in working with him, I was able to trust my own instincts, my own internal sense of authority. The previous year he had made a young woman first-year teacher's life hell, and try as he might, he wasn't able to have the same effect on me. While I first rejected his politicizing my classroom at every opportunity, I realized that every classroom is political; it's just that sometimes the politics are hidden. Since he thought he knew my politics, and since he himself was so political, I used this to my advantage to keep him off guard. No matter what he did—asking questions to challenge my authority, dominating discussions and thereby intimidating others in the class, making stereotypical statements about feminists, about women, about liberals—he couldn't narrow me down to fit his traditional conceptions. But through my readings of feminist theory, I was able to work with Jason. It gave me a multiplicity of perspectives, even on feminist issues, but it also helped me articulate, in a way students could understand, why rigid gender roles were inadequate and why they had too narrow views of the world.

By this point, my theoretical understanding had continued to grow with my graduate hours. Courses in multiculturalism, gay studies, and feminist theory all converged, blending into a set of ideas that were impossible to untangle. I realize that part of the authority I've developed has been in speaking out, in being a vocal activist and advocate. While I might have spoken up earlier, it would have been with trepidation and tentativeness, and I would have recanted quickly with any slight challenge—even a disapproving glance from a colleague. But now, facing situations over and over again in which I felt ethically and morally obligated to do something, to say something, I've gained confidence and effectiveness as a speaker in part because I am now informed and practiced in responding to homophobic, racist, sexist challenges.

"WHAT ARE YOU DOING IN YOUR CLASSROOM?"
THE NORTHEAST ENGLISH DEPARTMENT

Four years after I started at Northeast, we went from being a 10–12 school to becoming a 9–12 school. The enrollment rose from 1,400 students to over 2,000, and at the same time, 50 new teachers joined our faculty. As a result, teachers no longer had their own classrooms. In some ways, this created isolation, especially for those of us who began to teach in portable classrooms. But in many ways, as teachers began to share an office together, it provided opportunities for collaboration that had never existed before. The fact that we were physically together forced us to talk to each other. Suddenly there were other people to talk with, and we had the space and time in which to do it. And a group of new teachers were hired who came with perspectives about pedagogy, literacy, and issues of diversity that were similar to mine. Those elements laid the groundwork for creating a new sense of community for me.

When we came together in the same office, teachers new to our building were able to asked experienced teachers questions like, "What is English 10?" or "Why are you teaching this essay?" Those questions made me rethink and rearticulate my own ideas about teaching. It became clear that other teachers had questions similar to my own, and our visions for our classrooms were similar. We began to do more team planning. The power structure of the department shifted radically because the traditional "expert" teachers left. Paul was no longer there to dominate our discussions. As I finished my master's program, I now had a place and the people with whom to continue exploring my questions. I had a group of people whom I could trust with my questions without having them think I was an incompetent or failed teacher. I had a group of teachers who liked and wanted to reflect along with me.

Many things help make our community stronger, including food and fun. We often eat lunch together, and our department is known for the special food days we have. Occasionally we invite other departments, and often the administration stops by for a snack. We even have a "Martha Stewart week" each year when we have a craft table, a food table, and a day where we all dress like Martha Stewart. Some of the other things that have come out of this physical closeness to each other are the monthly English newsletter highlighting each of our most embarrassing moments of the month, an endless array of practical jokes, secret pals, and our annual Christmas party with white elephant gifts. Having our desks together in one room has allowed for a productive mix of professional talk and interpersonal engagement.

There are still tensions within our community, but now the issues get put out on the table, and we discuss them more openly and civilly. There are now not so many silences around our ideas about teaching, learning, and students. At department meetings we've had discussions about our composition program, our teaching of composition, and student failures. Although at times it's been tense and uncomfortable, still, we're talking and thinking. Currently we are piloting a textbook in our ninth and tenth grade classes, a piloting dictated by the district in the name of accountability. I need my Northeast community as I make sense of the textbook and the reasoning behind it. After nine years of inventing the things I do in English 10, the textbook feels fake, reminiscent of the old days when I was teaching other people's stuff without knowing why. I'm glad I have people with whom I can pose my new nagging questions.

WHERE WILL I FIND THE TIME?

It was in a feminist theory class that I first read Adrienne Rich's (1979) essay "When We Dead Awaken: Writing as Re-Vision." And Rich's words spoke directly to me:

> I was writing very little, partly from fatigue, that female fatigue of suppressed anger and loss of contact with my own being; partly from the discontinuity of female life with its attention to small chores, errands, work that others constantly undo, small children's constant needs . . . I wanted, then,

more than anything the one thing of which there was never enough: time to think, time to write. (p. 43)

This describes my life perfectly as, increasingly, the thing that eludes me is time. Time is the issue that keeps me torn between career and family. And my lack of time leads to something that I think women feel more strongly than men—the balancing act. Since the birth of my children, I have had to balance teacher/student/wife/mother/daughter/sister and being Toni. Even though my husband and I are both teachers, my time is structured differently than his. My husband helps a great deal with the day-to-day activities of our lives, but ultimately, I am the manager of the house: coordinating doctor and dental appointments, synchronizing the kids' schedules, making sure that bills are paid, that the dog goes to the vet, and that the endless array of tasks that confront daily living are all completed. Balancing this work with school has not been easy, and often my nagging questions are pushed aside for tonight's decision about what's for supper.

Lack of time also makes me feel torn when it comes to my own students. It has dictated the choices I make, especially when it comes to student writing, which leads to a seemingly endless black hole of response. With large class sizes, the papers are overwhelming, and I can't always rely on time at home to read them. It's also hurt connections I could make with students by limiting the amount of their activities I can attend. And this is so important: seeing them outside the classroom to get a more complete picture of who they are. I miss having the freedom to do this.

Lack of time spills over into another area, collaboration. I depend on talk with other teachers to help make sense of the daily act of teaching. I need them to vent to, ask questions of, hear versions of their teaching narratives, and to push me to ask critical questions of my practice. But it takes a concentrated effort to make this time in my teaching day, and often, when I get really busy with the day-to-day tasks, the first thing I eliminate is this talk time. It's easy to retreat behind the walls of my own classroom, and teaching in a portable classroom, I've found I can too easily isolate myself.

My greatest fear of all is that while people watch my daily challenges as I attempt to balance my life, they will stop asking me to participate in things necessary to my growth as a teacher. Upon returning to school on a Monday morning, my close friend and department chair said to me, "I didn't want to call you this weekend in case you were busy." She probably was right, every weekend is busy, but I was saddened by this lack of contact. Also, I was recently angry when a colleague, without asking me, made suggestions about changes in my teaching schedule. He has also told people that I'm not available to do things. While I know he's looking out for me, I'd like the chance to say no.

This fall I gave a presentation at a Youth-at-Risk Symposium about the need for supportive communities for gay youth. It felt so good to do this kind of "work," to spend a Saturday talking with others about issues at the core of our teaching. After the symposium, I felt invigorated and energized, having not participated in such professional talk and involvement outside my building for almost a year. I need these invitations to present and participate to continue, and I fear the "Oh, Toni's too busy" attitude will prevent this.

Lack of time has taken its toll on friendships, family relationships, and my effectiveness as a teacher. Drafting this chapter felt like an impossible task, writing it in the 15-minute chunks of time that my life currently allows. But in the last nine years, I've figured out that I need more than anything to be ever reflective on my practices as a teacher. I need this reflection in order to resist becoming complacent. I never want to be so sure of what I'm doing that I don't stop to ask questions. But then, that takes time.

7

Privilege as Possibility

John Skretta

Now I have decided that the succinct answer is always inadequate, and that the story of origin is always a complex saga.
—Phillipe Wamba, "A Middle Passage"

all I want is the truth/
just give me some truth
—John Lennon, "Give Me Some Truth"

We were meeting for the third time in six months. I was sitting in Dave's living room, listening to Dave and Joy while a lump grew in my throat and they pushed me to reconsider what was important for me to write about—as a teacher, as a person, as a thinker. Dammit. They were my *teachers*, they were my *friends*, and they still weren't satisfied with my chapter. I'd sifted through hours of transcribed interviews from almost a decade earlier, in which I had speculated on what it might mean to become a teacher. Now I was well into my fourth year teaching reading and English at Northeast High School. I had gone back to the transcripts and written an off-the-cuff account for them, a coming-of-age story about my life in educational institutions that sounded something like Dennis Miller meets Holden Caulfield. I thought they might let me walk away from it. I had convinced myself that I was okay with that, that I could live with a manuscript that maintained a tone of cynical detachment, allowing me to hover over my past without probing it. But Dave and Joy wouldn't let me live with a simplistic version of my story. They pushed me to dig deeper and say more, to seek the elusive truths of my past.

My personal and pedagogical history is a revisionist one. The story contained herein is one version from my personal rhetoric of possibility. I know now the importance of the developmental process. By *process* I do not mean a simplistic, reductive writing process that can be sequentially enumerated on an overhead and taught to somnolent freshmen. By process I mean something grander, something that subsumes everything we do, something that comes close to a life principle—a belief in constant examination and reflection as essential in our personal and professional worlds. I know now that if I cannot revise my own past by reconsidering what it means, then I am stuck with one version of the truth, and I deny myself the possibility of reimagining a better future for myself and my students. I don't want to live with my own story as it's already been told—and I don't want my students to live with the diminished life expectations that would result from them accepting someone else's version of their life stories. I want them to imagine what might be possible. So I work to grant them the privilege of mentorship.

I have been privileged with multiple mentors. The importance of mentors like Dave and Joy is not only that they have granted me access to discussions and invited me to become a decisionmaker in my own education or the education of others. Likewise, the importance of these mentors is not merely that they have helped me develop a voice that shapes practice and policy in schools. Instead, the most important thing my mentors have done is to measure me against my own ideals, to question me rigorously, and in doing so to be standard-bearers, modeling different, varied versions of who I might wish to become.

Through the mentorship of others within education, I felt valued within schools and grasped a sense of empowerment that has encouraged me to make an impact by making real what I envision as possible. As a teacher, I have helped create a school-within-a-school program for at-risk students, I have served on school- and district-level multicultural and curriculum committees trying to shape policy, and I have tried to push myself and my colleagues to reexamine our own boundaries and preconceptions about literacy and pedagogy through my presentations and writing.

The experiences noted above and my professional aspirations overall have not been about denying, walking away from, or forsaking my privilege as a white, middle-class male. I am not trying to atone for an abstract notion of sinfulness through being a beneficiary of society's privilege or apologize for my middle-class, mainstream origins. Instead, my story is perhaps best understood as a dialogue with privilege, an attempt at taking privilege to task and expanding its possibilities in order to become more inclusive and expansive for diverse others. If I push myself to share how privilege has functioned for my benefit and reflect on what it's meant to me, perhaps privilege can be put to work for others.

A CONTEXT FOR INTERPRETING PRIVILEGE

Most of the connotations privilege conjures up are negative, since granting privilege implies bias. Most people would probably be quick to deny they've experienced privilege because of this. But realistically, most of us have in fact been the beneficiaries of privilege at one time or another in our lives, because privilege is situationally conferred. As a white, middle-class, heterosexual male, I am constantly deriving the benefits of privilege, even on a small level. Unlike many of my African-American male students, I don't get singled out and followed around retail stores by security personnel. White privilege. Although my wife, Teresa, balances the checkbook and looks after our family's finances, we've noticed that during the ten years of our marriage, whenever we've had occasion to meet with bankers, loan officers, auto salespersons, and the like, their comments and questions are always directed toward me. Male privilege. I know I can walk into any store in this city and shop for high-ticket items—anything from camcorders to cars to couches, and no one will question my purchasing power, all because I dress and talk and look a certain way. Middle-class privilege. Privilege works in so many ways, the preceding being simple, minute examples. But privilege is also like that relative in the family no one likes to mention because he drinks too much, or got kicked out of the army, or did a stint in the pen—privilege invokes denial. Denial that one has ever had it, denial that one has ever benefited from it. I am admittedly reluctant to write about privilege.

For myself, at least, there is no small personal irony in contemplating privilege for the purpose of a teacher-change narrative that addresses my maturation and mutations as an educator. I do not come from an exceptionally privileged background, and I made a commitment to public education some time ago in no small part because I wanted to forsake a world of white male executive privilege and what I felt was a hollow promise of fulfillment through a corporate identity. I embraced public education instead with an idealistic belief in its power as one of the most fundamentally important functions of a democratic society—a zealous idealism that continues to motivate me even though I remain pragmatically aware that there's always some disparity between the real and the ideal.

My family is middle-class, probably more comfortably middle-class now than at any time in my father's work history because he is 57 and has reached the personal apex of a highly successful professional career in private industry. Dad is a corporate vice president of operations. My mother and father and three of my siblings live out on the East Coast—Massachusetts, Connecticut, New York. But I grew up in Iowa, and I think my wrestling match with privilege really begins with my father's story.

My father grew up on a family farm in northeast Iowa, one of five sons. His parents did not allow him to participate in any extracurricular activities at school because, as the oldest son, he had considerable daily chores—before school, after school, in the evening. He shared a significant responsibility in the daily operation of the farm and lived with an expectation of hard daily work from a very early age. These experiences instilled in my father an incredible work ethic, a powerful sense of self-reliance, and an unwavering belief that nothing much would ever get accomplished in life unless you "busted your ass" for it. He didn't believe in miracles or, for that matter, privilege. But he definitely believed in perseverance. Against his parents' wishes, he left the family farm and put himself through college at Iowa State University, earning an engineering degree. Then he entered the business world.

As a kid, you can imagine that my perception of my father as described above was that this was a pretty un-fun guy. As an adult today with a mortgage and a young son to think about myself, my view of my father is much more complicated. I admire him for much of what I couldn't understand or overtly contested growing up. I thought he was a real hardass. It's not much of a stretch to say that he was intolerant of imperfection. Some of that probably comes with the territory of working in industrial engineering, where "total quality" is the mantra.

One of the acute memories of boyhood was the rite of passage of learning to mow the lawn. Ribbons were not permitted; if you left any, you could expect a disciplinary tap on the head from his turquoise ring. It was that way with everything. Later on in our teens I remember Dad had assigned a summertime landscaping project at the house to me and my brother Fred. It was pretty labor-intensive, involving moving wheelbarrow after wheelbarrow of dirt from one area to another across the yard and leveling it off in the sweltering heat. At supper that night, when Dad requested a progress report on the project, I proudly declared we had hauled 20 wheelbarrow loads of dirt. His response was classic Fabian: "Who gives a damn how much dirt you moved around?! Is the job done, yes or no?" The job wasn't done. If Dad were a composition teacher, he wouldn't be a process-writing teacher. But he did impart privilege to us.

We were not *encouraged* to view life as a competition, we were taught that it was *inherently* competitive. Early in our childhoods, my father was not very supportive of the idea of us kids participating in extracurricular activities or even enrolling in swimming instruction over the summer.

Eventually his viewpoint came around to the notion that our involvement in these activities simply provided another avenue for us to demonstrate that we were among the competitive elite in any activity. Shortly after I began playing the saxophone, he showed me the payment book from West Music in Iowa City. He wanted to make it clear that if he was investing over $600 in an instrument, I had better get to be pretty damned good at it. I think that until I won a couple distinguished solo awards in jazz band, he was always a little frustrated that I never beat Lisa Hunter out for first chair.

Dad was even more extreme about sports. *Second place is the first loser. And if you win—well, look out, because no matter how big and tough you are, there's always somebody looking to knock you off. Never rest on your laurels. If you get lazy, you'll get blindsided. You're not giving a hundred percent unless you're giving a hundred and ten percent. You've gotta do more than you think you're capable of doing.* This may be pretty good advice if your goal is to inculcate a ferocious sense of competitiveness. It might also be why most of my closest friends refuse to play board games with me and have sworn off so-called recreational sand volleyball as well.

When we think of privilege, we tend to think of it in terms of self-indulgence and conspicuous consumption. Privilege is for people who can afford aesthetic titillation—tickets to the best show in town, whatever that show is, so long as it's exclusive. Privilege is also about exclusive ownership: demonstrating your financial clout with preposterously unnecessary expenditures, vehicles, clothing, gadgetry, all types of status symbols that are used to communicate to people in no uncertain terms that your portfolio is doing well. But that's not the sort of privilege I grew up with. My parents worked very hard to support six kids. My mother stayed home and did all the childrearing duties with the exception of discipline, where my dad presided as a kind of appeals court judge, handing out swift and certain punishment when called upon by Mom to do so. We weren't wealthy. To my extreme embarrassment, when we went to Hardee's for a night of fine dining, my dad would haul in a bag or two of generic-brand cheese puffs because they were cheaper than fries. We were never allowed to order beverages at restaurants because water was free. As a teenager, I had to perform scouting duty at new restaurants: "John, go in and ask for a copy of the menu. Check the prices to see if they're reasonable and come back out here." If the burgers were cheap, we piled out of the Suburban and into the cafe.

All that said, I cannot deny the role privilege has played in my life. But I owe it to my parents and my own sense of personal history to clarify that when I speak of privilege, I am not speaking of the kind of enormous socioeconomic status that the wealthiest few percent of our population enjoys. We didn't fly anywhere for vacations, we took three-day trips around Iowa and Illinois and stayed in roadside motels. Sightseeing consisted of watching the tugboats and barges on the Mississippi. We didn't always have the most fashionable clothes. We wore Sears Tuffskins, not Levi's.

From a socioeconomic standpoint, most of the privileges I benefited from were privileges that in the best of all possible worlds we would admit all young people are entitled to: food, shelter, clothing, health care, and parents who provided structure and support and a high level of concern about my upbringing. As a classroom teacher today, I am more aware than ever of how privileged I actually was to enjoy these basic elements of a quality life. I've worked with students who couldn't afford a winter coat (in Nebraska, something of a necessity), couldn't afford dental care, couldn't afford to not wear the same pair of jeans to school every day and endure the ridicule of other kids . . . and I've even worked with students like Todd, whose sister was beaten so badly by their drunken father that she couldn't attend school and Todd called her several times during the day to check up on how she was. I've spoken with apathetic parents about their runaway children, and I've spoken with hostile parents in denial about their kid's drug or alcohol use. Although I managed to imbibe a few times and sneak it past the parents during my high school days, for the most part my mother and father were suspicious and sleuth-like: I didn't get away with much, and I didn't try to get away with much.

Understanding the privilege I benefited from means understanding my father. My dad left a predictable, but to him unenthralling, future in agriculture in rural northeast Iowa so that he could pursue his education. The values my parents subscribed to and instilled in us were hard work, fair play, and a belief that through education, anything was possible. They believed in public education, from elementary right up through the state university system. I don't think it's an accident that not one of us six kids attended a private university; I remember that Dad would humor us by looking at the glossy color brochures and glancing at the tuition estimates and then always making it clear that we weren't *that kind* of privileged. But academics were still understood to be the level playing field of American opportunity. We were taught that through education, we could in fact become whatever it was we chose to be.

When I think of many of the kids I work with today at Northeast High School, I realize that the privilege I have been endowed with as a white, middle-class male is the privilege of perspective. The viewpoint my parents preached to us regarding education as a land of equal opportunity always had validity—for us. We were taught that the sphere of public education was competitive, but that it had one animating prin-

ciple: fairness. And when we questioned the fairness of a teacher's decision or grade, my parents would always be judicious, and were usually
more inclined to hear the teacher's side of the story than our own. School
was not regarded as a place where we were to socialize or question the
judgment of adults. It was a place where we were to demonstrate mastery
of the objectives and do so in an exemplary fashion. If we did this, it was
assumed that excellence as a person and a thinker would be the logical
result and "opportunity will come knocking," as my parents often repeated. C's were not tolerated because they were "average," and "average
people are a dime a dozen in this world."

It has taken me years of reading, reflection, and dialogue with diverse others to realize that the lived experience of public education is
very, very different from what I have just described for many, many
people. That's privilege. It's the privilege of being able to inhabit comfortably an institution with the sound awareness that the institution exists for
one's own benefit, that the system itself is animated by people who believe in your potential. Throughout the vast majority of my education—
elementary, junior high, high school, bachelor's, master's, and now further
graduate work—classrooms have been places where I have felt valued
and respected.

Unfortunately, schools don't value everyone. They don't send the
same message to all the children who walk in their doors. I grew up in
classrooms that reflected me in positive ways, but people of color were
either invisible or ignored. I grew up with a plethora of white male role
models—from history, from literature, from elsewhere. My high school
principal had come to our small town from another city that had a sub-
stantially more diverse student body. With a visible sense of relief and an
almost discernible hint of pride, he once described our student body as
"lily-white."

Some of the casualties of public education are inflicted on others by
a system that simply ignores the existence and value of those others. I
grew up in schools where it was considered permissible through the
school's silence to refer to some students as "scum" and "scuzzbuckets"
because they were suffering in poverty. I grew up in schools where "fag-
got," "homo," and "gay-wad" were common insults, part of the repertoire
of all males. And at recess in elementary school we would commonly
play a kind of football rumble game called "smear the queer" where everyone would gang-tackle whoever was unlucky enough to have the ball. I
don't recall any adult ever stopping us, ever asking us to question the
implied message of our supposedly innocent "playfulness." It would
have been unfathomable for an adult to simply tell us that such insults
were impermissible. Indeed, no one ever did.

GENDER AND CLASS PRIVILEGE

The most personal and immediate example of the disparate treatment schools administer on the basis of gender and class is the experience of my wife, Teresa. Knowing and loving Teresa is the way in which I have become most acutely aware of the fact that schools do not exist for the benefit of everyone, and that some kids succeed despite the schools they attend. Teresa is a product of the public schools of Lincoln, Nebraska, a graduate of the same high school where I now teach. She describes her own upbringing as "lower-middle-class or working-class." No one at Northeast much remembers Teresa from her time as a Northeast "Rocket," but that's not surprising. There's been a lot of turnover and none of the administrators and only a handful of the teachers on the current staff were here when Teresa was a sophomore. Today, Teresa is an attorney at Legal Services, a nonprofit organization assisting needy, low-income clients with matters regarding disability, family law, and juvenile court proceedings. Her commitment to Legal Services was a principle-centered decision based on her desire to make a difference.

As many bright young women do, Teresa succeeded in public schools in spite of her teachers. She recalls her early elementary experience as boring because her teachers did not recognize that she was gifted until she was assessed midway through third grade. In fact, an earlier teacher had recommended she be held back a grade. Then she was assessed and labeled as gifted, and found herself moved up a grade for several subjects. Her experience with being labeled gifted can be summed up in her statement that "after I was labeled, I wasn't doing anything differently but all of a sudden teachers were treating me more nicely." Throughout junior high school, she continued to perform exceptionally well in all academic areas. But, consistent with the experiences of many adolescent females, high school was very different for Teresa.

Although Lincoln High sent a counselor out to meet with Teresa and describe the program they offered for gifted students, Teresa chose to attend Northeast because many of her friends were enrolling at Northeast. At Northeast, Teresa endured three years of being systematically ignored. She never received any special services, counseling, or mentoring. Her counselor advised her only of the basic graduation requirements and never specifically advised her of postsecondary education opportunities. Teresa's mom and Teresa went over the undergrad application and requirements for the University of Nebraska to make sure she was meeting entrance requirements. At the same time that I was talking with teachers about my college choices and meeting with counselors about financial aid, Teresa and her mom were figuring it all out themselves, without any help from the school.

Teresa never felt valued by Northeast as a thinker: "After my first year at Northeast, I had earned an academic letter, but sports always got me more attention and I wasn't even very good!" She recalls only two types of teachers at Northeast: those who would pull her aside at the end of class to ask something like, "How ya gonna do out there tonight?" about volleyball or basketball, and the majority of teachers, who simply ignored her completely.

Naturally, Teresa became reluctant to participate in class. She would only answer questions when she became bored because no one else could figure the problem out or offer the answer. She was not provided with appropriately challenging activities and was not regarded as exceptional or even valued as an individual by her teachers. Despite consistently doing exceptional academic work and graduating near the top of her class, she received no special recognition. A close friend of hers always received more respect and recognition than Teresa. Why? "It came down to her dad was a college professor and everyone knew it and my dad worked at Ready-Mix . . . Draw your own conclusions."

Teresa's experience as a female from a working-class home typifies the kind of atmosphere many students from similar settings experience throughout high school. In her case, it's even more inexcusable because Teresa was already labeled gifted and was supposed to be receiving appropriate services; even then, educational theory suggested that gifted students needed a personalized educational experience with multiple mentors. She never had that. It's a common question to ask of people, "Who was a teacher you had who had a great influence on you or made a difference in your life?," as if we've all had those kinds of teachers. Teresa didn't.

If you quantified our experiences in public schools, on paper Teresa and I would look very similar. We were both high achievers academically. But my wife's experience, briefly summarized above, was qualitatively vastly different from mine. I was a joiner because I was encouraged to believe that I belonged. Although that was privilege at work, I didn't then recognize it as privilege. But as an adult in education, I realize today that privilege in schools is often best understood as an invitation to belong. I was always treated by individuals within educational settings as if I belonged there. At lunch during middle school, I remember that a small group of guys who played football and did well academically would sit around on the bleachers and chat with one of the school administrators. I never stopped to think that he didn't talk to just anyone, that as an administrator, he was signifying our importance by taking time from his day to come out on those nice fall afternoons and stand around chatting with us. The same themes continued through high school. I was president of the student council, captain of the track team, and elected by my class to speak at graduation. I was so convinced of the authority of my voice within school that I pushed it to the absurd limit of sponsoring a Twinkie-eating contest as student council president and calling the local media in to report about it. Afterward, the administrator even congratulated me on the carnivalesque nature of it all. Privilege? Teresa's experience in high school was so different from mine. She wasn't a lesser student; in fact, she was a better student, a sharper thinker. Her experiences in high school remain a source of bitterness and resentment to her, and motivation to me to ask myself as a teacher, "Whose voices am I valuing in here? Who am I hearing from? Who am I silencing through my curriculum or methodology?" If we want to level the playing field, those are the kinds of questions we have to ask. If we want to simply maintain the status quo, then we can just continue to perpetuate privilege.

OF HIPPIES AND POP CULTURE PRIVILEGE

Maggie Ellison was a chain-smoking, coffee-drinking, impassioned high school teacher of English, drama, and debate. I was fascinated and infatuated with Maggie and her histories—both real and rumored. Maggie had lived in California in 1967, the "Summer of Love." She seemed like a compendium of socially relevant knowledge. She had seen Bob Dylan, Janis Joplin, and Jimi Hendrix in concert. She'd supposedly seen the Doors perform at a beach band contest where they won the event with a rendition of "Light My Fire" before their debut album was even released. She viewed literature as a means of connection—a way of hooking into important social causes and activities. She would debate the merits of Bruce Springsteen's latest work with the same forceful analysis she brought to plays and poetry. She believed that literature and music were ways of dialoging with the world, of addressing injustice. She didn't make distinctions between high culture and low culture, but she definitely seemed to prefer the contemporary over the classical. For speech contest, she had us dressed up in black turtlenecks and reciting Ferlinghetti. Who cared that it was the mid-1980s and half of the speech judges we performed for probably interpreted our performance as parody? To me, it was real and Ferlinghetti was sending an urgent message.

Maggie was the first teacher I'd had who systematically incorporated elements of popular culture into her classroom. Although I'm sure some students viewed her liberal rhetoric as tiresome, I viewed it as a liberating antidote to the conservative, pro-Republican political recitations I heard at home. She loaned me Dylan's "Greatest Hits" on cassette and brought in her copy of Dylan's lyric book, which included ticket stubs from several concerts.

Although U2's Bono once said, "I don't believe rock and roll can really change the world," my own private adolescent world was definitely irrevocably changed by the pop culture forces of the 1960s. I started to spend lots of money from my job on amassing a large music collection, LPs and cassettes of everything from Crosby, Stills, Nash and Young to ZZ Top. My first, preliminary attempts at understanding what the Vietnam War really meant to America didn't come from history books or memorizing discombobulated facts for social studies. They came from songs like Creedence Clearwater Revival's "Fortunate Son" and Country Joe and the Fish's "I Feel Like I'm A-Fixin' to Die Rag." Whenever Woodstock came on public television, I watched it religiously, waiting for Hendrix's inspired, concluding performance.

I am certain my parents didn't appreciate everything about the new self I started to try on once Maggie began to unlock pop culture and the 1960s to me. Maggie was the first educator I developed a close relationship with who helped me push the envelope on privilege and question why it wasn't granted to everyone. She was the first voice I'd ever really heard that was challenging the status quo, asking us to start to think about the injustices some people experienced. I took Maggie's example with all the zealotry of the newly converted. By midway through my sophomore year of high school, my dad was frequently yelling at me to "Turn down that damned long-haired hippie-ass noise!" I started reading *Rolling Stone,* in addition to occasionally wearing headbands, tie-dyed T-shirts, and bell-bottom corduroys.

As a teacher, I have attempted to follow Maggie's example to some degree. I want my students to know that I am in touch with and value the contemporary culture, that literature and language arts aren't simply about the recitation of stale ideas from long-dead authors, but that they are vibrant, real, and immediate. I have taken calculated risks in the classroom in order to help kids make more tangible tie-ins to the curriculum, including developing units on media literacy, movie criticism, and even using *Beavis and Butt-head* to teach caricature, parody, and satire in an accessible way. Maggie's example continues to inspire me. Ironically, however, this too is another indication of my privileged experience as a high schooler. My work with Maggie was largely through speech and drama, outside the traditional classroom setting. She singled me out early in high school as someone who could make a real contribution to the drama program, and I played large parts in numerous productions for three years. Another invitation to belong.

PRIVILEGE AND THE PRINTED WORD

Most of the students I work with do not have much of an identity as readers. A survey I administered to almost a hundred of my freshmen across three different sections of English indicated that many of them "never" or "only seldom" choose to read on their own. The vast majority of the reading they do is directed by others, and the texts are assigned. Absent some kind of significant intervention that proves to these kids that their own life interests can be sustained, enlivened, and invigorated through books, many of these students will become adults who are complacent readers or, worse yet, nonreaders.

As I stated earlier, my parents were passionate about the value of education. Books were always understood to be an indispensable part of that education. My dad was a true believer when it came to the value of book learning. How could he not be? The education he had so assiduously acquired at Iowa State University had opened the door for him to the lucrative and highly competitive arena of big business in high-tech manufacturing, working with companies like Rockwell and Norand.

We regularly visited public libraries growing up, and books were cherished gift items even as young children. Like many boys, I went through a phase where I consumed sports biographies like so much popcorn. Educational theorist Frank Smith (1988) has written at greater length and more articulately than myself on the amazing, life-enriching power of membership in the "literacy club." Suffice it to say that membership in this club should not be a privilege, it should be a right, something all children are entitled to, something all adults ought to be expected to join.

Perhaps one of the reasons more people are not passionate readers is because opening oneself up to a book might mean emerging from that book a changed person. As Robert Scholes (1989) wrote in *Protocols of Reading*, "reading . . . is not the whole of action but a part of it, remaining incomplete unless and until it is absorbed and transformed in the thoughts and deeds of readers" (p. x).

One of the paradoxes of my own growth as a young reader was that my parents willingly purchased books for me that caused me to question some of the beliefs they had labored so hard to instill. In addition to things like the beautifully bound triple-volume set of Shakespeare's complete works that was a pretty safe bet, they also bought gift books for me simply because I requested them: Kierkegaard's *Fear and Trembling*, a trilogy of novels by Sartre, a couple of volumes by Nietzsche. I think there was a somewhat innocent belief on my parents' part that if a book didn't seem too sensational or bizarre on its face, or better yet, if the author was dead, then the subject matter within couldn't be too unsettling. But it was through reading Nietzsche that I began to question my Catholic upbringing, and it was through Kierkegaard that I felt that the individualism of Protestant Christian belief was perhaps more attuned to my heart.

My own reading history reflects both the influence of my family, where I was taught to believe that the written word was the final one regarding any sort of scholarship, and the influence of my schooling, where I was always valued by teachers as a swift and fluent reader. The only unpleasant recollection I have from my schooling regarding reading would be junior high, when my voice would skip or drop octaves when I was instructed to read aloud.

Another English teacher, Robert Hastrich, was particularly important in terms of modeling what I thought an exemplary reader looked like: he was self-consciously erudite, with a staggering ability to reference authors and works and paraphrase or quote them in a manner that seemed encyclopedic to me. He was constantly recommending authors and works to students, saying things like, "Until you read Fitzgerald's short story 'The Diamond as Big as the Ritz,' you just won't understand the glittering imagery of *The Great Gatsby* [1940], so stop whining about it." He introduced me to Vonnegut's *Slaughterhouse Five* (1969) and the holy trinity of existential literature: Beckett, Camus, and Sartre. He put us on the spot right up front in class by asking us what we'd read over the summer. Having been recently inspired by Maggie, I proudly declared that I'd read *No One Here Gets Out Alive* (1980), the biography of Jim Morrison, American poet! Robert laughed uproariously until, still convulsed with laughter, he began to poll other students. Unlike Maggie, Robert wasn't shy about making value judgments about literature and dismissing most of pop culture as trendy and banal. But just like Maggie, Robert invited me to become a reader, to belong to the same literate world he inhabited. I remember him pulling Dante's *Inferno* (trans. 1954) off the library shelf and saying, "You're a good Catholic altar boy, aren't you? Here's some required reading!"

When I think about the way my own development as a reader has evolved over the years, I know that I am seeing one of the benefits of privilege. First, I was privileged to belong to a family where books were idealized as the ultimate storehouse of all things worth knowing. Second, the books I chose to read *and* those I was asked to read in school, from Shakespeare to Updike to Vonnegut, were almost universally by white males, so I saw myself reflected in a myriad of positive ways through the examples of these authors. I don't think we should be quick to dismiss the message this sends to readers: to me, it made it not only possible but plausible for me to envision myself as a writer, as someone who put words on paper, who belonged to the tradition T. S. Eliot (1917/1992) referred to when he wrote that "No poet . . . has his complete meaning alone. His significance, his appreciation is the appreciation of his relation to the dead poets and artists. You cannot value him alone" (p. 761). Talk about the privilege of membership! For me, the invitation to literature was often personal, often conversational, from recommendations from Maggie and Robert to informal discussions in the school library with other like-minded voracious readers whose mutually shared interest in reading philosophy created the basis for our friendship. Not surprisingly, all of these fellow philosopher fanatics were white males—Greg, Ben, Brian, and Bob. So although it might seem unique or even strange that I graduated from high school having read a fair share of philosophy in addition to the current and classical authors I'd been exposed to or discovered myself, I don't think there is anything particularly unique about it. Instead, this is another indication of privilege.

Through privilege, I felt a sense of entitlement about literature and even the supposed "great ideas." I felt as if that tradition was mine to assume. Although most people correctly consider reading Kant and Nietzsche to be formidable tasks, as a 17-year-old I was tackling the stuff with other 16- and 17-year-olds. We felt it was our right to do so. It didn't matter that there was a lot in the books we didn't understand; what we did understand was enough to confirm in us that we belonged, that there wasn't anything we couldn't read and comprehend. I look back on that time now and I am staggered by the supreme and perhaps slightly misguided confidence I had as a reader, because so much of it was just bravado. But so many of the students I work with today are very intolerant of ambiguity in reading. They won't wade into readings they view as formidable, word and phrase pronunciations they are unsure of they will simply declare "Whatever!" and sometimes they will even resort to the most condemning phrase of the adolescent reader: "This sucks!" I try to teach my students that no text is beyond their ability to understand, to appreciate, to critique, if they can build appropriate strategies for making sense out of it. I try to empower them to discover themselves as readers so that they too can experience the privilege of membership in the reading/ literacy club. If students' reading lives are devoid of the experience of reading and mastering texts that might at first seem difficult and laborious, and if students are not encouraged to read about the topics and themes they are most passionate about, then we will perpetuate privilege for a few in literacy instruction. And until all students see themselves reflected in the authors and characters of the works we ask them to read, all students will not be able to see themselves as talking back to those books and becoming a part of that tradition Eliot wrote of.

PRIVILEGE AND MENTORSHIP

There is a rhetoric of caring in public schools that is virtually ubiquitous. In the school system I teach in, words and phrases like "feeling tone" and "student-centered" are used as a subjective means of helping to define a teacher's approach to the learning process and inviting others to participate in a dialogue that will lead to school improvement. One such word that has been very common in my four years at Northeast High School is "personalization." "Personalization" is one of those terms that sounds ominously technical and jargony while simultaneously eluding a precise definition. In essence, my understanding of personalization is that it is the mission of educators to recognize the inherent worth, potential, and individuality of all our students. This might be partially achieved through something as simple and routine as standing in the hall and greeting students during passing periods or merely addressing students by their first names in the classroom. Although these sound like baseline sorts of expectations for teachers, in reality many teachers find this a struggle when they are working with perhaps over 150 students each day and have to move from one wing of the school to another to get to their next teaching assignment (within 5 minutes) in a school that works with nearly 2,200 students.

I am a product of smaller schools where teachers knew everyone by name. Early on, I attributed some of my sense of the lack of personalization at larger schools to the simple disparity in numbers between schools the size of Northeast and schools the size of my high school, where there were only about 75 students in each graduating class. I worked to get involved in projects such as a school-within-a-school for at-risk students so that I would have the opportunity to get to know my students on a personal, individual level and, I felt, better motivate them to be successful learners. This is one of the most significant reasons why I still very much enjoy teaching reading classes, where the class enrollment lid is only about 16 students. It creates a much more legitimate possibility of actually building meaningful relationships than in those classes where teachers are routinely faced with nearly 30 or more kids. My motivation is not entirely altruistic, either. It seems to me that one of the most rewarding aspects of teaching is the opportunity to get to know so many wonderful young people and hear their stories.

Small schools and small schooling experiences are not always personal, however, as I have learned by listening to the stories of others. What I once naïvely felt to be merely the mathematical result of smaller classes and lower student-to-teacher ratios is, I think, probably more the result of privilege than a simple difference in numbers.

As a student whose identity and individuality were valued by schools, in no small part probably because my identity reaffirmed to those in education the value of their work since I strove so hard to please my teachers and parents, I was the beneficiary of multiple mentorships throughout my schooling. As a professional who continues to work within the system of public education, I continue to benefit from the privilege of multiple mentorships.

The logical culmination of any school's attempt at personalization must be mentorship. Knowing your students by name might be a tentative start, but making a commitment to helping a student or numerous students become the people they dream of becoming by opening doors for them or sharing the wisdom of experience with them through advice or anecdotes is infinitely more meaningful. My wife didn't have mentors until graduate school in sociology. Why? It's inexcusable. My public school district makes active efforts to recruit minority teachers while at the same time a disproportionate number of our students of color, especially African-American males, are struggling academically. I've often thought that perhaps if all of us teachers worked harder as a district at taking care of our own we might have more excellent minority teacher candidates several years later. I have sat through interviews with student candidates for the school-within-a-school program I helped develop for students at Northeast who are behind on their credits and in danger of dropping out. I'm always depressed at the number of these articulate, insightful 16-year-olds who, when asked to talk about a teacher who has made a positive difference to them or was especially memorable, have to reach all the way back to first or second grade or, worse yet, simply can't think of anyone who impressed them as caring much. I find my wife's experiences confirmed again and again in the voices of these kids, struggling to find a place to belong at the same school she graduated from a dozen years earlier.

Ultimately, mentorship cannot be dictated. It is something that is chosen, voluntarily, and it works best when there's a coalescing between mentor and mentee of purpose or passion. Historically, mentors have not looked for unlikely candidates. Instead, logically, they select those who seem most suitable, most apt to carry on a teacher's sense of mission. I have never had to venture very far to find mentors; I have always been blessed and privileged to find people in positions of power or authority who were willing to venture a bit out of their way to assist me. Without mentors, how could anyone navigate the perilous waters of academic discourse and find a measure of success? As Mike Rose (1989) writes in *Lives on the Boundary*, "To journey up through the top levels of the American educational system will call for support and guidance at many, many points along the way. You'll need people to guide you into conversations that seem foreign and threatening" (p. 47). Without that guidance, participation is almost precluded. If you cannot participate, you cannot develop your own voice and talk back to that system of education. And the most powerful form of mentorship is that where the mentee is granted the privilege of speaking, of being a valued voice within the discourse of the institution—the rhetoric of power.

In 1990, I was working my way through Teachers College at University of Nebraska-Lincoln when I was invited to be a part of a research study of preservice teachers that Joy Ritchie and Dave Wilson were conducting. To a certain extent, I recollect that the purpose of the study was to survey us, to check our feelings and thoughts about English/language arts teaching as preprofessionals and use this information to document certain things, like our growth processes. The act of actually being interviewed and invited to expound upon my own development as a literate person was one of the most empowering experiences I have ever been a part of. Primarily, the experience was validating in that I had a sense of, "Hey, they're asking me, therefore they must figure I know!" Secondarily, it was a validating experience because I achieved a greater awareness and sense of autonomy as a thinker about and practitioner of literacy. Through the interviews as a part of Joy and Dave's project and as a student in courses such as Women's Literature and Literature for Adolescents, I began to develop a much more refined and committed sense of myself as an aspiring educator. In short, I became more proficient in academic discourse.

In "Reflections on Academic Discourse," Peter Elbow (1991) writes that

> the use of academic discourse often masks a lack of genuine understanding. When students write about something only in the language of the textbook or the discipline, they often distance or insulate themselves from experiencing or really internalizing the concepts they are allegedly learning. (p. 137)

It seems to me that Elbow got it at least half right. First of all, expanding on Elbow's notion of academic discourse as essentially written, I would argue for a more expansive notion of institutional rhetoric—the power and privilege of being invited to speak, to talk back to, and to dynamically impact the institutions of education. Second, I think Elbow is absolutely correct when he states that using this (what I'll call) institutional rhetoric "often masks a lack of genuine understanding." But I think being able to try on institutional rhetoric, to play at academic discourse, is a necessary precursor to eventually becoming someone who utilizes academic discourse and institutional rhetoric to dynamically and positively impact things like curricular decisions and reserved reading lists, or to respond effectively to a peer who questions one's teaching methodology, and so on. In short, I would suggest that teachers cannot become effective participants in the high-stakes battles of competing educational ideologies unless they are first permitted and in fact encouraged to play with institutional rhetoric, to talk with others about their tentative beliefs, to dream about what it might be possible to achieve as a teacher. As Mike Rose (1989) put it when describing some of his graduate school experiences, "I was surrounding myself with a discourse of possibility rather than succumbing to images of defeat" (p. 79). Without empowering preservice teachers to embark on that discourse of possibility, we inevitably surrender ourselves to simply creating more of the same.

The interview process as a subject of Dave and Joy's study became my discourse of possibility. Or, as Dave and Joy have said elsewhere, "Our protocol became our pedagogy." Confession: I lied during the interviews. Well, I didn't lie insofar as I claimed to have achieved certain things I hadn't, but I intentionally packaged myself as someone who knew. I made a conscious effort throughout the process to sound articulate, intelligent, erudite. I tried to avoid responding impulsively. Most of the questions we were asked were higher-order, referential questions inviting lots of open-ended speculation. So rather than shrugging and admitting ignorance (which might have been technically correct a time or two!), I theorized wildly. I made up theoretical paradigms on the basis of what I'd read. I had no practical classroom pedagogical experience to draw upon; I simply culled stories from my own history as a student. But the act of being asked to speak, of being treated as someone whose opinions mattered without having those opinions constantly evaluated or scrutinized, helped me to tell my story and connect the pieces of that puzzle into a critical typology of teaching. It made me feel privileged, this playing at institutional rhetoric until I began to feel a sense of ownership and investment within it.

There is no substitute for building valued relationships among colleagues and among those one aspires to be like. A teacher can envision in his or her head what an effective and liberatory pedagogue might look like, but how could that compare to actually knowing an incarnate example—a person who walks the walk? Because of the multiple mentorships I have been privileged to benefit from, I have been able to assume a voice of authority within institutions that has helped me become a critical pedagogue rather than a teacher who simply surrenders to conformist notions of schooling. If a teacher cannot envision how a lesson, a curriculum, or an approach to reading in a classroom might be *different*, how could that teacher imagine how it might be *better*? The only way is through building real relationships with practitioners who are actively exploring alternatives and manifesting the traits one wishes to acquire. Early on, Maggie Ellison and Robert Hastrich were those people for me. Later, Dave and Joy and Ruth Kupfer became those people for me.

PRIVILEGE AS MORAL MANDATE

I was waiting for my seventh-period reading class to begin the other day, thinking about the theme of privilege and how my awareness of my own privilege had led me here, to Room 155 and my work with struggling readers. Anyone who has spent any amount of time in a high school reading classroom knows that for many if not most of these students, there are issues quite apart from literacy that have wreaked havoc on their schooling. My reading kids are not the children of privilege, and they do not reflect my own experience in schools. I imagine that the Advanced Placement students here at Northeast might have experiences that resonate more with my own past, but I really like the kids I get to work with, if for the simple reason that their lives are filled with challenges different from those I faced.

Today, Shaun walks in wearing his leather jacket, baggy pants, and Aerosmith T-shirt. Room 155 is a kind of sanctuary for Shaun. He often shows up early so we can quiz one another on rock music trivia and listen to music. Today he has brought in a new Ted Nugent disc. We sing along to "Cat Scratch Fever" and talk about what a great guitarist Nugent is. Later that hour, Shaun gets a call slip to go to the nurse's office. His probation officer has showed up to administer a urine analysis to screen for drug use. Shaun isn't nervous. "I'm not usin', man." He walks out.

Ryan walks in and sits on top of a desk by the window. He shivers in his thin Jeff Gordon NASCAR T-shirt. No coat. He hasn't eaten any lunch, as usual. I don't know if he just refuses to eat in the cafeteria because it's uncool or if his parents never turned in the forms, but we've developed a predictable routine instead of the free or reduced lunch in the cafeteria. "Got anything for me?" "Well, let's see, I got some pretzels left and an apple. . . . " "Cool!"

Emmit shows up, late. It's the first time I've seen him in a month. His head is shaved, and he's wearing his baggies and a Brett Favre jersey, looking hard. "Look, man," he pulls me aside, "I know I'm failin' 'cause I'm over the fifteen absences, but . . . " He says he hasn't been to school because a rival gang is looking for him, and they've threatened to take his life. So he's stayed home the last month playing Nintendo 64 and glancing out his windows, getting more and more school phobic. My middle-class instincts kick in, and I inevitably make an ass of myself, unwittingly demonstrating my privilege: "Did you contact the authorities? Should we go to the school resource police officer and explain the situation to him?" Emmit starts shaking his head, "No, no, no, this shit's been a long time comin'. What are you, stupid? I told you 'cause I thought you was cool. I can't talk to no cops! Damn."

Bruce is pumped that Emmit is in attendance. Bruce just moved here from Washington State and he wants to hang with Emmit. He takes a seat next to him and tries to start a conversation. Emmit seems passive about Bruce's gesture of friendship.

Amber is stressed about the upcoming winter break. She explains that her mother has been out of work since September, when she had surgery for cancer. Now they're down and out. They haven't lost their home yet, but it's looming on the horizon. They'll be having a charity Christmas dinner in a church basement. "It's not even our church. I feel weird about it."

These are some of my reading students. Not all of them have the privilege of living with even the basics I'd like to think all kids are entitled to: safety, adequate clothing and nourishment, parental structure and support. As their teacher for one hour a day, I can't make it all better. I can be open and inviting and supportive. I can grant them the privilege of being someone who cares enough to know them by name and hear their stories while I push them to learn under less than ideal circumstances. But I'm not there to be paternalistic, to condescend, or to assume that I know all the answers or that my life is in some fundamental way better than theirs because I've been privileged. I know that the scope of my impact as their teacher might be limited. Perhaps, as with Ryan, it's the one hour a day he always attends because Ryan thinks I'm "cool" (or so his IEP manager tells me). And occasionally I can have a more sustained impact beyond that hour: Like Corey, who called me the other day. He'd been released from the Omaha Correctional Center and wanted me to know that he had finished his GED while inside.

> I just wanted you to know that you made a big difference to me because you didn't get all judgmental and shit when I got busted, you just tried to help out and let me know that I always had the potential to do the right thing. And now I'm doin' it, gonna be goin' to community college.

I cannot walk away from my privileged past and pretend to know in any fundamental way what many of my students endure on a daily basis any more than these kids can simply step into a new life by succeeding in a reading class. What I can do is offer students a sense of hope by putting the power of privilege to work for them in limited ways. I can help them through the attendance appeals process, I can offer advice to them on their English classes, I can talk to them about strategies for meeting with an administrator when they're facing a disciplinary referral. I can be real and approachable. I can hear their voices.

The school I work in has a reputation in town. It's considered a tougher school with a more resistant student body. We have greater diversity and more lower socioeconomic status kids than the other schools. There are a number of teachers at this school who inevitably would go elsewhere if they could. But there are also many teachers at my school who are doing exciting things in an attempt to address the needs of our students. They are using their voices to talk back to the institution and help it change in positive ways. These teachers work on gender equity and multicultural issues, they commit their time to the safety committee or help the reading committee figure out what the best possible reading program would be for our students. They are real and accessible people to their students. They even know some of their students' parents by name. These are the people who understand that we have an obligation to extend the benefits of privilege to others, in whatever fashion we can.

At Northeast, there are many ways we gauge success with students, and some of those measurements might be more incremental than others. For a student on the verge of withdrawing from the school community, like Ryan, consistent attendance is a sign of success. For another student like Jessica, making the honor roll the semester after she gave birth to her daughter was a sign of success worth celebrating. These are two of the students I have tried to grant some privilege to—by extending a personal invitation to build their sense of belonging at school, by befriending and advising them. Not by any artificial measure or mark in the gradebook, but through building a collaborative, personal relationship like those relationships others have offered to me: the privilege of invitation.

8

Retracing My Journey Toward Self-Acceptance and Effectiveness as a Lesbian Teacher

Ruth Kupfer

> Difference is that raw and powerful connection from which our personal power is forged.
> —Audre Lorde, "The Master's Tools Will Never Dismantle the Master's House"

> Well-learned distinctions between public and private make us believe that love has no place in the classroom.
> —bell hooks, *Teaching to Transgress*

During my work in graduate school, I had the opportunity to look back over my 20 years of teaching and take stock of the changes I had made in my pedagogy over that time. What I was able to understand after making that examination was that teaching for me had come to be not about controlling the manner and degree of students' intake of information, but about how I might facilitate and foster the construction of personal knowledge by individual learners.

I had not always understood that, however. For more than half of my career, I was one of those teachers who stood in front of the class to teach, who wrote objective tests over novels and required students to fill out study guides. "Frontal teaching," I have heard it called, the kind of teaching that required an authoritarian aura around the teacher at all times and a distance between teacher and student that ensured a hierarchical set-up necessary for student compliance. But even though a concern for my students as individuals and the building of personal relationships with my students was an important part of my work then, it came second to the maintenance of my authority.

Because of a period in my career marked by transformative reading and study and interaction with an extraordinarily skilled student teacher, I began to see my role in the classroom differently. I came to understand that the kind of control I had attempted to maintain was artificial and largely ineffective. I started to realize that the kind of learning I had always hoped my students would achieve was going to happen only if they were granted a large degree of autonomy over their own classroom experiences. So I moved away from traditional kinds of teaching and into the use of reader-response and process-writing methodologies, and as I did, it became clear to me that it was critical to build personal relationships with students. In a student-centered, cooperative classroom, where students teach each other and in which self-discovery is a primary goal, trust is a crucial element. Without trust, students are not prone to take the risks they need to take to become involved in experiences that produce growth, both in their literacy and their life skills.

I also came to realize that in the kind of classroom I was creating, student-centeredness did not mean the erasure of the teacher. Rather, it meant that I needed to play a role that more closely resembled that of a mentor, and one who very clearly demonstrated an authentic sense of self-identity, since that was the goal to which I wanted students to aspire.

So through the process of transforming the nature of my authority in the classroom and transferring control to students, I have come to believe that there is a level of intimacy that is necessary between teachers and students. It is the kind of intimacy that makes it possible for a teacher to know what is important in a student's life, and consequently what he or she might be prone to read or write; what keeps a student from coming to school on some days; what makes a student happy or upset. This kind of intimacy facilitates interaction between students and teachers in order to encourage and motivate students. Knowing these things makes it possible for me to make teaching decisions that are better informed and more effective than they would be if I relied exclusively on an authoritative, treat-all-students-the-same model.

For many years, I tried to find out this personal information about students by handing out interest inventories. But no one was likely to write on their interest inventory that her father beat her and her mother, or that he was racked with guilt about not wanting to spend time with his father in another city, or that her primary source of joy was her six-month-old baby. These are things that students tell me in their private journals, or in one-on-one conversations. And they write to me and talk to me this way when we have viable personal relationships.

When a student begins to realize that the content of her own life is appropriate content about which to write, or with which to construct entryways to and connections with literature, then authentic learning begins to take place. Her work becomes meaningful in a way that it wasn't before. And her life experiences are validated and honored in ways that help the student build and maintain a healthy self-esteem and a self-confidence that will lead to more and greater risk-taking in learning experiences.

How much and how well would this happen when the teacher is constantly maintaining a lie about herself? I am sure that it can happen to a degree, because I have been an openly lesbian teacher only for around a third of my 23 years in teaching, but I have been actively involved in relationship-building with students for longer than that. But masking parts of my life took its toll on me emotionally, and I am certain that the quality of my interactions with students now is more vital than it used to be. I don't think it's necessary to make an out-of-context announcement about one's sexual orientation to a whole class, or to discuss the details of one's life that aren't relevant to a given learning situation, and I have never done so. But I talk about my own life when it is relevant and appropriate to do so, and I answer students' questions honestly.

The effect of my candor about my sexual orientation is that lesbian, gay, and bisexual students may feel less alone, less isolated, and less misunderstood. I do not take lightly the scarcity of role models for gay, lesbian, bisexual, and transgendered youth, and I realize the responsibility I have to provide a positive image. Equally important is that for heterosexual students, seeing me as a lesbian breaks down the stereotypes they have come to believe and helps them humanize and complicate their mental pictures of who lesbians are. My sexuality becomes an incidental, rather than the focus of students' perceptions of me. Some of these students also have gay and lesbian parents, siblings, aunts, uncles, and other family members. But perhaps most important of all, in the classroom where I am truthful, honesty becomes a valued standard.

When what happens in the classroom is honest and deeply relevant, many traditional classroom problems solve themselves. Truancies and tardies decline. Students develop respect for one another, resulting in increased and more effective communication with each other. Motivation increases drastically, because students are doing what they feel is important. It is an environment that takes a long time to build (many years for me!), but it is well worth the results.

FEAR AS A BARRIER TO EFFECTIVENESS

A great deal of the reading about lesbian and gay issues in the classroom that I have been doing lately tells me that the things gay and lesbian teens need most are role models, a community of their own to end the devastating isolation they feel, and a sense of safety at school. The lesbian and gay students with whom I work tell me the same things. I try to provide all of these things in my classroom and for my school community.

I use literature by and about gay and lesbian people in the English classes I teach. I have invited openly gay and lesbian speakers to POWER Club (People Outreaching for Women's Equality and Rights, the young feminist club I used to sponsor at my school) and the Gay/Lesbian/Bisexual/Straight Alliance (GLBSA), which I currently co-sponsor. I have organized student efforts to reduce and eliminate sexual harassment at our school, and I have worked with the administration to provide leadership for improving the school climate as it is affected by sexual harassment. I do not allow students to use gay or lesbian hate language. I have identified myself as a lesbian to my colleagues and my administrators. I come out as a lesbian to the students in my Women's Literature classes, the GLBSA, and to individual students as the need arises.

I am happy to be able to say all of this now. But things weren't always this way for me as a lesbian teacher. At different points in my teaching career, ignorance, fear, and shame kept me from providing students with the gay/lesbian-positive environment I try to create now. For a long time I kept my identity secret, and fear colored my response to lesbian and gay issues when they came up in my classroom.

But as detrimental to gay and lesbian students as my feelings of internalized homophobia were, a greatly limited effectiveness with *all* my students was also a product of that homophobia. My belief that dishonesty about my being a lesbian had to be maintained was just one part of my badly flawed vision of who I should be as a teacher. It was integral to maintaining the distance I thought should exist between teachers and their students.

I know now how wrong that idea is. But before I could understand or construct the intimacy between teachers and students that is not only appropriate but necessary, I had to retrace the journey that brought me to an understanding of what my full acceptance of my sexuality had to do with my full effectiveness as a teacher.

COMING TO OWN MY LESBIAN IDENTITY

When I began my teaching career in 1976 I was not fully aware of my sexual orientation. As a matter of fact, I did not know that lesbians even existed until five years before that. I remember being 18 when I watched a television program that mentioned the term "homosexual" and I asked my mother what it meant. She gave me her standard answer: "Let's look it up in the dictionary." I don't remember that dictionary definition, but I do remember feeling surprised to find out that such a possibility existed. It was difficult to even imagine.

When I was a senior in high school I was dating a guy who graduated a year ahead of me. He was working construction and would buy me flowers when he won the check pool. He was a sincerely nice guy, a big red-haired Bohemian boy from South Omaha named Stan, but I broke off with him even though there was no one else I was interested in dating. I couldn't really explain why I stopped dating Stan. It could have been because I felt weird about making out with him. It could have been because he was too nice. At the time, I couldn't have told you.

I dated a couple of other guys after that, went out once or twice with each of them. One of them made fun of me in front of his friends because when he had tried to kiss me, my hands shot up in front of my face. I felt stupid about it when he was telling his buddies, but at the time it was just a gut reaction. I honestly didn't know why I did it. I didn't *want* to kiss him—I knew that. But I didn't think it was because he was a boy. I figured that there was some other boy out there who would be fun to kiss. So what?

As I was growing up I had physical feelings of attraction for girls, and I came to believe they were normal, that every other girl probably experienced them, too. I just figured that no one paid any significant attention to them. My first conscious feelings of sexual arousal were triggered by dancing with junior high girlfriends. I had a consuming crush on my junior high school gym teacher and later on the girl who sat in front of me in Honors English class in high school.

When I went off to college in 1972, I met a boy named Tom who was from a small town in northeastern Nebraska. He had a Pontiac GTO and a beard. I was fascinated. Four years later, I was married to him. He was *interested* in me, a girl who had not dated until I met that construction worker when I was a senior.

I had been a music nerd in high school, hanging out in the band room four of the eight periods in the school day. I had been popular enough to be elected president of the band and girls' sargent-at-arms for my senior class, but not popular enough to be asked out or included in the cool group of kids. I had also been a chubby kid, and when I started my senior year in high school, I became caught up in a pattern of eating (or not eating) that looks frighteningly like anorexia when I think about it now. The emotional distance between my mother and me that widened as she became more and more dependent on alcohol after my sister left for college exacerbated a drive to find approval. So after high school graduation I was anxious to create an identity for myself. Unfortunately, all of those conditions also led me to base my identity on a need for acceptance.

The point here is that I got married for the wrong reasons. I had no real frame of reference for understanding my sexual orientation at that time, and I had a critical need for acceptance. I had lived with Tom during my last three years of college, and when I began to interview for teaching jobs, I thought cohabitation would be outside of standards for teachers. I got married despite reservations of which I was fully aware, because I could not see any other options.

I got a job—my first teaching position—at a large high school in central Nebraska, and we packed up and moved there. A year into my marriage, my husband starting working on the 3:00 to 11:00 P.M. shift at the local regional mental health center, and I started spending after-school and evening hours with a woman who was also a teacher. As my feelings for Susan grew and crossed over a line into strong attraction, happily, her feelings for me did, too. Even though we engaged in a brief but intense affair, the word *lesbian* never crossed my mind.

Looking back on that now, it seems pretty strange that I didn't at least question my sexual orientation at that time, especially since Susan was involved in a long-term relationship with a woman she had met in college. She had also told me the story of her first lover, a girl with whom she had been romantically involved through high school. Susan told me that she used to sneak up the back stairs at her girlfriend's house late at night and spend the nights with her, doing more than sleeping. Yet at that time, Susan did not call herself lesbian, or even gay. I don't remember either of us ever using those words.

At the beginning of my fourth year at that first teaching position, I left my husband because of increasing feelings of discontent with my marriage, and I made plans to quit my job. The following summer I moved to Lincoln and got a job teaching in a junior high school. That fall my mother passed away, and my feelings of grief and loneliness led me to isolate myself most evenings in my upstairs apartment.

Shopping at a local health food store one day, I bumped into a guy I had gone to public school with back in Omaha. He invited me to come and play volleyball with a group of his friends who played every Tuesday night at a nearby church. I had never played competitive volleyball, so I suppose I decided to go just to get out of my little apartment one night a week. The folks at volleyball were not too happy that I was such a raw beginner at the sport they took pretty seriously, but somehow their disapproval seemed to give me the impetus to stay with it until I had practiced and learned enough to keep up with them.

After a year or so, one of the women who played asked me if I would like to join their city-rec volleyball team. I was flattered that she wanted me to play with them, and said I would. I had gotten the sense that some of the women who played on Tuesdays at the church were involved in relationships with each other, and as it turned out, all but one of the women who played on the city-rec team were lesbian.

After our games, the team would go out for beer at the local lesbian bar. On one such evening, I was sitting at the bar with a woman who was to become a long-time friend of mine. In all the years that I've known Marti I've never known her to mince words, and she didn't that night. I was about to take a sip of my beer when Marti said to me, "So are you a lesbian, or what?"

Up until that point, even though I had been involved in sexual relationships with four different women, I never called myself a lesbian. So I stammered, "Well, I guess so. I guess I'm at least bisexual." I was taking into consideration the fact that I had been married, and I didn't really understand what I do now about the reasons why I had been married. But from that point on, Marti's question rang in my head and I became determined to truly understand the answer.

My entrance into Lincoln's lesbian community was through that volleyball team and through that bar. The following summer I played softball on a lesbian team and met more women. Watching those lesbians— seeing how they interacted, how they presented themselves, how they lived their lives—I gradually became able to see and understand myself with more clarity than I ever had been able to before. Pieces began to fall into place; memories began to make sense. Finally I had a context for myself as a lesbian. Finally I was able to form an identity that truly felt comfortable.

LESSONS ABOUT THE CLIMATE FOR A LESBIAN TEACHER

I was teaching in a junior high school at the time that Marti asked me that now infamous question. In the spring of my second year there, a proposal to include antidiscrimination rights for lesbian and gay people in the city charter was put to a vote of the citizens of Lincoln. By this time I was in the early stages of understanding the political implications for lesbians of living in this part of the country, and I got involved in work to campaign for the passage of the amendment. I leafleted homes in my neighborhood and attended the city council meeting at which the issue was debated by members of the public.

As a part of this effort, it seemed to me that the likelihood of the amendment's passage could be greatly increased if the Lincoln Education Association (LEA), to which I belonged, was to endorse it. I visited a colleague in my building who was very active with the LEA and asked him how to go about asking the Faculty Representatives' Council to make a statement in support of the amendment. He suggested writing a letter to read at the next Council. I also asked him if he thought that the group would assume that I was lesbian if I read such a letter. He said he didn't think so.

It was the first time that I came out to someone I worked with, and I'm sure I was visibly nervous about it. As it turned out, I had picked a fairly good, although naïve, candidate, as I found out later that he had once read a kid the riot act for calling another colleague of ours a "fag." But now I know that this advisor was wrong about part of his advice: If a person makes a statement in support of lesbian and gay rights, almost everyone will assume that person is lesbian or gay.

At the time, I didn't know any better. I wrote and delivered my letter to the Faculty Representatives' Council on shaky knees, and after some discussion my proposal was defeated. A man who was a particularly powerful leader in the LEA convinced the group that it would be more important for us to endorse the gubernatorial candidate we supported, and that an endorsement of the gay/lesbian rights amendment would destroy our credibility. Ironically, I found out later that this LEA leader was himself a gay man.

Thinking back about all of this now, I realize that both of us were doing what our environments called for. Without an antidiscrimination amendment, neither he nor I had any job protection. In the climate of disapproval that existed for gay/lesbian rights (the amendment was defeated by a two-thirds margin), the loss of a teaching job was a real threat. So it made sense for him to remain closeted, and even to speak against my proposal. But for me, at that stage of my sexual identity, it made sense to begin to speak out to address the larger environment for lesbians and gays. In my efforts to enhance my self-actualization, I was anxious to explore every facet of what it meant to be lesbian, including what it meant for my public life.

Even though I was becoming an activist in the work for gay and lesbian civil rights, it didn't mean that I was comfortable being out in every part of my life. For the little while when I operated under that false notion that a person can speak out for lesbian/gay concerns and not be pegged as lesbian or gay, I spoke out in the teachers' lounge and in my classroom and thought no one would make any assumptions. But when I began to understand that most people think that only a lesbian or gay man would care about lesbian/gay issues, it began to make me more nervous to speak out. Not that I stopped doing it—I didn't. But maybe that was because I was trying to justify myself in a culture that says that either I don't exist or I'm sick.

Another incident that opened my eyes to the environment that existed for me as a lesbian teacher occurred a few years after I began working at Lincoln High School. I had worked with a teacher named Sue Ellen for four or five years, and during that time we got involved in some discussions about political things, including feminism. One time Sue Ellen had told me that the local feminist paper I was helping to produce would be much better if only we would stop publishing articles by and about lesbians. According to her, we were hurting our credibility by allowing "them" to take up space in the paper. I had also heard stories about her homophobia directed toward students and community members, and I had witnessed her verbal attack on an openly lesbian psychologist and an openly gay community activist whom I had invited to speak to students at a lunchtime forum. So I knew that at any given time she was likely to act on her homophobia.

One afternoon Sue Ellen showed up in my room after we had argued in the teachers' lounge earlier in the day. She came into the lounge angry about something else that had happened, and she took her anger out on me, yelling that I had a hidden agenda for my Women's Literature students, and that I was trying to make clones of myself out of them. I quickly figured out that she was referring to a lesbian student in my class who was also in one of her classes, and I suppose this student must have been outspoken about her lesbian feminism, as she often was. I guess Sue Ellen couldn't imagine anyone being a lesbian without being recruited, so she was accusing me.

When she came into my room, she baited me for a while, trying to get me to answer some question that would confirm her suspicions that I was lesbian. When I wouldn't do it, she finally said,

> Look. I know you're a lesbian. You need to make sure that you don't meet with students outside of school, or be caught alone with a student. If you get yourself in trouble, I will be among those who support your being fired.

I was stunned. I told her that my personal life was none of her business, that I had never spent time with students outside of school (which was true), and that she could find the door. Afterward I was furious. I went home and spoke to friends about what had happened, but I said little to anyone at school. But my anger just continued to grow, and I finally told the assistant principal a couple of weeks later. Luckily she was supportive and understanding, having experienced one of Sue Ellen's attacks herself (for a different reason). She told me that if it ever happened again, to let her know.

The whole incident left me angry and hurt. It also opened my eyes to the sentiments that surrounded me in my workplace each day. If Sue Ellen were bold enough to be overt with her homophobia and her threats, I had to believe that there were others who shared her feelings and would act in like ways if they were ever given the opportunity. But the biggest damage Sue Ellen and her ilk did was subtle and insidious. The fear she created fed my internalized homophobia, fueled the place inside of me that still harbored doubts about whether teaching was a rightful place for lesbians who wanted to be open about their sexual orientation.

Looking back now that I am completely out as a lesbian teacher, it seems odd that I let myself feel so afraid. I knew it was important to include lesbian and gay characters in the literature I brought into the classroom, but when I led discussions about it I got so nervous that it often made the talking go badly. I knew that it was wrong to allow kids to call each other derogatory names like "fag," but I got scared after confronting their behavior.

What was I most afraid of? Despite what Sue Ellen had said, and because my behavior was never sexually inappropriate with students, there was never any direct threat of being fired. Perhaps it was more the fear of ostracism that froze me. As more and more of my colleagues figured out that I was lesbian, a few stopped greeting me in the hallways. It hurt, but no one I was close to or really cared about rejected me. What really frightened me and sickened me was experiencing how my own students could ostracize me.

TOWARD CLAIMING AN IDENTITY AS A LESBIAN TEACHER

A few years ago a young man in one of my classes began to harass me at school. Leon had figured out I was lesbian, and he seemed to have a desire to control all of his teachers and command attention. (I found this out later from other straight teachers Leon had.) The harassment ranged from modeling stereotypical gay behaviors visibly during class to see what my reaction would be to baiting me by asking questions about gay/lesbian issues or about my personal life. The class was well aware of Leon's behaviors and well aware of his motives. When the harassment turned into sexual harassment, I took Leon to the office, wrote him up, and he was suspended.

In the disciplinary conference with the vice principal, Leon confirmed that his behaviors were motivated by his belief that I was lesbian. I acknowledged that I was indeed a lesbian, and the vice principal made it clear that what Leon was doing was not only unacceptable in our school, it was also illegal. When Leon came back from suspension, his behaviors were completely appropriate and the problem of his harassment was solved. But it left the rest of the class in ruins.

This group of students—75 of them—rotated through a block of three classes together, so they were unusually close, and there were clear lines of communication among them. I am certain that what they witnessed in class and what they told each other came to affect the way they saw me and responded to me. Many became quiet and withdrawn. A few stopped returning my greeting at the door. I began to dread coming to school each day. My effectiveness as a teacher was greatly diminished.

Last year when I put together my teaching portfolio, I looked back over the teacher evaluations that these students wrote about me. Over and over they made statements about how I treated boys differently than I treated girls. They complained that I was too strict with the boys and let the girls get away with things. I believe that whatever they focused on concerning my classroom behavior, they saw me through the prism of a lesbian doing these things. Their socialized homophobia told them that I was a man-hater, and so any attempts on my part to confront nonproductive behaviors of male students became a part of that picture for them.

That group of students graduated last year, but throughout their time at my school, there were many who would not make eye contact or speak to me in the halls. Without my ever directly telling a student about my orientation, students I had never met knew about me. A friend of mine named Cara, a girl who lived for many years in my neighborhood and was a stepdaughter of a close lesbian friend of mine, told me this story: Cara was in the local Kentucky Fried Chicken store when she was a seventh grader two years ago. She and her friends were flirting with the high school boy behind the counter. Cara found out that he went to the school where I teach and she asked if he knew me. He said he did, and did she know that I was a lesbian? Cara, bless her ornery heart, widened her eyes in amazement and said, Why, no! She had no idea. She laughed a good laugh when she told me this story.

I laughed, too. Looking back at what happened that awful year when that big bunch of sophomores figured out I was lesbian, I realize that many of my own behaviors contributed to students' reactions. When I blushed or got shaky when Leon was harassing me, I was telling students that I had something to be afraid of or embarrassed about. When I never openly confronted what was happening in front of the whole group, I was telling students that what was happening was not to be spoken about, but was something to be kept hushed and secret. I was telling them that I had something I was ashamed of.

A significant part of the conflict with Leon was my coming out to another administrator, Dr. Sterns, who suspended him after learning about his behavior. Although I was friendly with Dr. Sterns and we had developed a good working relationship, an appropriate opportunity to come out to him had never presented itself.

But the momentum created by my anger and frustration about Leon's actions on the day that they crossed the line and became sexual harassment carried me right into Dr. Sterns's office. Without thinking about what the consequences might be, as I told him that Leon was harassing me because he perceived me to be lesbian, I added that indeed I was a lesbian. He looked a bit shocked, but did not allow any feelings he may have had about this news to affect his handling of Leon's case.

Afterward, though, I took the opportunity to ask for a meeting with Dr. Sterns so that we could talk about the implications of what had happened. We sat in his office on a sunny spring afternoon and I told him that I wanted him to consider what it meant to be a lesbian or gay teacher in a public school.

The first statement Dr. Sterns made to me was this: "I know you, Ruth. You are one of the best teachers we have here. I know that what happens in your life outside of school doesn't affect your work here at all." My heart sank.

Dr. Sterns had reduced the question to one of sexual practice. Inherent in his remarks was the idea that being lesbian was deviant, and must be kept very distant from the classroom. So I tried to explain that my sexual orientation was not a part of me that could be isolated as only sexual acts and separated from the whole of who I was, and that attempts to fragment myself in that way would be harmful. He was forgetting that none of my straight colleagues were expected to segment themselves and hide away all the suggestions of their heterosexuality—their family photos, wedding rings, bouquets delivered on Valentine's Day. But he was not able to grasp the idea that every aspect of my life is affected by who I love and who loves me, and his attitude went unchanged.

And what a dangerous attitude it was. It was simple: keep your sexual practice—and your *identity*—out of your classroom, and no problem would exist. It is insulting, first of all, to imply that the possibility would even exist of my bringing information about my sexual practice into my classroom. But it also ignores all of the threats to my work that exist because of both external and internalized homophobia.

Did my administrator and my colleagues think that as long as I kept my sexual orientation hidden, the threats to lesbian and gay teachers and gay-positive curricula made by the powerful religious right wouldn't affect me? Did they think that I had lost my effectiveness with my class because I had not kept my identity hidden? Did they think that as long as I hid, which shame would easily enable me to do, I would be a whole person? Did they think that fragmented people with secrets, who told lies, were the best teachers? Did they understand how much energy it takes to manage all the work of concealing a fundamental part of your life, by constantly changing pronouns, avoiding students' questions, remembering what lies were told to whom, while all the time being fearful that others have figured you out anyway, just because of your haircut or the fact that you never wear a dress and are 40 years old with no children and no husband? What were they thinking?

And what was I thinking? Up until that point, when I had to defend myself to Dr. Sterns, I hadn't understood those implications either. But I began to see that as long as I maintained a split identity and acted ashamed, I wasn't the kind of teacher—or human being—I wanted to be.

THE PRICE OF CONCEALING MYSELF FROM STUDENTS

Years ago, I attended an intensive workshop, the purpose of which was to explore and unlearn oppressive beliefs and behaviors. I attended because I was deeply involved in antiracism work. The other participants were mostly friends of mine, a dozen women who were either in the Lincoln Women Against Racism discussion group of which I was a part, or who were lesbians and straight women I knew from the community. One of the participants was a woman named Diana who had been in one of the first sections of Women's Literature class I had taught at Lincoln High a year or two before.

The workshop began with a simple exercise. All of us stood against one wall facing an open space. As the workshop facilitators requested, we crossed in groups to the other side. They asked the women of color to cross the room, turn, and face the rest of us. As we gazed at each other, we began to feel the effects of enacting the divisions that existed between us that daily are ignored, and we began to feel what it must be like to be on the other side of the room. The women of color came back, and the facilitators called for different groups of women to cross, one by one: women with disabilities, women from alcoholic families, women who had been in abusive relationships, women who were lesbians. As we moved and saw, the distances between us went from being abstract to being physical and real. We couldn't ignore them any longer. We began to feel what the distances meant for each of us.

More short exercises followed, each one designed to get us to move from our heads into our emotions with regard to oppressing and being oppressed. We took a break and had a bite to eat, and when we reassembled we were told about the final exercise. All of us sat in chairs theater-style, facing the two facilitators. One by one they asked each participant to come forward. As the rest of us looked on, the individual at the front would be invited to tell the story of the burdens created by oppression with which she was struggling.

The women of color were called up first. Some of them told stories that were horrible and wrenching. One young African American woman who had grown up in Omaha told about the times—twice—when her father had been shot. She wept as she told the stories, and I did, too. I thought about how I had known this young woman but had never stopped to think about how life had been made harder for her because of the racism that she was faced with every day.

Another African American woman told of the ostracism she felt in the Lincoln lesbian community. Other women stood up and told stories about being estranged from their families, being hurt unintentionally— but hurt, nonetheless—by the privilege and ignorance of their friends, being an outsider in almost every arena of their lives.

Eventually it was my turn to be called up to the front. As I rose to walk forward on uncertain legs, I had no idea what I would say to the rest of the group. The facilitator, a woman named Ana whom I had known for a time, put her arms around me and let me talk to her alone. She told me that I could tell her what was really painful for me, what I was dealing with and needed to unburden. To my own surprise, what I whispered to her was that as a lesbian I felt estranged from my students who were also lesbian. What came pouring out was a great sadness about not feeling able to acknowledge my sexuality to lesbian students, and not being able to build relationships with them in ways that honored who we were or accessed what we had in common so that we could use that as a basis for growth.

As I talked with Ana, I realized that it was the presence of Diana that unlocked these feelings. She asked me if I wanted to tell Diana, and at first I said no. Ana gave me a couple of minutes, talking to me about what I was feeling, and asked me again. I suppose because I felt I had nothing to lose by taking the risk, I turned and told Diana about my feelings. She came forward and hugged me, a sign of her empathy and I hope of her understanding.

I wish I could say that after that experience I made up for my estrangement from Diana, and that we went on to develop a friendly relationship. It didn't happen. It would be too much like a fairy tale to expect that it would after the extensive socialization we both had experienced that told us to maintain a distance between us. But the experience I had at that workshop was just one of many which helped me to understand that distances between me and my students, especially those created and reinforced by homophobia, were not only detrimental to my teaching effectiveness, they were devastating to my self-esteem.

Another experience came years later when, during my Women's Literature class's reading of Gloria Naylor's *The Women of Brewster Place* (1982), a young woman stayed after the period ended to talk with me. She told me that she had been apprehensive that day when we began our discussion of the chapter entitled "The Two," which is about two lesbians in a long-term relationship who move into an apartment at the Brewster Place housing project. She said that when lesbian or gay issues came up in her classes, she was often deeply hurt by students' homophobic remarks, because her mother was a lesbian. As she told me about her mother's life and the discrimination and hateful treatment her mother had endured, I began to feel as if I would be the consummate hypocrite if I kept mute about my own sexual orientation, which would have been easy to do. But when the opportunity presented itself for me to respond to her stories, I told her that I understood her feelings, and that I understood what her mom had gone through because I was a lesbian myself.

We talked for about an hour that afternoon, and although we never spoke about it again, I was glad that we had had that conversation, and I hoped it made her feel as if she had an ally at school. At the very least, it helped me to know that I could come out to a student and the sky wouldn't fall.

So gradually I began to let go of my anxiety and my feelings of shame, and as I did, it was easier to take risks about being open about who I am. I have become increasingly comfortable just being myself, mentioning details of my personal life to classes or individuals when it is appropriate. I even started letting go of the fear of rejection by kids that would make my teaching ineffective. Taking those risks has facilitated relationship-building with students, making the learning environment much more comfortable and safe and more full of potential for growth— theirs *and* mine.

FIRST STEPS: BEING PRESENT FOR A LESBIAN STUDENT

Five years ago, I was pleased when I read my Women's Literature class list of students at the beginning of the year and saw the name of a young woman with whom I was familiar because of her athletic accomplishments at Lincoln High. I remembered watching Sandy play basketball on the varsity team when she was a ninth grader and thinking to myself, *I'll bet that girl will figure out she's a lesbian someday.* It was just something about the way she looked and the way she carried herself, not to mention the way she played ball. But that wasn't the reason I was happy to have Sandy in class; I'm nuts about women's sports, and I was just happy for the opportunity to get to know someone whose accomplishments I had admired on the basketball and volleyball courts.

About two-thirds of the way through the class, kids were reading books they had chosen for themselves. Sandy and Lori, another student, were reading Fannie Flagg's *Fried Green Tomatoes at the Whistle Stop Café* (1987), the story of two women, Idgie and Ruth, living during the 1930s who have been thrown together by fate and have come to build a family life together.

One day, Lori came up to me, breathless, shouting, "Ruth and Idgie were lesbians, weren't they?" She said that Sandy didn't think they were, but *she* did. I went with Lori to find Sandy, and we talked about possibilities. Could the two main characters have been lesbians? What *is* a lesbian? There were no sex scenes between the two women in the book; were there other things about Ruth and Idgie and their relationship we could look at to answer the question? We talked about it for about 20 minutes.

Afterward I wondered what I would have said if I had read *Fried Green Tomatoes* when I was in high school. I would have had absolutely no context for even questioning whether Ruth and Idgie were lesbians. I was glad that I had the chance to help provide some of that context for Sandy and Lori.

I would see Sandy in the halls and around school the semester after our class together ended, and she was always friendly. I would ask her how basketball or tennis was going, and she would give me a brief report. When she graduated in May, I was a little sad to think that I would be losing touch with her, that we never had the chance to really talk or become friends. But it was like that with lots of students I came to especially like and admire—we just lose touch.

One Sunday that following summer, Liz, my partner at that time, came home from playing basketball. We played with a group of our lesbian friends every Sunday at 10:00 A.M., outside in good weather and in the school gym when it got cold. That Sunday I had stayed home for some reason, and Liz told me that they had played a couple of games when they became aware of the presence of a young woman standing outside the fence watching them. When they asked her if she wanted to join them, she practically leaped the fence, Liz said. Then she proceeded to kick everybody's ass. I thought to myself, *Hmmm. Could that have been Sandy?*

Sure enough, the next Sunday, when we got to the courts, it was

Sandy who was there. It felt funny playing basketball with her, mostly because I am a very inexperienced player, having only really started to learn the game in my late thirties. But it also felt odd socializing with someone who had been in one of my classes. Over the years I had developed an unwritten rule for myself: keep your school life separate from your nonschool life. That came about, I told myself, because I wanted to leave the stresses and responsibilities of school behind. But I am sure now that it had just as much to do with my internalized homophobia, that sense that to avoid the threat of problems, I should never have students to my house or do things with them outside school.

But here I was. Basketball was sacred to me because it was a time when I could count on both being with other lesbians and participating in a team sport, which I dearly love. I was definitely not going to stop playing. And it became clear that Sandy was not quitting, either.

As time went on, Sandy began to build a friendship with Liz. They started to do things together, and Sandy started coming over to our house to hang out with her. At first it felt funny to have her there, and Liz and I talked it over and decided that we weren't going to change anything about how we acted at home just because she was there. As time went on, I got more and more used to her being over, and more comfortable with crossing over into friendship, leaving our teacher–student relationship behind.

Eventually, Sandy told us that the reason she started hanging out at the basketball courts where we played was because she could see that we were lesbians, and she wanted to be around us. She was becoming aware of her own sexuality, and she wanted to be a part of a lesbian community.

Now that we have successfully developed a peer relationship, I am very grateful and happy that I was able to make the transition. I am glad that my former partner and I were able to provide a little help to Sandy in finding the community she was looking for. But mostly I am glad to have freed myself from my self-imposed restrictions so that I could get to know someone as wonderful as Sandy.

When many of my lesbian friends and I talk about our younger days when we were coming out, the stories are of underage drinking in bars like one called "The Cave," or of disappointing and destructive relationships we got into because we didn't know any better. Sandy, on the other hand, is making strong and admirable decisions for herself, not rushing into things before she is ready and being up front with everyone in her life about who she is and the choices she is making. She would be an excellent role model for all of the high school–aged youth I know.

In October of the second year after Sandy started coming to Sunday morning basketball, she and I drove to Omaha together to attend the

National Coming Out Day celebration there. We had a good time to-gether, checking out the Omaha lesbian climate and seeing what kinds of organizations the Omaha gay/lesbian community had to support them. After our fabulous dinner out at Taco Bell (all that Sandy could afford), we went to the concert by Cris Williamson and Tret Fure at the With-erspoon Concert Hall that evening. I had gone to my first concert by Cris Williamson, one of the founders of the women's music movement, with Susan, my first love from years ago during my first teaching job. Now here I was, nearly 20 years later, with a friend who wasn't even born when I went to that first concert. It felt like coming full circle to me—remembering my coming out as a lesbian and finally being in a place where I could fully accept who I am and what that means to me as a teacher. It was wonderful to share with Sandy the powerful and comfort-able feeling of being surrounded by lesbians, totally safe, and completely content with my identity.

CONNECTING MY PERSONAL AND PROFESSIONAL IDENTITIES

Experiencing this intergenerational friendship with Sandy has helped me break down my barriers to becoming friends with other students. More importantly, I developed two significant friendships with students who were aware of my sexual orientation from the outset. The best part about this for me is that it signaled an end to my fragmenting of myself—I en-tered these relationships as a whole person/teacher. These students are now in college. Sophie is preparing to graduate in the spring, and Amy is in her sophomore year.

I got to know Sophie when I helped her and some other women students found the POWER Club at my school. The purpose of the club was to promote an awareness and understanding of feminism and gender equity at our school, and Sophie was a student who was very interested in these issues. Even though she was never enrolled in any of the courses I teach, Sophie and I spent many a Thursday afternoon after our POWER Club meetings talking about feminist issues, and over her three years at Lincoln High, we got to know each other pretty well.

During her senior year, Sophie and her family learned that her mother had a terminal illness. Having already lost both my parents to illnesses, I felt comfortable talking to Sophie about what she was experi-encing: fear, powerlessness, grief. When she left for college, we continued our conversations via e-mail. After her mother died, I believe I provided a safe outlet for Sophie to express her feelings of mourning and loss.

In the process of these conversations, I used examples of my own experiences to try to provide a window of understanding for Sophie. So I spoke and talked to her of my own life. I talked about my relationships naturally, since information about them fit into the context of our talking or writing. Perhaps because the content of our communication over several years was so frequently about emotions, and perhaps because impending death makes other fears irrelevant, it became natural at some point for me to tell Sophie that I loved her, often ending my e-mails that way.

Last summer when she was home from college and we went out for breakfast to catch up with each other, Sophie told me something that now seems ironic. She said that a classmate of hers had suspected us of being involved in an affair when she was still in high school. I was shocked when Sophie related this; even if I didn't have as a cardinal rule to never become sexually involved with students, the fact is that I am never sexually attracted to students. But more than that, it saddened me that the level of intimacy that we did share was interpreted that way. I have a feeling that this is not especially unusual, either; I suspect that since the notion of a teacher loving her student is taboo, it suggests to some that the nature of that love would bring about an even greater taboo. Even more ironic is that Sophie now tells me that I am one of a handful of women she thinks of as mother figures.

Nevertheless, I did, and still do, love Sophie, an introspective, intense, sensitive young woman doing the work of creating herself amidst pains of loss and growing. Should I hide my love for her to maintain a distance that does not serve a teacher and a student years after we are no longer in our student/teacher roles? How would that serve her? How would it serve me?

Amy knew about my sexual identity from the first day I met her, as we worked together within the context of the Gay/Lesbian/Bisexual/Straight Alliance (GLBSA) at our school. With her more than with any other student, I have been myself—not only truthful but natural in the process of building a friendship. Amy is one of the most articulate and intelligent students I have known, so getting to know one another came largely from the analytic conversations that I so enjoyed during and after our GLBSA board meetings.

Although Amy, too, experienced a family tragedy during her senior year, and I counseled her about that and other personal questions she posed to me, our relationship was characterized more by our honest exchange of ideas, conversation, and humor than by any sense of mentorship. Our friendship continues, too, now that she is across the country in college, through phone calls, e-mails, and visits when she returns home for holidays. We started a tradition of sharing meals when she was a senior in high school. She came over for home-cooked meals my partner, Mary, and I would fix, and later when Amy became employed during the summer we went out to eat so she could repay us the hospitality we had shown her. Amy talks to both me and Mary on the phone when she calls from college, and she e-mails each of us. Amy is continuing the lesbian activism she began in high school in her work in college and sees it as a possible part of a career for herself.

The quality of my friendship with Amy at this point in my teaching life means that my irrational fears about my sexual identity—the ones that caused me to be intimidated by homophobic colleagues and harassing students, and the ones that caused me to censor myself—are completely gone. Oh, I still have healthy fears about what it means to teach in a school district, city, and state that do not have anti-discrimination protection laws for lesbians and gay men. As a matter of fact, I have changed the names of all of the students to whom I have referred in this writing in order to avoid any conflicts stemming from a reader's misinterpretation of my intended message. But I don't let imposed fears paralyze my effectiveness in my classroom with students who need to see me being honest in order to do the best work they can at creating themselves through literacy.

My life partner, Mary, is a wonderful woman who has worked to overcome any qualms she had about accompanying me to school events, like games and plays and even our Pride Prom for GLBSA members. Her job is one at which it is not safe to be completely out, so when she does take risks by accompanying me—"the *lesbian* teacher"—she inspires my admiration. The GLBSA members know her by name, ask about her, and speak to her when they see her. But when a student from one of my General English classes asks me who she is, there are still times when I might say, "She's a friend of mine." These are the times when I am heeding the advice of a good friend who told me that I don't always have to set myself up for a struggle if I see one coming, that I don't have to fight every battle with people who aren't ready to look at their own beliefs.

FEELING AT HOME IN MY IDENTITY

A couple of years ago, a reporter from the Lincoln city newspaper called me. She was doing a story about women's studies classes in high schools and wanted to talk about my Women's Literature class. One of her questions was about why I had initiated the class, and I told her that it was because women students had the need to see themselves in the curriculum, and that doing so would improve their self-esteem and bolster their confidence. I said that having a forum to discuss the things that mattered in their lives would make learning more meaningful and would validate their own lives. I told her that these conditions in a classroom are excellent for nurturing the literacy skills of women and their male supporters.

Walking home from school that day, I thought about that answer, and what I realized was that it was the teacher in me talking. Underneath that answer, which I still believed in, I knew that the real reason I initiated a women's literature class was because *I* needed it. I needed to work in a forum that validated who I was. As altruistic as I might have been, and as beneficial for students as it has turned out to be, underneath it all, I was doing it for myself.

That's where I find myself now. I have to be honest about every aspect of who I am for myself. That this will provide a positive role model for students on various levels is a wonderful side effect, that this will increase trust and risk-taking in my classroom is beneficial, but beneath it all, feeling at home within my identity is something I have to do to be fully alive. It's really for me.

9

Toward Supporting Resistance and Revision

Coming to voice is not just the act of telling one's experience. It is using that telling strategically—to come to voice so that you can also speak freely about other subjects.

—bell hooks, *Teaching to Transgress*

The stories Toni, Carol, John, and Ruth have composed and revised over the past few years have taught us even more about how to examine and understand the interconnections between the personal and professional development of teachers. And they have prompted us to look again at ways in which narrative can become a critical instrument for naming, resisting, and revising the multiple and varied ideologies that inflect the lives of teachers. Most fundamental in coming to critical consciousness is the act of naming and telling one's story. But as Carol and John so strongly assert, this act of constructing one's own narrative is not enough. It is equally crucial, as Freire and Macedo (1987) point out, to historicize and contextualize one's experience in order to see how experience and knowledge are shaped *in* social relations and *by* the very discourse that constitute the telling.

Why do narratives of personal and professional identity, narratives of personal learning and teaching, work in this way? As Jerome Bruner (1986) and others have shown, every act of writing or telling involves constructing and therefore interpreting past experience and present rhetorical context. Stories are interpretive acts, and they are never single-voiced but instead are dialogical, shaped by previous history, by present emotional and rhetorical context, by the potential listener as well as by the teller. They also open up the possibility of reinterpretation and "re-vision," coming to our lives with new eyes, as Adrienne Rich (1979) describes. Bruner (1986) says that narrative, unlike "logico-scientific" lan-

guage, inhabits a realm "of potential, of possibility, of uncertainty, contradictions and silences" (1986, p. 11). Narrative, then, creates multiple potential meanings and even contradictions, and therefore narrative creates
spaces for rethinking and resisting old interpretations. This process
makes possible the recognition that cultural narratives about who one
ought to be and how one might live are not monolithic or homogeneous.
Each of us resides in multiple locations by virtue of our gender, religion,
ethnicity, race, sexual orientation, and physical characteristics. When individuals begin to see the multiple and often conflicting nature of those
narratives, it becomes possible to hold them up to scrutiny, to critique
them, to break their hold over us. But more than interpretation and critique are possible through narrative. In this process of resistance and revision, action can occur. Narrative is never passive, never just interpretive
and reflective. Knowledge emerges through narrative when it is used
strategically and connected in an ongoing dialogic between "telling" and
"doing," between narrative, reflection, and praxis.

   Narrative's revisionary and deconstructive potential for strategic action is demonstrated in the stories Ruth, Carol, Toni, and John tell. In
writing and rewriting her story, Carol, for example, articulated and exposed the tensions and contradictions between converging narratives of
selfhood. In the convergence of these narratives, she found new understandings and the possibility of resisting and revising old narratives, indeed of renaming herself. But more than that, she has begun to use narrative to nurture her students' development as well. She believes that
students, too, must be invited to tell stories, to compose their experience
within a supportive framework for critically analyzing those stories. "Stories serve as the windows through which we discover our core beliefs and
understandings and examine our constructs of the world," Carol says in
an earlier version of her story. Carol has also developed a valuable heuristic of questions to use in looking critically at our own stories and those
around us:

> What is the larger context? What obscures meaning? What struc-
> tures are in place that contributed to this event? What do I learn
> from this experience? What lesson is there for me? . . . Why did . . .
> [I] pick these stories? What do these stories say about who . . .
> [I am] and why . . . [I] think, feel and act the way . . . [I] do? What
> beliefs and social discourses shape the telling of these stories?

Carol has turned her own processes of resistance and revision into a critical pedagogy for her students.

   Toni's process was different than Carol's in that she had to come to trust her own nagging questions. She came to trust them as her graduate courses allowed her to engage in dialogue with theory and her own lived experience as a woman, a student, a teacher. For Toni, doubt has not been replaced by certainty—she has not become Paul—instead, doubt serves as a catalyst for action, moving her toward new relationships with students and colleagues and toward an activist role in her school. Toni does not set herself up as some ideal, transformed teacher; she acknowledges that the very process of drafting her story for Chapter 6 highlights the compromises she continually has to make because of the ways in which her professional life as a teacher interacts with the exigencies of her personal lives as mother, wife, woman, and learner. Telling her story, following her nagging questions, takes time that Toni does not always have.

John, too, has used narrative to move to action. For him it began with our interviews in his role as one of our research participants and continued with our ongoing challenges to him "to dig deeper, to say more." John came to see "constant examination and reflection as essential in our personal and professional worlds." He says:

> I know now that if I cannot revise my own past by reconsidering what it means, then I am stuck with one version of the truth, and I deny myself the possibility of reimagining a better future for myself and my students. I don't want to live with my own story as it's already been told—and I don't want my students to live with the diminished life expectations that would result from them accepting someone else's version of their life stories. I want them to imagine what might be possible. So I work to grant them the privilege of mentorship.

Part of what John has discovered in telling and retelling his story is his own privileged status and the powerful role mentorships have played in his own development, providing him with what he calls a "discourse of possibility." John now works to develop this same possibility for his students.

In Chapter 8 Ruth exposes the contradictions between her self as teacher and as lesbian woman, and the contradictions between teaching students to explore and connect their identities in reading and writing when she was suppressing her own identity in the classroom. Ruth has used telling and examining her own story to redefine what it means to be student-centered. She has revised her teaching to become a less controlling and authoritarian teacher, less focused on students' intake of information and instead fostering students' constructions of meaning/ideas. But in the process of moving toward this new version of student-

centered pedagogy, she also argues that the teacher's own identity must
not be erased. She asserts that in order for students and teachers to engage in the risk-taking necessary for meaningful learning, teachers have
to be honest about bringing all of who they are into their classrooms. As
Ruth wrote in reflecting on an interaction with one of her administrators:

> Did Dr. Sterns think that as long as I kept my sexual orientation
> hidden, the threats to lesbian and gay teachers and gay-positive cur-
> ricula made by the powerful religious right wouldn't affect me? Did
> he think that I had lost my effectiveness with my class because I
> had not kept my identity hidden? Did he think that as long as I
> hid, which shame would easily enable me to do, I would be a
> whole person? Did he think that fragmented people with secrets,
> who told lies, were the best teachers? . . . What was he thinking?

Ruth goes on to acknowledge the ways in which operating from her own
need have not always been in opposition to being student-centered:

> . . . I knew that the real reason I initiated a women's literature class
> was because *I* needed it. I needed to work in a forum that vali-
> dated who I was. As altruistic as I might have been, and as benefi-
> cial for students as it has turned out to be, underneath it all, I was
> doing it for myself.

Storytelling and reflection have allowed Ruth to bring together her personal and professional identities, claiming her own place in her student-
centered classroom.

FROM RESEARCH METHODOLOGY TO CLASSROOM PRACTICE

The stories from Carol, Toni, John, and Ruth offer us a discourse of possibility for teacher development, for reimagining ways to support the revision of teacher practices and identities. In undergraduate and graduate
classes—like Composition Theory and Practice, English Methods, and
the Nebraska Literacy Project—we have begun more systematically to
invite prospective or practicing teachers to tell and reflect on two kinds
of stories. Some of these stories address their own personal and literacy
development, both inside and outside school; others, in teaching journals,
describe and reflect on the dynamics of their classrooms and their students' lives.
    These stories become a kind of primary text in these classes, enabling

preservice and practicing teachers to uncover their unspoken assumptions; examine the contradictions between their pedagogies and their experiences; complicate their understandings of literacy, learning, and teaching; integrate their examined experiences into their working conceptions of literacy and learning; grow in understanding who they are and how they have become who they are; develop intimacy; and build community. They also provide teachers with a sense of their own authority to resist and revise the powerful scripting narratives of the culture and schools so they can begin to compose new narratives of personal and professional identity and practice.

As a result of our work with teachers in this study, and as we focused more deliberately on the issues that confront teachers as they negotiate the cultural and institutional narratives of teaching and selfhood, we decided to try to create a collaborative group of teachers to support one another's development through reflection within a supportive community. In the fall of 1992, with funding from our university, we, along with Robert Brooke, invited 17 middle-level and secondary English teachers from eastern Nebraska to participate in a collaborative professional development project. In addition, two English Department graduate students and we three university faculty members (two from English and one from education) participated. We brought these teachers together across institutions and grade levels to attempt to decrease their isolation and build a collaborative community in which teachers could observe and reflect on their own teaching, tell stories of their own personal and professional development, and share those with others.

The group met once a week during the fall semester, continued to meet during the spring semester every other week, and then met monthly for the next two years, with some members dropping out and others joining. During the fall, we each wrote a weekly reflective observation of a particular classroom event and shared these informal writings in small groups during our meetings; we also asked people to form journal partnerships to provide each other with sustained opportunities for response. On another occasion we assigned ourselves to write about individual students—for example, "a student who troubled, excited, or intrigued" us. As the first semester progressed, teachers' own needs and agendas began to shape our work together.

The teachers decided to organize our time together in the following way: (a) quiet writing and reflection, (b) interaction in small groups about our writing, (c) discussion of in-common professional reading, and (d) large-group sessions to debrief and synthesize the issues about which we were writing and talking. Teachers shared professional issues with which they were wrestling in their districts and buildings (interdisciplinary team teaching; expectations about literacy and learning from other teachers, administrators, and parents; school politics; interactions with individual students; plagiarism; top-down curriculum initiatives). And inevitably our discussions brought our personal lives into the picture. Teachers talked about their children's experiences in school, shared stories about loved ones, and set goals to get more exercise and healthy food into our lives.

The teachers decided that our final group "product" from the fall seminar should be an anthology of excerpts from our writing during the semester. It included "mini-case studies," such as "Mike's Story: Working Through My Anger," in which Amy wrote: "The more I look at Mike, the more I'm seeing. I'm losing the frustration and anger. It's not that my expectations will lessen, but I can see him as a real person beyond being my student." In, "Keeping a Teaching Journal: Reflections on Reflecting," Terry wrote:

> What is in my teaching journal? Stories—stories about my students like Matt, who present daily challenges to me; stories about my teaching strategies—how my writing workshop is sputtering, choking, and evolving; stories about my own teaching attitude—how tired I am or what kind of essays are driving me nuts. As I read through the entries, I see my teaching life unfold, but how does this reflection make a difference? . . . Now I have an ongoing dialogue with myself about how I have been teaching. The act of writing sharpens my perceptions and helps me discover ways to change or adjust. I have also discovered I hold the answers to my own questions . . . More than anything, keeping a teaching journal helps me focus on the classroom and some individual students and confront myself honestly and without risk about what works and what doesn't. At first that confrontation made me somewhat defensive. I wasn't so sure that after 16 years of teaching I wanted to question myself so much . . . Now I find myself composing sentences and paragraphs in my head.

At the beginning of the next semester, the group again negotiated its use of time and set some specific goals for ourselves. Two projects emerged in addition to our ongoing reflection. One of them was to offer a seminar for preservice teachers entitled "The Realities of Creating and Maintaining Nontraditional English Classrooms." Undergraduate preservice teachers submitted questions in advance, and our teacher group worked to develop an evening that would help the undergraduates get some answers to these questions and provide them with a sense that some Nebraska teachers were creating alternatives to the traditional English classrooms that many undergraduates had experienced in their own high school careers. This gave the experienced teachers in our group an opportunity to think about what they were doing and why and how, and affirmed that they did have a kind of expertise that they didn't always feel.

The second project also developed in response to something the undergraduate preservice students were doing. As a part of their teacher preparation, these undergraduates were asked over the course of several semesters to articulate their informed beliefs about learning, teaching, and the language arts. These belief statements were then mailed out to cooperating teachers before the university students showed up for practicum or student teaching, so that the cooperating teacher had a sense of the kind of classroom the student was hoping to create. The teachers in our group reported feeling embarrassed that they hadn't, maybe even couldn't, articulate the beliefs that underlay their own practices. "We need to write our own informed position statements," one teacher insisted.

This second semester of the project gave teachers opportunities for questioning, reflection, and storytelling within a supportive community. Teachers were continually asked to tell and analyze the stories of their own lives both inside and outside classrooms. This two-semester intensive project spawned a number of other activities that continued far beyond that year. Several teachers wrote articles for *NEBLAB*, the *Nebraska English Language Arts Bulletin*, based on their reflective writing in our project. Teachers and university professors initiated or continued teaching journal partnerships. One teacher who had already begun to organize a multicultural reading group called SEED (Seeking Educational Equity and Diversity) in her school used the project to further expand that effort, and many of the teachers in our project participated or began leading SEED groups in their own schools. Several of the teachers from our project ended up in our graduate courses or in summer institutes of the Nebraska Writing Project. One of the teachers co-planned and taught a multicultural literacy project the following summer with a university professor. And out of that literacy project, another teacher reading-writing group emerged that continued to meet once a month for three years. Many of the teachers who were in our collaborative professional development project also participated in that group.

Our efforts to create collaborative communities of reflective teachers had at least some success—not because of any dramatic strategies on our part. This success occurred simply because teachers felt supported and engaged by the opportunity to compose and critique the stories of their personal and professional lives and to share them with others. Recently teachers have asked us when we are going to organize such a project again. One teacher said, "I'm jealous that I didn't get to participate in that group. Those folks still talk about it. I'd like to have the opportunity now."

Narrative has emerged as a crucial strategy in our work with preservice and inservice teachers and with graduate students. A requirement for the completion of the master's degree in curriculum and instruction is a summative work, a project that pulls together students' graduate coursework and their classroom experience. Many students recently under our supervision have drafted their teaching autobiographies in an attempt at understanding how they have become the teachers they are and at gaining some control over the teachers they will become. Earlier drafts of Ruth's and Toni's chapters were written as summative works.

Our use of narrative has been equally important with our undergraduate students, both in English and in teacher preparation classes. As a result of our study of preservice teachers and initially from students' response to Mike Rose's *Lives on the Boundary* (1989), several years ago we began asking students to compose their own autobiographies as writers and readers in their composition theory and reading theory and practice classes. We recognized that those experiences, whether articulated or not, had enormous impact on students' reception/connection with the theories and practices we were presenting and engaging in during those classes. Examining their own experiences allowed us all to move those experiences out of the closet and into the light of the classroom for examination and reflection. We ask students to describe important incidents, people, and events in their development as readers and writers. Often these narratives turn into 10- or 15-page histories that reveal the important sites of their literacy development in home, church, and community and the differences between self-sponsored and school-mandated forms of literacy.

The first assignment in methods class is to "describe the best teacher you've ever had and tell a story that illustrates why you revere that teacher." Students have written about revered teachers who were in fact abusive—teachers who failed any paper that had two or more misspelled words or a single run-on sentence, or teachers who led students through a routinized semester-long research project and claimed to have what students come to see as phony high standards, telling students, "Someday you'll thank me for this." Our students talk about some of their revered teachers as being incredibly knowledgeable. But when they unpack that statement, they see how the teachers often used their knowledge to oppress or control them and to keep them from developing their own understandings of a given text or the process of writing. More common are stories about a teacher who "cared about me as an individual." In those cases we attempt to understand how we knew that, what the teacher did to demonstrate that, and whether others might have felt cared for as well. In subsequent classes, we attempt to uncover the assumptions about teaching that are implied by their stories, often then critiquing those assumptions. It's a matter of bringing these assumptions into the light of day. Students carry these assumptions into our classrooms and into their own future classrooms, and the opportunity to analyze and critique them is crucial to the possibility of resisting and revising these narratives.

In graduate seminars and summer workshops for teachers, we have used similar prompts to help teachers reexamine their own literacy and educational history and the influence it has had on their assumptions about teaching and learning. In the orientation for new graduate teaching assistants in English, we use many of these same strategies. Doctoral students in English often seem especially entrenched and invested in traditional narratives of English and teaching that suggest that their role as college teachers is to mandate high standards, to be rigorous and intellectual, to promote a fixed conception of literature and writing, and to weed out those who don't measure up. They are sometimes the college version of the 1950s English schoolmarm, yet armed with sophisticated theory. Their very success in graduate school has in some cases depended on their buying into a version of that model. Others come with less traditional notions of English and teaching. Many creative writers, for example, understand the value of process pedagogies; and other, more experienced graduate teaching assistants have used collaborative and interactive pedagogies in their classes. But often even they have not had opportunities to examine the assumptions that underlie their practices, nor have they been exposed to the theories and practices of writing, rhetoric, and literature that might further complicate their teaching. At the same time, they have often not practiced these strategies in their own development as writers. Sometimes they are worried about theorizing about their writing or reflecting on their own writing processes, fearing that "thinking about it too much" will spoil the magic or mystique of the artist/writer. In fact, sometimes graduate students are very resistant to the reflection and investigation we are asking them to do.

Because of our work with preservice teachers, we have gained further understanding of the sources of our graduate students' resistance. We realize that to some degree, we're asking them to forego developing an identity as professor that may be central to their motivation for pursuing doctoral studies in the first place. As a way to mitigate this resistance and to displace the problems of our authority as their professors, we now organize graduate teaching assistants into peer teaching groups, facilitated by a more experienced T.A. These groups meet each week to compose and examine the stories of their teaching and to help each other negotiate the personal and professional issues they are facing as beginning Ph.D. students. These groups have proven to be an invaluable element in their ongoing development as teachers, providing support for continuing reflection on teaching beyond the semester-long seminar and orientation. We conclude the semester by asking T.A.s to submit an emergent teaching portfolio and to compose a statement of teaching philosophy. Although these will have an important professional function as students seek jobs in the future, they often are further sites for composing and reflecting on their teaching. Sometimes even resistant students come back to us in subsequent semesters saying, "I realize that I've missed the opportunities for reflection and conversation about teaching that we had in the seminar, and I'd like to keep that as part of my intellectual and professional development."

USING NARRATIVE FOR CHANGE

Despite our efforts to reshape our teaching and our classrooms, we believe that the potential for teacher change—teachers revising their conceptions of and practices surrounding language learning—is not located in programs or classes that do something *to* teachers or give teachers new "methods" or information. Instead, change is made possible and becomes sustainable when teachers gain critical perspective on how their identities have been constructed by/in the culture and how cultural narratives of teaching have shaped their personal and professional subjectivities. When teachers use writing and reading to name and interpret their own histories, the narratives they compose can begin to reveal the contradictions and conflicts among their own complex subjectivities. Recognizing those contradictions makes it possible for teachers to resist and revise the hegemonic narratives of teaching and learning that position them as teachers and as individuals. In turn, they may more fully understand the social and political implications of literacy for students and help students use writing and reading to become self-reflective and critically literate citizens.

As a result of our exploration of narrative, we are calling for teacher education and reeducation that allows teachers to locate, name, and critique the position of teacher as constructed by the culture and by education more specifically, and to theorize that cultural construction of teacher in relation to their identity as writer, reader, and person. We are calling for teacher education that acknowledges that teacher change occurs when personal and professional identities are recognized as being inextricably linked. But narratives of self and of learning are not a panacea and, as the stories in this book suggest, are not effective in isolation. Teacher development requires that narrative be used strategically alongside sustained ongoing reflection. And as bell hooks (1994) reminds us, a community is required—not just for safety, but because community can sustain commitment, can nurture individual and community agency, and can thus result in action.

We have seen how much prospective and practicing teachers are at risk—at risk of perpetuating restrictive notions of reading and writing that do not take into account the complexity of language or the inextricable links between language learning and the fundamental personal and social development of human beings; at risk of operating with reductionist visions of education that seek merely to domesticate students to prescribed roles; at risk of taking on a role as teacher that is a mere caricature of authority and control, but one that inevitably leads to a severely diminished intellectual and professional identity.

We must understand clearly what we are asking teachers to do in expanding their understandings of teaching and learning. We are asking them to engage in a radical relearning process that has powerful personal and political repercussions and risks. Rather than just adding on ideas, they must reconceive and reconstruct their knowledge—and perhaps their identities—and in doing so struggle against the fundamental beliefs and habits of mind of their experience, of our society, and of the local communities into which they move.

This task may be difficult. But we also see enormous possibilities in our students and colleagues and in what we continue to believe can be the transformative learning power of narrative—stories told and reflected on within supportive communities.

References

Althusser, L. (1971). Ideology and ideological state apparatuses. In Althusser, *Lenin and philosophy, and other essays* (B. Brewster, trans.). New York: Monthly Review Press.

Apple, M. W. (1982). *Education and power.* London: Routledge.

Applebee, A. N. (1981). *Writing in the secondary schools: English and the content areas.* Urbana, IL: National Council of Teachers of English.

Applebee, A. N. (1989a). *A study of book-length works taught in high school English courses* (Report Series 1.2). Albany, NY: State University of New York, Center for the Learning and Teaching of Literature.

Applebee, A. N. (1989b). *The teaching of literature in programs with reputations for excellence in English* (Report Series 1.2). Albany, NY: State University of New York, Center for the Learning and Teaching of Literature.

Applebee, A. N., Langer, J. A., & Mullis, I. V. S. (1986). *The writing report card: Writing achievement in American schools.* Princeton, NJ: Educational Testing Service.

Atwell, N. (1987). *In the middle: Writing and reading with adolescents.* Portsmouth, NH: Heinemann.

Saint Augustine. (trans. 1991). *Confessions.* Oxford: Oxford University Press.

Bakhtin, M. M. (1981). *The dialogic imagination* (C. Emerson & M. Holquist, Trans.). Austin: University of Texas Press. (Original work published 1975)

Bauman, R. (1977). *Verbal art as performance.* Rowley, MA: Newbury House.

Behar, R. (1993). *Translated woman: Crossing the border with Esperanza's story* Boston: Beacon Press.

Behar, R. (1996). *The vulnerable observer: Anthropology that breaks your heart.* Boston: Beacon Press.

Belenky, M. F., Clinchy, B. M., Goldberger, N. R., & Tarule, J. H. (1986). *Women's ways of knowing: The development of self, voice, and mind.* New York: Basic Books.

Bloom, B. (1956). *Taxonomy of educational objectives: The classification of educational goals.* New York: Longman.

Britzman, D. (1991). *Practice makes practice: A critical study of learning to teach.* Albany, NY: State University of New York Press.

Bronner, S. (1998). *Following tradition: Folklore in the discourse of American culture.* Logan: Utah State University Press.

Bruner, J. S. (1986*). Actual minds, possible worlds.* Cambridge, MA: Harvard University Press.

Butler, J. (1990). *Gender trouble: Feminism and the subversion of identity.* New York: Routledge.

Calkins, L. (1983). *Lessons from a child: On the teaching and learning of writing.* Portsmouth, NH: Heinemann.

Cochran-Smith, M., & Lytle, S. (1993). *Inside/outside: Teacher research and knowledge.* New York: Teachers College Press.

Dante Alighieri. (trans. 1954). *The inferno* (J. Ciardi, Trans.). New Brunswick, NJ: Rutgers University Press.

de Lauretis, T. (1984). *Alice doesn't: Feminism, semiotics, cinema, and fiction.* Bloomington: Indiana University Press.

Dewey, J. (1962). *The relation of theory to practice in education.* Cedar Falls, IA: The Association for Student Teaching.

Elbow, P. (1991). Reflections on academic discourse: How it relates to freshmen and colleagues. *College English, 53*(2), 135–154.

Eliot, T. S. (1992). Tradition and the individual talent. In H. Adams (Ed.), *Critical theory since Plato* (Rev. ed.) (pp. 761–764). New York: Harcourt Brace Jovanovich. (Original work published 1917)

Emig, J. (1971). *The composing processes of twelfth graders.* Urbana, IL: National Council of Teachers of English.

Fitzgerald, F. S. (1940). *The Great Gatsby.* New York: Scribner's.

Flagg, F. (1987). *Fried Green Tomatoes at the Whistle Stop Café.* New York: McGraw-Hill.

Freire, P. (1986). *Pedagogy of the oppressed.* New York: Continuum Books.

Freire, P., & Macedo, D. (1987). *Literacy: Reading the word and the world.* South Hadley, MA: Bergin & Garvey.

Giroux, H. A. (1983). *Theory and resistance: A pedagogy for the opposition.* South Hadley, MA: Bergin & Garvey.

Gitlin, A., Brighurst, K., Burns, M., Cooley, V., Myers, B., Price, K., Russell, R., & Ties, P. (1992). *Teachers' voices for school change: An introduction to educative research.* New York: Teachers College Press.

Goffman, E. (1959). *The presentation of self in everyday life.* New York: Doubleday.

Graff, G. (1987). *Professing literature.* Chicago: University of Chicago Press.

Graves, D. (1983). *Writing: Teachers and children at work.* Portsmouth, NH: Heinemann.

Grossman, P. L. (1987). *A tale of two teachers: The role of subject matter orientation in teaching.* Paper presented at the annual meeting of the American Educational Research Association, Washington, DC.

Grossman, P. L. (1988). *Learning to teach without teacher education.* A paper presented at the annual meeting of the American Educational Research Association, New Orleans.

Grossman, P. L. (1990). *The making of a teacher: Teacher knowledge and teacher education.* New York: Teachers College Press.

Grumet, M. R. (1991). The politics of personal knowledge. In C. Witherell & N. Noddings (Eds.), *Stories lives tell: Narrative and dialogue in education* (pp. 67–95). New York: Teachers College Press.

Handelman, D. (1990). *Models and mirrors: Towards an anthropology of public events.* Cambridge: Cambridge University Press.

Haraway, D. (1988). Situated knowledges: The science question in feminism and the privilege of partial perspective. *Feminist Studies, 14,* 3–15.

Harding, S. G. (1991). *Whose science? Whose knowledge?: Thinking from women's lives.* Ithaca, NY: Cornell University Press.

Heath, S. B. (1983). *Ways with words: Language, life, and work in communities and classrooms.* Cambridge: Cambridge University Press.

Hegi, U. (1994). *Stones from the river.* New York: Scribner.

Heilbrun, C. (1988). *Writing a woman's life.* New York: Norton.

Hennessy, R. (1993). *Materialist feminism and the politics of discourse.* New York: Routledge.

Hoagland, S. (1991). Some thoughts about "caring." In C. Card (Ed.), *Feminist ethics* (pp. 246–253). Lawrence: Kansas University Press.

Hollingsworth, S., & Cody, A. (1994). *Teacher research and urban literacy education: Lessons and conversations in a feminist key.* New York: Teachers College Press.

hooks, b. (1990). Choosing the margin as a space of radical openness. In b. hooks (Ed.), *Yearning, race, gender, and cultural politics* (pp. 145–153). Boston: South End Press.

hooks, b. (1994). *Teaching to transgress: Education as the practice of freedom.* New York: Routledge.

Hopkins, J., & Sugarman, D. (1980). *No one here gets out alive.* London, England: Plexus.

Hynds, S. (1997). *On the brink: Negotiating literature and life with adolescents.* New York: Teachers College Press.

Jalongo, M., & Isenberg, J., with Gerbracht, G. (1995). *Teachers' stories: From personal narrative to professional insight.* San Francisco: Jossey-Bass.

Jarratt, S. (1991). Feminism and composition: The case for conflict. In P. Harkin & J. Schilb (Eds.), *Contending with words: Composition and rhetoric in a postmodern age* (pp. 105–123). New York: Modern Language Association.

Kliebard, K. M. (1973). The question of teacher education. In D. McCarty (Ed.), *New perspectives on teacher education* (pp. 8–24). San Francisco: Jossey-Bass.

Kozol, J. (1967). *Death at an early age; The destruction of the hearts and minds of Negro children in the Boston public schools.* Boston: Houghton Mifflin.

Lather, P. (1986). Research as Praxis. *Harvard Educational Review, 56,* 257–277.

Lennon, J. (1971). Give me some truth. On *Imagine.* Los Angeles: EMI Records, Ltd.; manufactured by Capitol Records, Inc.

Lightfoot, S. (1983). The lives of teachers. In L. S. Shulman & G. Sykes (Eds.), *Handbook of teaching and policy* (pp. 241–260). New York: Longman.

Lorde, A. (1984a). The transformation of silence into language and action. In A. Lorde (Ed.), *Sister outsider: Essays and speeches* (pp. 40–44). Freedom, CA: Crossing Press.

Lorde, A. (1984b). The master's tools will never dismantle the master's house. In

A. Lorde (Ed.), *Sister outsider: Essays and speeches* (pp. 110–113). Freedom, CA: Crossing Press.

Lortie, D.C. (1975). *Schoolteacher: A sociological study.* Chicago: University of Chicago Press.

McEwan, H., & Egan, K. (1995). *Narrative in teaching, learning, and research.* New York: Teachers College Press.

McWilliam, E. (1994). *In broken images: Feminist tales for a different teacher education.* New York: Teachers College Press.

Middleton, S. (1992). *Educating feminists: Life histories and pedagogy.* New York: Teachers College Press.

Myers, M. (1996). *Changing our minds: Negotiating English and literacy.* Urbana, IL: National Council of Teachers of English.

Naylor, G. (1982). *The women of Brewster Place.* New York: Penguin Books.

Neumann, A., & Peterson, P. (1997). *Learning from our lives: Women, research, and autobiography in education.* New York: Teachers College Press.

Noddings, N. (1984). *Caring: A feminine approach to ethics and moral education.* Berkeley: University of California Press.

Plato. (trans. 1960). *Gorgias* (Walter Hamilton, Trans.). Baltimore: Penguin Books.

Plato. (trans. 1973). *Phaedrus* (Walter Hamilton, Trans.). Harmondsworth, England: Penguin.

Pratt, M. B. (1984). Identity: Skin, blood, heart. In E. Bulkin, M. B. Pratt, & B. Smith (Eds.), *Yours in struggle: Three feminist perspectives on anti-Semitism and racism* (pp. 11–63). New York: Long Haul Press.

Pratt, M. B. (1995) *S/HE.* Ithaca, NY: Firebrand Books.

Rich, A. (1979). When we dead awaken: Writing as re-vision. In *On lies, secrets, and silence: Selected prose, 1966–78* (pp. 33–49). New York: Norton.

Ricoeur, P. (1983). *Time and narrative.* University of Chicago Press.

Rief, L. (1992). *Seeking diversity: Language arts with adolescents.* Portsmouth, NH: Heinemann.

Rose, M. (1989). *Lives on the boundary.* New York: Penguin.

Rosenholtz, S. (1991). *Teachers' workplace: The social organization of schools.* New York: Teachers College Press.

Salvatori, M. (1994). Pedagogy and the academy: The divine skill of the born teacher's instincts. In P. Sullivan & D. Qualley (Eds.), *Pedagogy in the age of politics* (pp. 88–99). Urbana, IL: National Council of Teachers of English.

Schell, E. (1998). *Gypsy academics and mother teachers: Gender, contingent labor, and writing instruction.* Portsmouth, NH: Boynton/Cook.

Scholes, R. (1989). *Protocols of reading.* New Haven: Yale University Press.

Scott, J. W. (1992). Experience. In J. Butler & J. W. Scott (Eds.), *Feminists theorize the political* (pp. 22–40). New York: Routledge.

Smith, F. (1986). *Insult to intelligence: The bureaucratic invasion of our classrooms.* Portsmouth, NH: Heinemann.

Smith, F. (1988). *Joining the literacy club.* Portsmouth, NH: Heinemann.

Sunstein, B. S. (1994a). *Composing a culture: Inside a summer workshop with high school teachers.* Portsmouth, NH: Boynton/Cook.

Sunstein, B. S. (1994b). Teachers' tales as texts: Folklore and our profession. In

A. Trousdale, S. Woesthoff, & M. Schwartz (Eds.), *Give a listen: Stories of story-telling in school* (pp. 99–111). Urbana, IL: National Council of Teachers of English.

Thoreau, H. D. (1854). *Walden.* Boston: Ticknor.

Tolkien, J. R. R. (1988). *The hobbit.* New York: Houghton Mifflin.

Turner, V. (1986). *The anthropology of performance.* New York: PAJ.

Vinz, R. (1996). *Composing a teaching life.* Portsmouth, NH: Boynton/Cook.

Vonnegut, K. (1969). *Slaughterhouse-five, or, The children's crusade, a duty-dance with death.* New York: Dell.

Waller, W. (1932). *The sociology of teaching.* New York: Wiley.

Wamba, P. (1998). A middle passage. In C. C. O'Hearn (Ed.), *Half & Half: Writers on growing up biracial and bicultural* (pp. 150–169). New York: Pantheon.

Wasley, P. (1994). *Stirring the chalkdust: Tales of teachers changing classroom practice.* New York: Teachers College Press.

Weedon, C. (1987). *Feminist practice and poststructuralist theory.* London: Blackwell.

Wilson, D. (1994). *Attempting change: Teachers moving from writing project to classroom practice.* Portsmouth, NH: Boynton/Cook.

Witherell, C., & Noddings, N. (1991). *Stories lives tell: Narrative and dialogue in education.* New York: Teachers College Press.

Yee, M. (1991). Are you the teacher? In C. M. Hurlbert & M. Blitz (Eds.), *Composition and resistance* (pp. 24–31). Portsmouth, NH: Heinemann-Boynton/Cook.

Zeichner, W. M. (1983). Alternative paradigms on teacher education. *Journal of Teacher Education, 34*(3), 3–9.

About the Authors

Joy S. Ritchie is an associate professor of English and Women's Studies in the Department of English, University of Nebraska-Lincoln. She has taught high school English in North Carolina and Nebraska. She has published articles on rhetoric, composition, and feminist theory and pedagogy, including "Feminism and Composition: Inclusion, Metonomy, and Disruption," in the 50th-anniversary volume of *College Composition and Communication*. With Kate Ronald, she is also co-author of *Available Means: An Anthology of Women's Rhetorics*. She teaches undergraduate and graduate courses in composition theory and pedagogy, rhetorical theory, and women's literature.

David E. Wilson is an associate professor of English education in the Center for Curriculum and Instruction, University of Nebraska-Lincoln. He has taught English and journalism in public and private high schools in Missouri, Afghanistan, Pennsylvania, and Iowa. In addition to journal articles and book chapters, he has authored *Attempting Change: Teachers Moving from Writing Project to Classroom Practice* (1994). He teaches undergraduate courses in English education and graduate courses in teacher development, teaching writing, literary response, and language and learning.

Ruth Kupfer is a reading and English teacher at Lincoln (Nebraska) High School and holds a B.S. and an M.A. in Curriculum and Instruction from the University of Nebraska-Lincoln. She co-sponsors the Gay/Lesbian/Bisexual/Straight Alliance at her school, founded a club for student feminists, and in 1988 established the first women's literature class taught in a Nebraska high school. She is interested in ways in which public education can be a tool to empower disenfranchised students and promote social justice. Another of her narratives appears in *One Teacher in Ten* (1994).

Carol MacDaniels is a doctoral student at the University of Nebraska-Lincoln. Her research interests include teacher identity formation, educational reform movements, and rural education. She is also an adjunct instructor in Composition at Peru State College. Her essay "Reflection on Telling Stories: A Response to Resistance, Revision, and Representation" appeared in *English Education,* and she is the co-author (with Gerry Cox) of *Guide to Nebraska Authors* (1998).

Toni Siedel has taught at Northeast High School, in Lincoln, Nebraska, for nine years and holds a B.S. and an M.A. in Curriculum and Instruction from the University of Nebraska-Lincoln. Some of her work at Northeast includes serving on multicultural and equity committees, co-sponsoring a Gay, Lesbian, Bi-sexual, Straight Alliance, and developing and implementing a women's literature course. She has also presented at regional and national conferences on the importance of narrative and on the needs of gay youth.

John Skretta has a B.A. and M.A. in English from the University of Nebraska-Lincoln. He teaches English and reading at Northeast High School in Lincoln, Nebraska. Skretta has published articles in *English Journal* and a chapter in *Reading Stephen King.* At Northeast, he has helped design and implement a school-within-a-school for credit-deficient students. He has served on multicultural and reading committees at the school and district levels. Skretta's current work includes teaching reading and coordinating his district's reading graduation demonstration exam.

Index